About the *A*

Robin Esrock is a bestselling author, journalist, TV host, public speaker and producer. His stories and photography have appeared in major publications on five continents, including *National Geographic Traveler*, *The Guardian*, *The Chicago Tribune*, *South China Morning Post* and *The Globe and Mail*. Robin has been profiled as a travel expert by *60 Minutes*, ABC, *The Sydney Morning Herald*, MSNBC and *The Wall St Journal*, and he was honoured as Master of Ceremonies at the Explorer's Club Annual Dinner in New York. The creator and co-host of the 40-part television series *Word Travels*, Robin has been seen by millions of viewers in nearly two dozen languages on National Geographic and Travel Channel International. He is the bestselling author of *The Great Canadian Bucket List* and *The Great Global Bucket List*. Robin lives in Vancouver, Canada, with his wife and two children.

Online: robinesrock.com
Twitter: @robinesrock
Instagram: @ausbucketlist
Facebook: facebook.com/australianbucketlist
Follow Robin's Australian Bucket List blog at www.aussiebucketlist.com

THE GREAT AUSTRALIAN BUCKET LIST

ROBIN ESROCK

ONE -OF-A- KIND TRAVEL EXPERIENCES

Affirm press

This book is dedicated to Australian kids of all ages, including Phoenix, Amber, Ricky and Amy, and as always, to Raquel and Galileo. Life holds many adventures. Dream big.

Published by Affirm Press in 2018
28 Thistlethwaite Street, South Melbourne, VIC 3205.
www.affirmpress.com.au
10 9 8 7 6 5 4 3 2 1

A catalogue record for this book is available from the National Library of Australia

Title: The Great Australian Bucket List / Robin Esrock, author.
ISBN: 9781925712117 (paperback)

Printed and bound in China by 1010 Printing

Contents

VICTORIA   1

SOUTH AUSTRALIA   43

AUSTRALIAN CAPITAL TERRITORY   91

NEW SOUTH WALES   107

TASMANIA 153

QUEENSLAND 197

PAPUA
NEW
GUINEA

*Arafura
Sea*

*Coral
Sea*

Darwin

INDIAN
OCEAN

Broome

NORTHERN
TERRITORY

QUEENSLAND

Cairns

Alice Springs

WESTERN
TERRITORY

Brisbane

Coober Pedy

Byron
Bay

SOUTH AUSTRALIA

NEW SOUTH
WALES

AUSTRALIAN
CAPITAL
TERRITORY

Perth

*Great
Australian
Bight*

Adelaide

Sydney

Canberra

VICTORIA

Melbourne

*Bass
Strait*

Launceston

TASMANIA

Hobart

Introduction

*'One day you will wake up and realise there won't be any more time to do the
things you've always wanted. Do it now.'*

Paulo Coelho

Many years and miles ago, my life wasn't going as planned. My career in
the music industry was soul crushing, my friends were all getting married,
I had too much energy and, even though I was young, it felt like so many
opportunities were passing me by. One morning on my way to the office, a
car ran a stop sign and slammed into my bike, resulting in a swan dive over
my handlebars and a cracked kneecap. This was, by far, the luckiest break
of my life.

The excruciating pain of a broken knee translated into a $20,000 insur-
ance settlement – the kind of money that, if applied *very* sparingly, could be
used for a one-year backpacking adventure. Even light brushes with death
can remind you that it's time to start living. Inspired to travel, I booked
a round-the-world ticket to visit 24 countries on five continents, sold my
possessions, and said goodbye to my bewildered friends and family. The fear
of dangerous situations, ill health, and all the silly things that keep one glued
to the couch terrified me as much as anyone. Yet I was determined to visit
the places and do the activities that had always captured my imagination; in
effect, to tick off my bucket list.

Nobody knew what a bucket list was in 2005. While the term is ubiquitous
today, it only entered popular culture with the 2w007 film of the same name.
Starring Jack Nicholson and Morgan Freeman, the movie wasn't particularly
good, but it gave us an instantly memorable and corny catchphrase for a
powerful human desire shared across all ages, interests and cultures. What
holds us back from chasing our wildest dreams? And what constitutes a
bucket list adventure anyway?

Almost immediately, I found myself drawn to one-of-kind experiences,
those memorable activities and destinations you simply cannot find
anywhere else. They should always make great stories and, importantly,
be available to everyone. Using these criteria, I began writing about my
journey on a blog. Taking a friend's advice, I then pitched a story to a

newspaper, and the travel editor bit. Website traffic boomed, and more editors of more major publications picked up my 'gonzo' travel stories, in which I'd say yes to any adventure and jump in headfirst. On my return home, I had morphed into a fully fledged travel writer, the seemingly perfect combination of passion and job. I soon realised travel writing is a lifestyle, not a career. Low on the journalism totem pole, I was making little money but was invited on exotic trips around the world. One day I'd be sleeping on a friend's couch, the next in a five-star hotel in Central America! This absurdity, coupled with the public's fascination with travel journalism, led me to the idea of a TV show. The stars aligned once more, and my National Geographic/Travel Channel series *Word Travels* was my ticket to continue ticking off my bucket list in 36 countries. After the series wrapped, I continued writing for papers and magazines and published my bestselling *Great Global Bucket List,* a book about my favourite adventures in 110 countries on all seven continents. I also wrote a bestseller about travel across my adopted home of Canada. I found that Canadians largely took for granted the wonders in their own backyard. Too often they looked abroad for travel inspiration, and dismissed unique and grossly underrated local experiences. Sound familiar?

The Great Australian Bucket List is not a guidebook. We are drowning in information online, and there's no shortage of websites, apps and publications to tell us *how* to travel. Very few, on the other hand, tell us *why* we should travel in the first place. What might we feel, who might we meet, and what might we learn? I travelled to every Australian state and territory on a feverish quest to unearth the most unique experiences in the country, spanning nature, culture, history, food and active adventure. My experience as a professional traveller allows me to recognise when something is truly worth doing before you die, and I'm honoured to share my *personal* journey with you. Oh yes, travel is as personal as your brand of underwear! Your interests, fitness level, age, mood, appetite, finances and grip on reality are likely entirely different to my own. Tracing my footsteps, you're bound to meet different people, experience different weather and gravitate towards different highlights. It couldn't, and shouldn't, be any other way. Travel, like life, is not a race, and nobody has the right to judge the best of everything, except for themselves. It's important to remember that each adventure is your own, and wherever you are is where you're supposed to be.

Crafting a national bucket list is a big responsibility, and one I do not take lightly. I am but one writer – limited by time, energy and budget – and so you'll likely notice glaring omissions. How could I leave out X, gloss over Y, and not get to Z? I completely agree, but with any luck I'll be able to add new stories to future editions, and definitely to the companion website. As such, I expect *The Great Australian Bucket List* will continue to grow; this is a nation blessed with a full and rich bounty of unique experiences, a country of remarkable people and places, and one that requires a lifetime to explore.

Despite the inevitable backlash, I believe bucket lists are living documents, and a force for positive inspiration. They appeal to all ages, educate us, and as we increasingly isolate ourselves behind our glowing screens, they create meaningful cross-cultural bonds. Whether you're in high school or a retiree, a family, a visitor, or just setting out on your own life adventure, I hope this book tunes you in to the possibilities that surround us. Sometimes, that's the only lucky break we ever need.

robin@robinesrock.com
www.robinesrock.com

How to Use This Book

Practical information shifts with far more regularity than print editions of a book. *The Great Australian Bucket List* includes plenty of information, but very little about prices, accommodation and restaurant options, the best times to visit, and how to get to each adventure. That's why I've created an extensive online companion to the inspirational guide you hold in your hands. Visit *www.aussiebucketlist.com* and you will find all the information you need to follow in my footsteps, along with videos, photo galleries, official links, prize giveaways and the chance to weigh in via social media. In our digital age, I believe inspiration belongs on a page and information belongs online. Each chapter concludes with a direct link to the companion site, although you'll need to register first. It's free, quick and easy (and automatically enters you into Bucket List prize draws). Just remember to add the book code **GIRTBYSEA** when you register to unlock all the experiences.

Disclaimer

Tourism is a constantly evolving industry. Hotels change names, restaurants change owners and activities may no longer be available at all. Records fall and facts shift. While the utmost care has been taken to ensure the information provided is accurate, the author and publisher take no responsibility for any errors, or for any incidents that might occur in your pursuit of these activities.

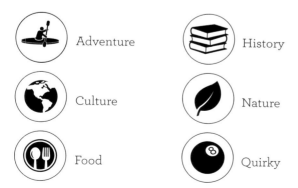

Adventure

History

Culture

Nature

Food

Quirky

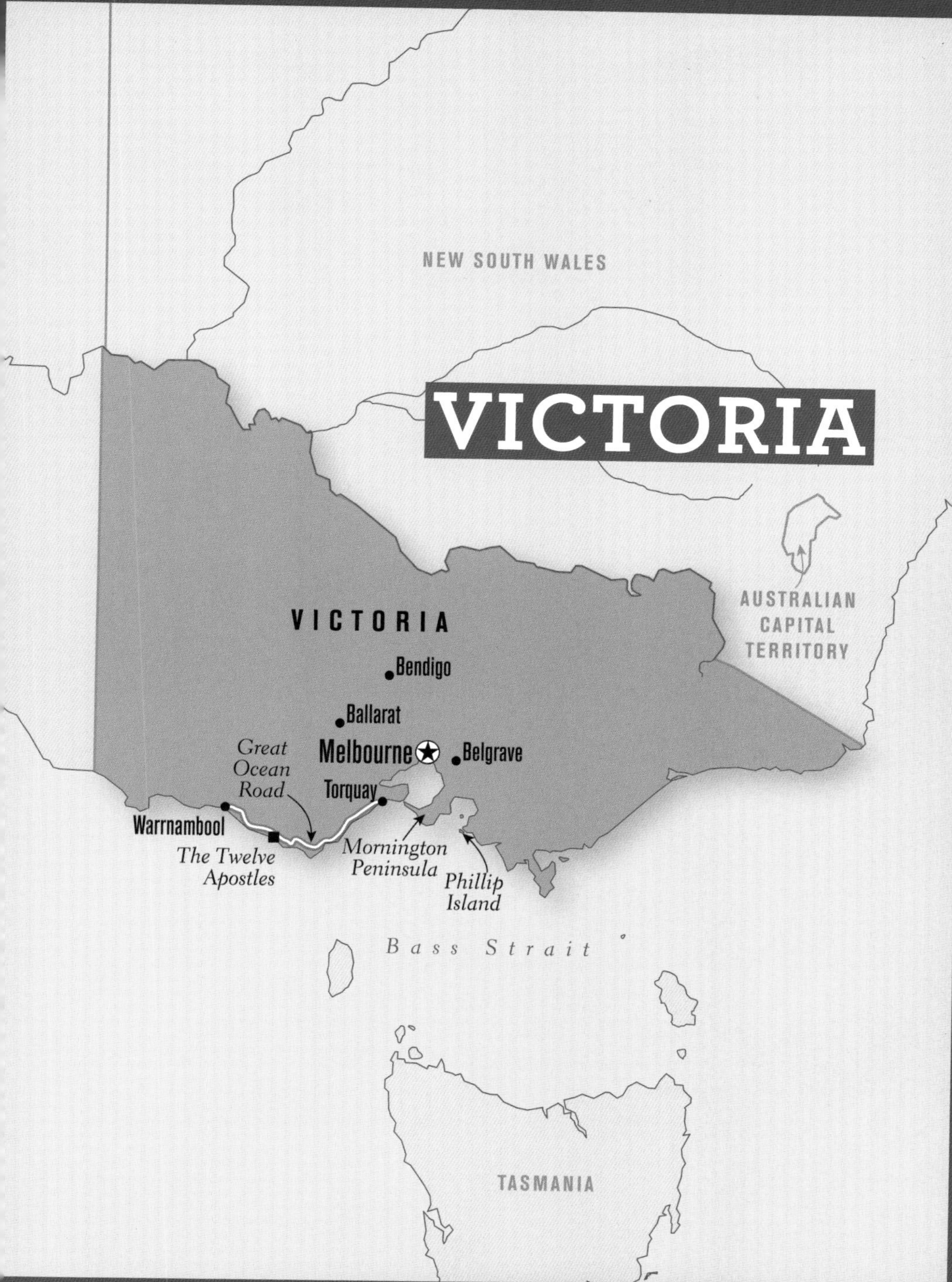

NEW SOUTH WALES

VICTORIA

VICTORIA

AUSTRALIAN
CAPITAL
TERRITORY

● Bendigo

● Ballarat

*Great
Ocean
Road*   Melbourne ✪ ● Belgrave

Torquay ●

Warrnambool ●

*The Twelve
Apostles*   *Mornington
Peninsula*

*Phillip
Island*

Bass Strait

TASMANIA

ALL PLAYERS

MELBOURNE

Cheer at a Major Sporting Event

Some talk of Lords and Sydney, and e'en the Astrodome
Of Manchester, Old Trafford and the Coliseum of Rome
But of all the world's arenas — where'er they made be found —
There's really none that can compare with the Melbourne Cricket Ground
Dr Donald Cordner, former president, MCC

Nearly 90,000 spectators quieten down as an English fast bowler begins his run. It is the first day of the Boxing Day Test, and the opening Australian batsman has slowly edged his way to 99 runs, the very brink of a memorable first-class century. Australia has dominated the Ashes this year, and with the series locked up, the crowd hungers for drama. As the sun bastes the field of the nation's most glorious stadium, the locals get ready to celebrate.

Melbourne is home to Australia's biggest sporting events: The AFL Grand Final, the Australian Open, the Formula 1 Australian Grand Prix and the Melbourne Cup. In the most sports-mad city of the most sports-mad country, no other arena commands such reverence as the Melbourne Cricket Ground, affectionately known as the MCG. The nation's largest stadium is the birthplace of Australian football, international test cricket, and the one-day international. Although Australia is blessed with world-class stadiums from Perth to Brisbane, most visiting tourists wouldn't be able to name them, or associate them with more than one event. Most visitors certainly wouldn't line up like I did for a 75-minute behind-the-scenes tour to explore the Melbourne Cricket Club (MCC) Long Room, the Cricketer's Viewing Platform, the state-of-the-art Ron Casey Media Centre, or the grounds of the hallowed arena itself. We're divided into groups that leave from the entrance of Gate 3 every ten minutes. There are Brits, of course, but also fans from India, South Africa, the United States and even China. Operated by volunteers from the MCC, Australia's oldest sporting club, the tour leads us at a brisk pace through the stadium. In the members-only pavilion, a guide points to a photo of Sachin Tendulkar with the late, great Sir Donald Bradman. An Indian dad lines up his young son for a photo. 'Sir Don was the greatest cricketer the world has ever known!' he tells the boy, who is clearly awed by such information.

The MCC is a private club with 103,000 members worldwide and a waiting list that spans several decades. Members pay an annual subscription that gets them into all MCG events, with a quarter of the stadium's seats reserved for them, should they be required. The Members Pavilion smells like polished wood and old money, adorned with portraits of former legends and leaders, and a massive 7-metre-wide, 2-metre-high tapestry depicting famous sporting characters and events in chronological order. It's fitting for a palace that weaves together the dreams of both elite sports stars and the fans who celebrate them. A dream that, sometimes, can turn into a nightmare.

The opening batsman surely felt the sharp claws of Destiny on his pads and, in a moment of

indecision, softly hits the ball into the hands of a waiting English fielder. Having endured several frustrating Tests under the studded shoe of the dominating home team, English supporters explode like a grenade. The infamous Barmy Army cannot believe their luck: a star Australian batsman caught out for 99. The majority of the crowd are in disbelief. On the first day of a five day Test it's not the most significant wicket to fall, but the MCG crowd has always been among the nation's most empathetic, a 13th man comprised of 96,000 parts. Shoulders slumped, the batsman takes the long stroll back to the pavilion while the English team celebrate their change of fortune.

'The MCG is a shrine, a citadel, a landmark, a totem. It is to this city what . . . the Eiffel Tower is to Paris and the Statue of Liberty is to New York.' I read local sports journalist Greg Baum's words downstairs in the MCG's National Sports Museum. As the museum showcases the legacy, stories and artefacts of Australian sporting history, I hoped it would answer a question often asked around the world: Why are Australians so good at sport? With a relatively small population, Australia often finds itself in the Top 5 medals table at the Olympics, and has won the Cricket World Cup more than any other nation. Over the years, Australian men and women have peaked in international surfing, swimming, tennis, golf, athletics, netball, field hockey, cycling and many other disciplines (as for Aussie Rules football, there's no point having another nation compete, so I guess they just don't bother). All this is celebrated through the museum's outstanding exhibits, divided into different collections, with Halls of Fame, short films and a fun interactive gallery where I discover I'm horrendous at netball, Aussie Rules, soccer and cycling. In the adjacent MCC Museum, I'm greeted by an elderly volunteer named Pat, who looms over me as former AFL players are wont to do. I ask him why Melbourne is the nation's sporting capital, and not, say, Sydney.

'Oh, Melburnians will watch anything!' he replies. No other city has so many major sporting stadiums – the MCG, Melbourne Park, Olympic Park, Flemington Racecourse – so close to the

Australia's Sporting Bucket List

Attending any of the events below is well worthy of a chapter in one's life story.

The Ashes

In our fast-paced world, the slow build-up of drama, heroes and narratives between the English and Australian cricket teams – those great sporting rivals – engages the entire nation. It is held at least once every two years, when the highly symbolic Ashes urn (said to contain the remains of a burnt cricket bail) was first presented to the losing English team in 1882-83.

AFL Grand Final

The pinnacle event of the most popular sport in the country – Aussie Rules – the AFL Grand Final sees the MCG pulsing with an electric atmosphere on the last Saturday in September.

The Melbourne Cup

The whole of Victoria grinds to a halt on the first Tuesday in November for the country's most prestigious thoroughbred horse race. Part of the four-day Spring Racing Carnival, it is the richest two-mile handicap in the world.

Australian Open

Serving up two weeks of action at Melbourne Park every January, the Australian Open is the first of the annual Grand Slam tennis events, and holds the record for the biggest crowds of all the slams.

Bledisloe Cup
Rugby Union's biggest grudge match, between Australia and New Zealand, is a best-of-three series that dates back to the 1930s, although it is now part of the four-nation Rugby Championship.

State of Origin
This best-of-three rugby league series between longstanding rivals NSW Blues and Queensland Maroons is reportedly the most watched domestic sporting event on TV.

Formula 1 Australian Grand Prix
The nation's oldest motor race has been held in Melbourne's Albert Park since 1996, with hundreds of thousands of spectators and visitors attracted to the roars of Formula 1 engines.

Sydney Hobart Yacht Race
No sailing event attracts as much media attention as this 630-nautical-mile race, which kicks off annually on Boxing Day.

CBD and accessible via public transport. According to the *Herald Sun*, visitors to Melbourne are three times more likely to watch a sporting event in Melbourne than in another city. Several years ago I visited Melbourne Park on a short three-day visit to the city, and ticked the Australian Open off my bucket list. It was my first Grand Slam and the enthusiastic, welcoming and supportive crowds were more memorable than the tennis. On another visit, I signed up for the 10-kilometre run attached to the Melbourne Marathon, and finished with an elated sprint into Australia's Sport Temple itself. Seats in the MCG that morning

were mostly empty, but I imagined what it must be to triumph when they are full. Triumph, or fail miserably.

Cricket, they say, is a funny old game. Before the Aussie batsman has walked off the field, a video replay flickers on the giant, high-definition scoreboards. The English team are still hugging each other, the stadium awash in cheers and chatter. Hang on a moment! Is the bowler's foot over the line? Slow motion now . . . and, YES! It's a no-ball! From the nosebleeds to the VIP grandstand, the players box to Level 1, Bay M57, Row AA seat 12, the crowd goes berserk with joy. A few minutes later, the lucky batsman scores an easy single, caps off his century, and runs deep into the pitch, leaping high into the air with emotion. We've *all* swung from hero to zero to hero. Just another bucket list moment then, inside the world's greatest sporting stadium.

START HERE:
aussiebucketlist.com/mcg

Discover a Laneway Masterpiece

R.I.P MALCOLM YOUNG

A young waiter eats his lunch on the laneway steps behind his restaurant kitchen. It's just another afternoon, just another shift. He rests against a wall that is stained and cracked with time, dust and neglect. Centimetres from his *pad thai* bowl is a black and white stencil depicting a cartoonish gloved hand holding a rat by the tail.

'Hey, do you know this is a famous piece of street art?' I ask him.

'It is?' he replies, somewhat curious.

'It's a piece by the legendary French street artist Blek le Rat,' explains my street art guide, Meyer Eidelson. 'It's a message to Banksy, who himself was inspired by Blek le Rat. If it was on paper, it would be worth tens of thousands of dollars.'

Instead, it's on a back alley wall in downtown Melbourne and, tonight, someone might paint over it.

Melbourne's Most Iconic Laneways and Arcades

....

Centre Place: For the bluestone floor and hole-in-the-wall restaurants.

Degraves Street: A bustling, cafe-lined laneway which feels like you've just stepped into Paris.

Block Arcade: The elaborate architecture – said to have been inspired by Milan's famous Galleria Vittorio Emanuelle II – transports you back to another century.

Hosier Lane and AC/DC Lane: If you only have an hour and want to see what the street art fuss is all about, these are the two lanes you need to visit.

Royal Arcade: Australia's oldest surviving arcade has high glass ceilings and the famous statues of Gog and Magog at the southern end.

Hardware Lane: A foodie favourite, this lane is chock-a-block with restaurants and bars, whose al fresco dining areas take up much of the red-brick footpath.

In just under a decade, Melbourne has become one of the world's most important centres for street art. Building on the city's long tradition of counter-culture, Melbourne authorities have encouraged artists to express their creativity in the narrow laneways that carve up the CBD grid. Since the first legal permit was issued in 2007, street art has become an attraction that generates millions in tourism income. It might look like creative anarchy run amok, but there are formalities and etiquette, and a street ethos that Meyer finds both gratifying and ephemeral.

'This is art for the people,' he tells me. 'Not locked up in some gallery. You can't buy it or sell it. This is art that can exist for a day or might stay up for years. The street decides.' To some degree, so does the city.

Street art is characterised by paste-ups (stickers); murals and paintings; sculptures and installations; writing and graffiti; and yarn bombing, where coloured wool is wrapped around trees, posts or street furniture. It is legally permitted in just 20 of the Melbourne CBD's 200 laneways. Every day, young artists vie to

establish their reputation, some-times blanking out someone else's work with their own creative vision. Meyer explains that if a building owner consents, art can appear just about anywhere. If they don't, it is considered illegal, with stiff penalties for those caught spray-paint-red-handed. Still, famous underground artists with street names like Sunfigo, Adnate, Sync, Lush, Swoon and Phibs might prefer an illegal lane where their art will remain hidden, and likely stay up longer. Some artists are paid well by businesses to produce incredibly vivid and expensive murals. Meyer

pulls out a map that illustrates the Golden Mile – the most visited street grid in Australia – and the most popular laneways for promi-nent street art. The lanes look like lines on a circuit board, program-ming the inner city with its globally renowned urban culture.

The most popular place to see street art in action is Hosier Lane, accessed off Flinders Street opposite Federation Square. It is a riot of colour, with tourists posing against giant neon murals. Clearly, street art has been a successful urban strategy for the city. Hosier Lane has been used in various

people – only here, they share lane space with tourists and Instagrammers. Artists themselves jostle for space, deface each other's work and ruin hours of hard labour with a few seconds of snarky tagging. In a messy world of politics, culture, ego and art, few are expected to paint within the lines.

Off Flinders Lane, we turn down AC/DC Lane, where street art is permitted against the walls of the legendary rock 'n' roll club Cherry Bar. Meyer points out hidden gems and the stories behind them. He's a fantastic gallery guide, more so because his gallery is the street. As a writer and historian, he has published more than a dozen books about Melbourne, and his company, Melbourne Walks, hosts regular and custom walking tours. Having visited the world's finest galleries – the Louvre, the Hermitage, the Bardo, the Met, the Tate – I've found you often remember the stories far more than the art itself.

We round the bend, taking pictures of an enormous sponsored work that climbs up half a building. Meyer has been recording street art for many years and, while he is saddened when a personal favourite

films over the years, the kind of inner-city alley that can't be faked by Hollywood. Once voted among the world's top free attractions, Hosier Lane has also seen no shortage of controversy. In 2010 the local council painted over the Banksy originals, and today a glitzy boutique is cashing in on the crowds – directly opposite the offices of an organisation that supports at-risk youth. As with other back alleys in major urban centres, there are homeless

is painted over or wrecked, he believes the beauty of street art is in the act of creation.

'Here sit the rarest and most expensive art pieces in Australia.' He points out the last two remaining Banksy stencils in Melbourne's laneways, two rats on opposite posts of an unassuming doorway. There used to be seven stencils accredited to the world's most famous and secretive street artist. Five have been destroyed by the city to accommodate new businesses.

'They should be in the National Gallery of Victoria,' says Meyer. 'I'm hesitant to tell people exactly where they are, because some troll will just want to destroy them.'

I take a few photos and permit myself to touch a piece of priceless Banksy street art. It is accessible, it is real, it is in your face, and it is now. I can't say I had the same experience when I saw the *Mona Lisa*. We continue into Chinatown and look at art scrawled onto the walls of Croft Lane. After three hours of strolling through laneways and arcades, there's little doubt that street art represents the creative energy beating at the very heart of Australia's cultural capital.

START HERE:
aussiebucketlist.com/streetart

Test Your Nerve In Cell 17

MELBOURNE

I don't believe in ghosts, but I do believe I took a photo of one. On a late-night ghost tour in one of the most haunted houses in spooky Savannah, Georgia, I waited for fellow tourists to clear out of a salon so I could get a clear shot of a large mirror, the only original piece of furniture in the house. Nobody was in the room with me, *especially* not a small woman dressed in 18th century garb who mysteriously appeared in the bottom corner of the mirror when I checked my photos back at my hotel. Gotcha! Ghosts are notoriously allergic to cameras, so I was pretty excited to have another go during a ghost tour inside the Old Melbourne Gaol on Russell Street.

In a country with no shortage of brutal convict history, there's a tangible creep factor visiting the cells and gallows that dispatched notorious figures like bushranger Ned Kelly, murderer (and possible Jack the Ripper) Frederick Bailey Deeming, and 131 others. It's especially palpable at night, when the lights are dimmed, the daytime tourists have cleared out, and writer Trevor Poultney is leading a group of two dozen tourists through the gaol. He informs us that he doesn't need to make up any silly ghost stories to frighten us, since the gaol has plenty of real-life tales to do the trick. In fact, the gaol's consistent paranormal activity inspired Trevor to start the ghost tours in the first place. Of course, nothing has been proved and there's no guarantee you'll actually see anything. I ask two couples in my group why they feel it is a good idea to spend a Saturday night in a dark, haunted 19th century prison block. Both reply that it is a birthday present. Price of a Ghost Tour: $38. Scaring the crap out of your spouse: Priceless.

A purple early evening glow still permeates the cellblock when Trevor begins.

'It's dark in here, and it's going

to get darker. Keep in a tight group, as it's less likely you'll be picked off.' He's joking of course, but he's also a great storyteller, adding just enough bite to his words to keep everyone on edge. It's a ninety-minute tour, mostly conducted outside the cells since they are too small, too dark, too claustrophobic and too damn spooky to spend much time in. Trevor begins with the tale of a site supervisor locking up the museum for the night. Suddenly, she felt someone kick her in the leg. Heavy doors began banging, chains rattled, and she heard groans and screams. Much of the weirdness tends to emanate from Cell 17 on the second level, although no records exist explaining why this would

be the case. Trevor tells us that prisoners were often moved around, documentation has vanished, and conditions were notoriously horrific.

At the rear of the first level, we sit around the lit-up death mask of Ned Kelly, the most infamous bushranger in Australian history. Alongside replicas of the handmade armour Ned wore during his famous shoot-out with the law, Ned's head is the museum's most famous attraction. Gad is it creepy! After the lifeless bodies of the condemned were removed from the gallows, it was common practice for prison officials to shave their heads and cast their death mask for research. It was part of a discredited 19th century practice called phrenology, which believed science could

Australia's Most Haunted Places

There's enough paranormal weirdness in Australia to fill several books (and indeed they have). If ghosts are the kind of phenomena that get you excited, here are more notorious sites worth visiting:

- Fremantle Arts Centre, WA
- Port Arthur, TAS
- Monte Cristo Homestead, NSW
- National Film and Sound Archive, ACT
- Boggo Road Jail, QLD
- Old Adelaide Gaol, SA
- Beechworth Asylum, VIC
- Old Fannie Bay Gaol, NT

physically determine the motivations of criminals and lunatics.

Ned's head looks peaceful enough as Trevor whips out his tablet to show us the three types of ghost photos the jail receives from visitors. There are the fakes, easy to spot and silly to attempt. The second are from people seeing things that simply aren't there, an easy but sincere mistake given the numerous shadows and effects of using a camera flash. 'You paid good money. It's an atmospheric building. We're very suggestible. Of course we want to see a ghost, why else would we be here?' he explains. Out-of-focus, blurry images *do* make great ghost photos, but the apparition is almost always in the eye of the beholder. But, as my own photo from Savannah testifies, not always. The third photos are the anomalies, the ones with no feasible explanation. Trevor shows us the spectre of a man with a hat standing outside Cell 17. We see the wraiths of a woman and child hovering on level three. Visitors who have not taken a ghost tour claim to have physically encountered these people during the day, with some even asking them for directions. At the gallows on level two, the very spot where 129 men and four women took their last breath, Trevor shows us the one photo that continues to freak him out. His own feet appear at the top of the image beneath the rope ... but he was with the visitor who took the photo on the opposite side of the building.

'I think it's a peaceful building,' he whispers. 'Do I believe in ghosts? Things *happen* here, and that's as far as I'll go.'

We have fifteen minutes to roam about freely before the gaol closes. We enter cells to gaze at the haunting death masks of dispatched prisoners, feeling an icy chill lick our necks. We read about the torrid history and conditions of the prison, which operated between 1842 and 1929. Not many visitors are brave enough to enter Cell 17, because Trevor has done a bang-up job spooking us about it. This is where the belligerent man with the hat appears. Where guests *feel something* pushing on them. Where breath gets laboured, and electronic devices go on the blink. This is the one cell guide dogs refuse to enter. With nervous giggles, a few of us walk into Cell 17. With our imaginations in overdrive, the sense of dread in

the cell is unmistakable. I took plenty of photos, of course, and I've poured over them in search of an apparition. As much as I want to believe in life beyond the shadows, I did not strike ghostly photographic gold in the Old Melbourne Gaol. I did, however, encounter a fascinating cultural and architectural history, entertaining stories, unforgettable characters, and a true one-of-a-kind experience. What more could you ask for on a great night out in the city?

**START HERE:
aussiebucketlist.com/
melbournegaol**

Climb Down a Mine Shaft

BENDIGO

Ever feel claustrophobic? Like a lift is too small, the ceilings too low, and you need a little more space to breathe? Then skip to the next chapter, because this one is *definitely* not for you. Everyone else, let's put on our overalls, thick flannel shirt, hard hat and headlamp to tick off the deepest underground mine tour in Australia. For this bucket list experience, you simply cannot get any further down under, Down Under.

My guide today is Ken Bice, a fifth-generation miner with deep Cornish roots in Bendigo. He's serious, strong and deeply committed to sharing Victoria's gold mining legacy, including the nuts and bolts of the mineral's extraction. As we put on gear provided to each guest for Central Deborah Gold Mine's Nine Levels of Darkness tour, Ken discusses Bendigo's rich mining history. Gold was first discovered here in 1851, on what was then a remote sheep station. News of the lucky strike quickly led to a massive rush that attracted more than 40,000 people in just under a

year. It didn't take long for the surface gold to be panned out, but visiting Californians recognised the landscape's potential for a substantial underground gold reef. Once they started blasting tunnels into the quartz rock they discovered the world's richest gold reef, and by the 1880s Bendigo was one of the richest cities in the world. Some 780,000 kilograms of gold have since been mined in the region. I could go on with other fascinating factoids, but we're here to get deep and dirty.

'This is still a working mine, using the same equipment dating back over a century,' explains Ken. He shows us the unnervingly low-tech machinery that operates the shaft lift, with an operator using a clock-like indicator to manually brake us at the right level. Four of us squeeze nose-to-nose into a cage to be lowered to level six, passing the tourists on the family friendly mine tour on level three. In the cage, we are close enough to smell each other's breath, and there's no room for pudginess. It strikes me that miners have to be physically adept merely to get to work, never mind the arduous task of hauling out the rock. It's a relatively smooth descent, which comes to a sudden halt at our destination. Ken rings a bell to confirm our arrival with the lift operator, and we exit into a cave-like room called a plat. From here small teams of miners branched out to drill holes, fill them with dynamite and tunnel in. The rock was pushed out on rudimentary rail lines by a cart (called a truck), and the work continued until the gold ran out, assuming they found some. Ken explains that miners are paid by metres of successful tunnelling, not by the amount of gold they extract, and they get paid regardless of whether they're hauling out waste rock (called mullock) or solid gold. Every step we take into the tunnel took a small team of men painful hours to bore, and we're going to be taking *many* steps. Meanwhile, water drips down from the surface and has to be pumped out or the tunnels get flooded. Dank, dark, wet and cool. It doesn't take too long before sunlight feels like a distant dream.

Ken demonstrates how up to a dozen sticks of dynamite, and later gelignite (both invented by Alfred Nobel, the guy behind his namesake peace prize), are inserted into drilled holes. Fuses, called rat's tails, are connected and lit. Miners take cover, count the blasts, and begin clearing the rubble. A good trucker will push up to 50 or 60 trucks a day loaded with 500 kilograms of rock. In this mine, every 1000 *tons* of rock produced just 500 *ounces* of gold. There was no time to slack off and barely enough to eat on crib break, mining slang for a light meal. Over Cornish pasties, Ken points out that around 40 per cent of Bendigo's early settlers arrived from Cornwall, where the tin and pewter miners were regarded as the best on the planet. We follow their example and descend the adjacent escape shaft to level nine, using steep iron ladders which run alongside the cage lift. I'm pretty lean, but I can barely squeeze into the shaft. Securely attached to a fall line, we descend single file, yelling 'clear!' at each of the 10 narrow platforms along the way. A light shower sprinkles my hard hat, and my gloves get soaked. Stepping down a slippery ladder 228 metres below the surface is not the time to panic. Clear! Clear! Clear! There's no room for a camera, and three points of contact must be on the ladder at all times anyway. Suffice to say it's a relief to finally arrive on level nine, where there's enough room on the plat to just barely stretch out.

Ken shares more stories and history about the region, the lifestyle and the techniques of ancient and modern mining. It would currently cost about $2000 an ounce to extract the gold that still sits in the surrounding reef, but new technology and rising gold prices may mean Bendigo's booming yesteryear can once again become a reality. Mining is obsessed with speed and efficiency, and has evolved from the tap and barrel method – which took hours to drill holes into the rock – to modern mine drills that take mere minutes. Ken positions a hydraulic drill and invites us to give it a go. The noise and vibration is intense. As for any real dangers, accidents are exceedingly rare. Turns out that the number one killer of Bendigo miners in the 19th century was the inhalation of silica, a dust that shredded the lungs of miners as they chiselled their way forward. This is why water in a mine is so important, along with the quality of ventilation. I follow Ken into a passage that gets hotter, darker and seemingly more desperate as we go further.

'What a way to earn a living!' I exclaim, pressed up against a wall.

'People needed to eat,' explains

Ken. 'And it *was* enormously satisfying, to see what you've accomplished, to be the first person ever to step foot here and discover something new.' The simplicity of the task, the brutal physicality, and a camaraderie that determined both your level of compensation and survival bonded men of all stripes.

Ken gets a sparkle in his eye. 'Speak to the old timers and they'll tell you there was no other place they'd rather be.'

We squeeze back into the cage and ascend quickly enough for my ears to pop. Midday sunlight stings my retinas once we reach the surface, where we strip off our damp overalls in the mine's original change rooms. Although never as profitable as other mines in Bendigo, the Central Deborah Gold Mine has done a wonderful job restoring and conserving the city's mining history. The on-site museum, original stamping press, shaft machinery, equipment and tunnel tours take you as deep into Victoria's Gold Rush history as you'll ever need to go. It's a tight squeeze on the Nine Levels of Darkness tour, but there's plenty of space on our bucket list for this captivating underground adventure.

START HERE:
aussiebucketlist.com/minetour

Other Bucket List Mine Tours in Australia

Coal Industry Centre – Singleton, NSW
Learn all about coal mining close to the world's biggest coal-export port, which ships the black stuff from the Hunter Valley's 40-plus coal mines.

The Super Pit – Kalgoorlie-Boulder, WA
Although you won't go underground here, you can learn all about the site of Australia's largest open-cut gold pit mine at the visitor centre.

Hard Times Mine – Mount Isa, QLD
This million-dollar facility takes you 25 metres underground, where you can air drill into the rocks for lead, zinc, silver and copper.

Port Hedland – Pilbara, WA
Iron ore from the world's biggest single open-cut mine journeys along the world's longest privately owned rail network to the world's biggest iron ore port. Giant rocks, giant equipment and a giant experience are on offer at the Port Hedland Visitor Centre.

Soar Above The Twelve Apostles

GREAT OCEAN ROAD

They say the Great Ocean Road is among the world's most beautiful coastal drives. Whoever *they* are, they're wrong. It *is* the world's most beautiful coastal drive, period. The 243 kilometre coastal track, built by soldiers returning from WWI and dedicated to their fallen comrades, is more than just a highlight on the Australian National Heritage List. It is more than just the world's largest war memorial, or a road link between holiday, surf and historical towns. For this is not the *Nice* Ocean Road, or even the *Cool* Ocean Road (we've all driven a few of those). It is *Great*, and you can only truly appreciate what that means when pilot Emma McDonald swings a figure eight above the limestone sentinels known as the Twelve Apostles. Seated in an open-air cockpit as the turbulent Southern Ocean crashes into cliffs, I was literally and, yes, *figure-eightively*, blown away.

For most bucket listers, the Twelve Apostles will be the climax of a road trip that offers enough eye candy for your retinas to start demanding insulin. Commencing in Melbourne, I officially enter Route B100 in the popular surfing town of Torquay, home to Australia's National Surf Museum and iconic surf break Bells Beach. The Surf Coast section of the Great Ocean Road has many attractions like this, and they can keep you busy for a couple days to a couple weeks. Today, crowds are packed into Anglesea for a public holiday beach market, with traffic jammed on either side of the attractive seaside town. Moving on, the road snakes and twists along the coast, making one appreciate the many lookout spots that allow faster traffic to pass and photographers to have a field day. It swings inland by Great Otway National Park, lush with forest and waterfalls. Navigator Matthew Flinders called the next section of the road a 'fearful coastline' – a region known today as the Shipwreck Coast. Hundreds of ships were destroyed here, which is why you won't find boat tours of the Twelve Apostles, Loch Ard Gorge, London Arch and the Grotto, but you will find parking lots with lots

of tour buses. Walking trails take you to the cliff edge or down to the beach, but the winding nature of the road makes it difficult to absorb the true greatness of this coastline. This explains why helicopter tours do a roaring trade; but why tick off one bucket list experience when you can tick off another at the same time? This is how I come to be seated in the open-air cockpit of Adventure Flight Co's single engine 1964 Grumman Ag Cat bi-plane.

'Those must be the Twelve Apostles!' I gulp into my microphone over the roar of the engine up front. It's hard to speak when the wind has stretched a permanent smile on your face.

'No, that's the Bay of Islands,' pipes back Emma, seated in her pilot cockpit behind me. 'Less busy than the Apostles, just as spectacular. Ready for a steep turn?'

When a bi-plane banks hard, it's like being on the world's highest rollercoaster. Your eyeballs take in the view but your stomach wants to see what the fuss is about, so you feel your guts snatching a glimpse from the back of your mouth. Luckily I'm suitably attired in a leather jacket, aviator hat and clear goggles as the plane travels at 70 knots up the limestone and sandstone coastline, carved by nature to aesthetic perfection. Tourists wave at us from various viewpoints and,

up ahead, I finally see the main attraction.

The Twelve Apostles refers to eight large limestone stacks that guard the coast, eroded and battered by the ocean. There used to be more; a large stack collapsed as recently as 2009. Over the years, the stacks have gone by various names – the Sow and Piglets, the Pinnacles – as have the individual sentinels themselves. I certainly can't begrudge anyone experiencing a spiritual moment when you see them from the air. Against a backdrop of windswept bays, beaches and towering cliffs, the stacks look otherworldly, like floating mountains. I've seen sea

The Drowned Apostles

In 2016, geologists at The University of Melbourne announced that they had discovered a range of limestone stacks preserved six kilometres off Victoria's southern coast, submerged beneath fifty metres of water. Rock formations like these would have typically eroded long *before* being submerged, so their existence is something of a mystery. Geologists think they might have been swamped after a dramatic rise in sea levels after the last ice age.

arches and sentinels in Iceland, the Galapagos, Thailand and Newfoundland, but they simply don't stack up to the location and majesty of the Apostles. Which is why the Great Ocean Road is more than just the world's most scenic road trip. It is an essential highlight on anyone's Great Australian Bucket List.

START HERE:
aussiebucketlist.com/
greatoceanroad

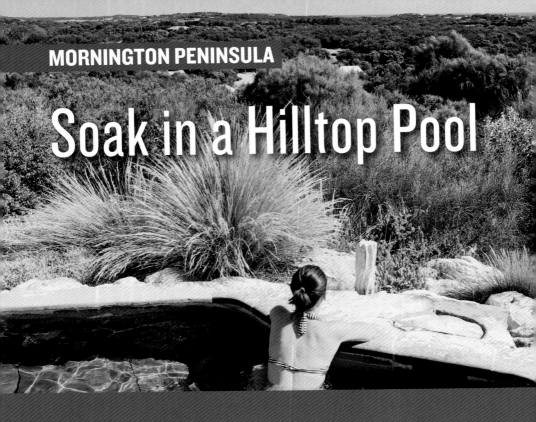

Soak in a Hilltop Pool

Ever dipped a piece of bread in gravy? Watched it soak up all that tasty goodness until it softens into a mush, ready to devour? At Peninsula Hot Springs, your body is that bread and naturally heated geothermal water piped from 637 metres below ground is the gravy. As for the dish on which this plate of relaxation is served: imagine 35 different bathing experiences, elegantly dotted around 42 acres of landscaped bushland. There are wading pools and plunge pools, family pools and hydrotherapy pools, a Turkish hamam and hideaway pools; basically, a pool for every taste and occasion. After a long-haul flight from the other side of the planet, these are the pools I want to be in.

The hot springs are the brainchild of two brothers, Charles and Richard Davidson. Many people travel abroad and wonder why incredible experiences – like, say, a Japanese spa retreat – aren't available at home. After living in Japan for a couple years, Charles not only brought home his Japanese wife, he also brought a vision to redefine the mineral bathing experience in Australia. In 2002, the brothers struck liquid *aaaaaah* deep below the surface of the very peninsula in which they grew up. They discovered naturally occurring sulfate alkaline hot springs with a pH level of 6.8, minerals like potassium, calcium, magnesium,

sodium ions and (thankfully) low amounts of stinky sulphurous gas. Essentially, the very stuff Japanese and European bathers have been crazy about for millennia. Beyond the therapeutic benefits for the body – hot springs are known to promote healthy skin, eliminate toxins, alleviate arthritis and reduce blood pressure – one finds the mental joy of peace, tranquillity and imagining your body as bread dipped in gravy.

Shaded by trees on a hot summer day, I alternate between several pools in the bathhouse, including a popular cave pool and stimulating hydrojet pool. My wife visited the nearby Spa

Dreaming Centre for an hour-long Peninsula Vine Massage, during which she was rubbed down with an antioxidant grape balm (another great use for the locally grown shiraz). I asked her to take mental notes about the experience for this chapter, but she emerged with a huge smile and dreamy look of love that husbands should just appreciate without asking for details and ruining the moment.

There's a whole category of travel journalism devoted to spas and, to be honest, there are only so many ways to describe soft music, fluffy bathrobes, ambient lighting, fragrant scents and people relaxing. Over the years, I've been whipped by birch leaves in Siberia and watched my hair freeze while soaking in a hot pool in a -40 degree Canadian winter. Three men covered me in hot oil for the Ayurvedic massage of my life in Goa, while in Taiwan a 'fire doctor' used open flames to rub the tension out of my back, leaving grill marks

Bucket List Thermal Springs in Australia

- Peninsula Hot Springs, VIC
- Hastings Caves and Thermal Springs, TAS
- Hepburn Springs, VIC
- Dalhousie Springs, SA
- Innot Hot Springs, QLD
- Mataranka Thermal Pool and Bitter Springs, NT
- Lightning Ridge Bore Baths, NSW
- Zebedee Hot Springs, WA

in the process. Georgian men have walked on my back in 17th-century domed bathhouses and, like many a backpacker, I've felt the hard elbow and knee of a Thai masseuse. From Mauritius to Budapest, I've done my share of the spa thing and therefore do not say the following lightly: With its creative vision, outstanding service, gorgeous location and wealth of treatment options, Peninsula Hot Springs is my bucket list spa of choice. As it's open until 10pm, you can visit late in the day for the chance to soak in the Hilltop Pool, admiring a peach-purple sunset as the stars begin to strobe over the fields and valleys. Take a deep breath. Be the bread. Feel the gravy.

START HERE:
aussiebucketlist.com/
peninsula-hotsprings

Pan For Gold

As far as we know, there are no time machines in Australia. No contraptions that, for a price, will transport you to another era. Fortunately, there *is* Sovereign Hill, where the dial is permanently set to the mid-1850s, when the Central Victorian town of Ballarat was booming. Thanks to one of the biggest gold rushes in history, Ballarat exploded into a 'Golden City' of more than 60,000 people after gold was discovered in nearby Buninyong in 1851. Lured by the prospect of striking it rich, diggers came from around the world: Europe, Asia and North America (whose miners became known as Balifornians). Within a few short years, the state of Victoria was providing one third of the world's total gold output, allowing Australia's colonial ruler Great Britain to pay off her debts and fund the greatest empire expansion the world had ever seen.

Gold deposits ran rich and deep. Diggers, along with those who had the foresight to profit off them, flooded in. Australia's population tripled in size as a result. By 1896, Victoria had produced a staggering 61,034,682 ounces of gold, which at current gold prices works out to around $80 billion dollars. Infrastructure boomed, particularly transport links from goldfield centres to the capital city of Melbourne. The gold rush was also instrumental in the development of Australia's national identity, where concepts like mateship and *a fair go* were forged above and beneath the surface.

Opened in 1970, Sovereign Hill has become one of Victoria's top visitor attractions. Spanning 25 hectares, the open-air museum is located in a suburb of Ballarat, about ninety minutes' drive from Melbourne. The museum recreates an 1850s mining town in painstaking detail, including a theatre, wheel-making factory, lolly shops, livestock paddocks, houses, mine facilities and various storefronts. All are staffed and brought to life by enthusiastic costumed re-enactors, who are eager to interact and share their characters' stories. My guide

Benjamin greets me on the busy Main Street. His long beard proves the strong connection between modern hipsters and 19th century gold miners. There's a wealth of information on offer, but I long ago discovered that memorable experiences arise from being able to interact with our surroundings – especially in a place like this. This is where Sovereign Hill excels. We start off in a photographic studio where my family is invited to dress up in historical costumes and pose for a black-and-white portrait that looks like the real deal. It's a great way to kick things off, literally feeling the past against our skin. For a moment, it feels like we've entered Westworld, an uncanny recreation of history where anything

is possible (although refreshingly not prone to rogue killer robots). Dozens of demonstrations take place throughout the museum at all times of day, ensuring there is always something to see and do. We watch the production of wagon wheels in a large wheelhouse factory using century-old machinery. Exploring some of the authentically furnished houses on Speedwell Street, we catch the Red Coats marching to the square, where they will fire their loud muskets to the squeals of tourists. At the Gold Pour, we learn how this precious yellow metal is extracted, watching it form and cool into a small, three-kilogram bar worth more than $160,000. My kids are more impressed with patting the friendly goats and chickens, and the Clydesdale

horses that pull passenger carriages around the streets. There are two mine tours on-site, and all visitors are encouraged to take up the pan and shake it for gold in the Sovereign Hill creek. It's hard work but a few sprinkles of gold dust collected in a souvenir bottle are ample reward. The scent of melting sugar permeates the sweet-making facility, where we watch traditional lollies like raspberry drops being

pressed. We are surprised to hear that, given the high price of sugar in the 1850s, sweets were an expensive treat reserved for adults. We catch a rehearsal in the theatre, where actors recite lines from a play about the famous Eureka Stockade, a seminal moment in Australian history.

'Daddy, when are we going to go back in the time machine to our time?' asks my four-year-old daughter. Popping into the modern bathroom or seeing a credit card machine in the bakery seems almost jarring. Granted, the overall experience is quite manicured and romanticised, but Sovereign Hill still weaves a wonderful historical spell. With the recent upsurge in the price of gold, mining continues in the Ballarat region and visitors might hear underground blasting from a modern gold mine nearby. Like all booms, the Victorian gold rush quickly ran its course. The vast majority of new arrivals did not find their fortune, but they did help forge a nation. The discovery of gold in eastern Australia led to the creation of vital national infrastructure, the abolition of convict transports and the establishment of political representation. Sovereign Hill gives us an intriguing glimpse into the past, one we can treasure long after returning to the future.

**START HERE:
aussiebucketlist.com/
sovereignhill**

Gold-panning Tips

- Fill your pan halfway to three-quarters full with silt. Pick out the bigger rocks, looking for nuggets as you do so.
- Find a spot where the river flows strongly enough to carry away the silt from your pan. Sit on a log or rock unless you're particularly flexible.
- Dip your pan in the water, using your fingers to sort the dirt and moss. Heavy gold will sink to the bottom of your submerged pan.
- Shake the pan while it's submerged, breaking up the silt even more, allowing any gold to sink and the silt to rise to the top.
- Tilt the pan downwards, shaking the pan some more.
- Submerge the pan again, shaking it up and down and left to right, allowing the river to wash away the lighter material. Tilt occasionally, rinse and repeat. Keep checking to see if any gold has sunk to the bottom.
- Use tweezers or a wet finger to extract your treasure.

Ride a Vintage Railway in the Forest

DANDENONG RANGES

Gather up your raincoats and tell the kids that Thomas the Tank Engine is expecting company. *Fffff! Fffff! Ffff!* There's something distinctly Hogwartian about stepping into a restored vintage carriage pulled by a narrow gauge steam locomotive. Especially when the train's open windows look out over the verdant fern gullies and farmlands of the Dandenong Ranges.

At just 762mm wide, the Puffing Billy Railway was built in 1900 to provide a low-cost rail system for the villages and hamlets of this pretty mountain community. Ironically, a low-cost narrow gauge system is limited in what it can transport. Together with the rise of horseless carriages – otherwise known as cars – and the construction of bigger railways nearby, the unprofitable Puffing Billy became increasingly obsolete. In 1954, a landslide blocked off a portion of the tracks and it was decided to shutter the operation for good. Like so many other small railways before it, Puffing Billy might have become an obscure footnote in Australian railway history, but then something funny happened on the way to the scrapyard. A newspaper reporter in Melbourne was looking for something to write about for his family column. Someone suggested he ask Victoria Railways if they'd run a farewell trip on Puffing Billy. In a curious case of a railway bureaucrat making a fun decision, the Railway agreed. Around 30,000 people showed up to bid farewell to the train, which was a little problematic as only 2500 passengers were able to get tickets. Another farewell event was held two weeks later and even more people showed up. Encouraged by the public's interest,

a preservation society was formed to operate and run the train on weekends and holidays. Despite a few ups and downs over the years, Puffing Billy has continued to roll as one of Victoria's most endearing attractions.

Today I've got a ticket to ride the train from Belgrave to Lakeview. One of the fifteen locomotives in operation pulls into the station, puffing steam from its coal-fired engine, as the nostalgic smell of soot fills the air. The conductors, station managers, porters, signalmen and stewards are all volunteers. One of the conductors tells me he's retired,

loves trains, meeting people and being in the Dandenongs. With 900 volunteers working at the railway, clearly he's not alone. Together they make the atmosphere fun and fitting for a leisure ride. Meanwhile, the restored and operational narrow gauge locomotives in use look like they've chugged out of the pages of a children's book.

Trainspotters will rejoice in the technical aspects of the steam engines: the boiler pressure; cylinder diameter; tractive effort; and maximum axle load. Since I'm not one of them, I'll merely describe the experience of gazing out the window as the train crosses

Race Against the Train

Are you faster than a not-quite-speeding train? Each year, The Great Train Race challenges thousands of runners to beat Puffing Billy in a hilly 13.5 kilometre race through the Dandenong Ranges. It's a challenging route that traverses tarmac, dirt roads and trails, with strict cut-off times. Top runners usually beat the train, but most participants will find themselves eating Puffing Billy's soot.

the scenic Monbulk Creek trestle bridge and steams into dense forest. Most passengers will take the one-hour trip from Belgrave to Lakeside, visit a tearoom, stretch their legs, and return. Others might continue onwards to Gembrook,

which takes just under two hours one-way. I chat to fellow passengers and volunteers, wave to cars and locals who live along the tracks, spot some wildlife and zone out to that ambling motion unique to old-world travel. The railway also offers dining experiences in fully enclosed carriages, as well as theme nights with murder mysteries, music, dining and dancing. As technology continues to make the world bigger-better-faster-smarter, it's easy to go off the rails. Kids, railway enthusiasts – and the rest of us, too – should relish every opportunity we get to take the slow train.

START HERE:
aussiebucketlist.com/puffingbilly

Watch the Penguins Parade

Each year, three and a half million people visit Phillip Island to watch the world's largest colony of little penguins emerge from the sea. This says bucketloads about the appeal of penguins to the general public, and to bucket listers in particular. For many visitors, this nightly spectacle is both the highlight of their trip to Australia and one of the reasons why they visit the country in the first place. What is it about these beady-eyed, pot-bellied flightless birds, graceful in the sea yet awkward on land? Perhaps we can trace the popularity of penguins to the documentary *March of the Penguins*. More likely it's because no other bird looks so distinctly human, and because they are so damn cute. Especially the blue-and-white-feathered little penguins, smallest of the species, weighing around one kilogram and growing just 33 centimetres tall. Having the nickname 'fairy penguins' doesn't hurt either, especially with kids.

Some 32,000 breeding adults live around Phillip Island, spending most of their time at sea before returning to the same nesting beach burrows at sunset. A highly polished conservation effort ensures that up to 3800 people can see the penguins each night, gathered in stadium-like seating or more exclusive areas, such as an underground viewing platform. Tonight, there's a tizzy of anticipation as the clock approaches 9pm. Visitors jostle for position, overtired kids are howling, and the wind blowing over the peninsula has a nip to it even after a warm summer day.

Most of us arrived this afternoon to explore other attractions on the bridge-linked island first. We strolled the raised treetop boardwalks to encounter Australia's most beloved marsupial at the Koala Conservation Centre. Lazily sleeping in the nooks of eucalyptus trees, the koalas were not the least bit bothered by the many selfie sticks and zoom-lens cameras. With my kids in tow, I stopped in at the lovely Churchill Island Heritage Farm, enjoying demonstrations of sheep shearing, cow milking and whip cracking. For visitors who

live in big urban sprawls, watching a sheep lose its wool (or a tourist accidentally whack himself with a whip) is certainly enjoyable. Phillip Island Nature Parks has done a cracking job filling up your time while you wait for the main event. At the western tip of the island is the Nobbies Centre, offering a network of coastal boardwalks, boat tours, an impressive Antarctica exhibit complete with augmented reality, and, of course, a restaurant and gift shop. One and a half kilometres offshore lies the Nobbies rock formation, as well as Seal Rocks, home to Australia's largest colony of fur seals. The views from here across Bass Strait are spectacular. Soon the tour bus engines fire up, as the crowds make their way to the Penguin Parade, five minutes down the road. The sun is setting, and the curtain is almost up for the main event. What are those shadows emerging from the surf? Is that? Could it be?

Penguins. Huddled together for safety, a group is walking up the beach with their comical waddling gait. Their pathways are well-trodden, and there's plenty of space for visitors to see them at close range. Since camera flashes or mobile phone lights can disorientate the penguins, all photography is prohibited during the parade. In our digital world, where nothing happens unless there's a photo to prove it, I enjoy this rare moment of collective now-ness, a bucket list experience that refreshingly must exist on everyone's internal memory card.

Penguins without the Crowds

Phillip Island packs in the crowds, but it's not the only place to encounter the world's smallest penguin in its natural habitat. You'll also find them waddling about in:

- Low Head / Lillico Beach / Bruny Island, TAS
- Granite Island, SA
- Penguin Island, WA
- Kangaroo Island, SA
- Manly Wharf, NSW

START HERE:
aussiebucketlist.com/
penguinparade

NORTHERN TERRITORY

QUEENSLAND

WESTERN AUSTRALIA

Coober Pedy •

SOUTH AUSTRALIA

NEW SOUTH WALES

Barossa Valley ■

⭐ Adelaide

Port Lincoln •

Penneshaw ■

Victor Harbour •

Kelly Hill Caves ■

Kangaroo Island

Fleurieu Peninsula

VICTORIA

Naracoorte •

Great Australian Bight

Mount Gambier •

SOUTH
AUSTRALIA

Stand Beneath a Snarling Lion

MONARTO ZOO

When I heard that Monarto Zoo had launched a lion cage experience inspired by and modelled on shark cage diving in Port Lincoln (see page 64), I admit I was a little sceptical. Lions in zoos don't do much but sleep and laze about in the sun, but claiming to be a world first, Lion 360 demands further investigation.

Located an hour's drive from Adelaide, Monarto is a 1500-hectare sanctuary billed as the world's largest open-range zoo, operated by the not-for-profit Zoos South Australia conservation charity. It is home to more than 500 animals, including the country's largest herd of giraffe, endangered southern white rhinoceros, chimpanzees, cheetahs and hyenas. Unlike your typical zoo, most of the animals are kept in massive enclosures, with visitors accessing them via buses or viewing platforms. Driving along the M1 from Adelaide and seeing expanses of grassland reminded me distinctly of the African bush; the fact that both regions lie on similar latitudes is one of the reasons why African animals thrive in the breeding programs at Monarto. The king of the bush – erroneously and too often called the *jungle* – is, of course, the lion. Few apex predators inspire such fascination with the general public. Lions are a symbol of strength and pride, courage and power. Throughout history, lions have adorned national flags and family crests, sports teams and military parades. Modern marketers use lion imagery to enhance their products – from homewares to cars. Typically, Australians have only encountered real lions in three situations: in a zoo enclosure, on a safari abroad, or on television (usually accompanied by the soothing tones of David Attenborough). Monarto Zoo's Lions 360 experience hopes to change that.

Zoos SA has constructed a special cage from which zookeepers and visitors get closer to fully grown lions than any sane human being would ever want to be. Monarto times its Lions 360 experience with the two daily feeding sessions, ensuring the big cats are

above our heads, staring at us like kids in a lolly shop. The novelty of being able to look up and see the belly of a lion right above me is quickly accompanied by the thought of said lion defecating on my head (the park assures me this hasn't happened . . . yet). Hearing a lion growl right near your face is not unlike standing behind a jet engine ready for take-off. It resonates in a distinctly primal manner, as hundreds of thousands of years of evolution kick in to remind me that hungry lions don't want a cuddle, and I should probably start running really fast. Of course, great care has been taken to ensure visitors are perfectly safe, something you'll want to remind yourself of when feeling the hot breath of a hungry lioness. In a homage to safari parks, a model Land Cruiser pokes out of the cage, so you can also observe the pride through a reinforced car window. At one point, a massive paw comes out of nowhere and slaps the window, scaring the scat out of my four-year-old daughter, who is at the driver's wheel. She never quite recovers, and the jury is out on whether the experience will lead her down the path of conservation, or give her a lifelong

active, curious and engaged. With careful consideration of the pride's diet and habits, handlers limit their meat, which is hand-fed through the cage with metal tongs. Having already ticked off shark cage diving, I didn't think the lions would inspire nearly as much awe or thrill. And then I walked into the cage.

Almost immediately, eight large lionesses approach us. We're advised not to place our hands or fingers anywhere *near* the cage itself, as the lions will be more than happy to remove them as part of their morning snack. Two lions hop

lion phobia. Certainly, no adult or kid will leave the cage unaffected, and you'll never regard these magnificent creatures in quite the same way again.

Once the feeding is over, the pride is content to stay close, observing us hairless apes gathered in a cage. This experience is a world first, and I expect safari parks around the world are taking note. Yes, the lions are encouraged to participate with food, but so are sharks for a cage diving experience. Yes, it's not a safari on the plains of Africa, but how many animal encounters put you in the cage while the animals can wander about? Yes, Monarto is technically a zoo, but it's also an important sanctuary that raises funds to support rangers in their constant fight against poachers. And yes, the Lions 360 experience is as bucket-list-worthy as cage diving with great white sharks.

START HERE:
aussiebucketlist.com/lions360

Adelaide's Urban Wildlife

Walking into the Garden of Unearthly Delights, it feels like I've stepped inside a neon circus, a warped rabbithole, a wild party and a steampunk festival. For thirty-one days during February and March, the Adelaide Fringe wows crowds with the world's second-largest arts festival (only Edinburgh is bigger). Thousands of performance artists descend on the city to perform in theatres, pop-up venues, tents, warehouses, galleries and bars. Kicking off with a lively street parade, the festival brings the city alive – buildings downtown are beautifully illuminated, and hotspots like the Garden of Unearthly Delights in Rundle Park host dozens of stages, food trucks, beer gardens and rides for the kids.

Dive in a Sinkhole

MOUNT GAMBIER

Anyone who dives or snorkels knows the importance of visibility. Many destinations will boast about 20 metres, 30 metres, or even 50 metres! That's an impressive distance, but nothing comes remotely close to what you will see in the spring-fed limestone ponds outside of Mount Gambier. It's the result of a rare geological phenomenon whereby the bones, shells and coral from millennia of marine life settled on the bottom of the ocean. The sea level dropped, and rain and a rising water table eroded calcium carbonate to create a labyrinth of underground caves and sinkholes. Something similar happened in Mexico's Yucatan Peninsula and in Florida, USA. Likewise, Mount Gambier offers the some of the best freshwater and cave diving on the planet.

The caves attract that rare breed of technical diver who enjoys the challenge of squeezing into tiny, dark places with a wafer-thin margin for human or equipment error. Cave divers from near and far have long explored South Australia's Limestone Coast and, thanks to the bold move of one of Australia's top cave diving experts, the subterranean and aquatic wonders of Mount Gambier have now been opened up for the rest of us too.

Reef 2 Ridge has only been open a couple weeks when I walk through the front door. Holding her nine-month-old daughter, Laura Main is on the phone booking dives. Her husband Rob is organising students for an advanced cave diving certification, dealing with walk-ins, *and* booking me in for a dive at a legendary local sinkhole. Sensing a clear demand for dives in the area, Rob and Laura packed up their home in New South Wales, drove to Mount Gambier, opened a store and, suddenly, what was once a local secret is now a must-do on the Great Australian Bucket List.

I am not a cave diver, but I've thought about submerging myself in a sinkhole ever since swimming in the impossibly cobalt-coloured water of Mexico's cenotes. You can see a similar colour at Mount Gambier's Blue Lake (see page 53). Limestone

sinkholes look like Mother Nature poured blue dye in an over-chlorinated swimming pool. It looks like an advert for overpriced mineral water. Fortunately, with just an Open Water certification you can join Rob and his team at Kilsby Sinkhole, a large, deep sinkhole located south of town on a private sheep farm. At more than 70 metres deep, it's been used by the Navy to test sonar buoys and by South Australian Police to train divers.

On the way to the site – which has strict access protocols – my divemaster, Ben, points out other sinkholes. All I see are endless, flat sheep farms, but we pull over to see a few holes in the ground filled with sparkling freshwater. When we arrive at Kilsby, Rob is putting several cave diving students through their certification paces. Like me, half a dozen leisure divers have been kitted out in full-length wetsuits for a descent in and around the light zone. With a constant temperature of around 16 degrees, the sinkholes lead into a spiderweb of tunnels that more experienced divers can explore, but we're here for a far less challenging adventure. We hop off the platform and descend far quicker than we would in saltwater. Initially, the lack of sediment and sea dust in the water is strange. I flipper over to my dive buddies before realising I'm already at 25 metres and my dive buddies are the other technical guys. Rob points me back in the right direction: up and towards the dancing beam of summer sunshine. I follow Ben over a lip of rock and watch other divers buoyantly enjoying a disco-ball light show as the sun's rays penetrate the water up to 40 metres. Even though Kilsby is devoid of any life, it's a moment that quickly leapfrogs some of my most memorable coastal dives.

'Kilsby is all about scale, but no life. Ewens is much smaller, but it's all about the life,' Rob explains back on the surface. We drive back to the dive shop, wolf down a pie and climb into the dive van for the short

drive to Ewens Ponds Conservation Park. Three basin-shaped ponds, each about 10 metres in depth, are connected by shallow channels. Constantly fed by fresh water that bubbles up from the limestone base, the ponds' clarity allows plants to grow fully submerged, some of which cannot be found anywhere else in the world. It's a deeply fragile ecosystem, home to the critically endangered Glenelg spiny crayfish and the endemic Ewens Pygmy Perch. A sign at the entrance invites scuba divers and snorkellers to enter, but swimmers and floatation devices are strictly prohibited.

After a quick tutorial on how to leave as small an impact as possible, I escape the midday heat by sliding into the water, lowering my mask, looking down and oh . . . my . . . God! You've seen green, but never like this. You've seen blue, but never like this. You've seen sunlight in water, but never like this. It's been only seconds, but snorkellers on the surface are already high-fiving. Our small group of divers descend, watching springs bubble and the sunlight breakdance on different leafy plants. Reeds glimmer with

reds and oranges, and one patch of plants looks like an enormous rocket salad. Back on the surface, our instructor Safari tells us it's about to get better. If the pools are a party of plant life, the channels that link them are a full-blown riot. A gentle current guides us forward for several minutes of full-sensory delight. Plants brush our masks and wetsuits, before we soft launch into the next technicolour pool. With the sun high overhead, nature is putting on a magical show.

The final channel is longer and denser with aquatic life, while the final pool teems with schools of fish. It's as rich a diving experience as you'll have anywhere, especially for those looking for something different. Plus, at only 10 metres deep, there's no worrying about decompression sickness or running out of air. Snorkellers of all ages will love it, too. This place is picturesque proof of the importance of visibility and I hope it's now plain for all to see: Mount Gambier, a small town in South Australia, offers some of the world's best bucket list dives.

START HERE:
aussiebucketlist.com/mtgambier

The Blue Lake

I've come across a few blue lakes in my travels, and a few more blue holes. Seeing Mount Gambier's Blue Lake for the first time . . . well, it kind of makes a mockery of everything else. The lake is blue-blood royal blue. A throat-flicking chilly blue. As blue as the mocking glare of an Ice Queen, as blue as a Smurf holding its breath. Expecting something a little more ho-hum, the first time I glimpsed it I almost drove my car (an Everest blue) off the scenic road that surrounds it. 'That's *blue*!' said my toddler daughter, who has a knack for stating the obvious. Sitting in the crater of a dormant volcano just a few minutes' drive from the city centre, the Blue Lake is up to 75 metres deep, and more than a kilometre wide. No-one is allowed to swim in it, as it supplies Mount Gambier with high-quality drinking water. It is only blue in the summer months (from December to March), when calcium carbonate in the water reflects the sun's blue wavelengths. The rest of the year it's a far less impressive grey. There are several viewpoints to admire this incredible lake, which – I'd like to remind you – is really, *really* blue.

Feast under an Apple Tree

FLEURIEU PENINSULA

Ben Neville brings out a silver tray loaded with thick slabs of Black Angus porterhouse steak on the bone, dry-aged for four weeks. My mouth would salivate, but it's been doing that all morning on the Fleurieu Peninsula, a fine region for fine living about an hour's drive south of Adelaide. Named in honour of a French explorer, the Fleurieu (which locals pronounce something akin to *Floorie-oh*) encompasses the world-renowned McLaren Vale wine region. Picture rolling farmland running into sunset-red cliffs that overlook the silver beaches of your dreams. Too many visitors merely drive through the region on their way to Kangaroo Island; but, as Ferris Bueller so endearingly reminds us: 'Life moves pretty fast. If you don't stop and look around once in a while, you could

Ben, a strapping and boisterous former rugby player, doesn't want you to miss it either. His personable Off Piste 4WD Tours take you right into the heart of the region and if it feels like you're being shown around by a proud local, that's because you are. Prior to studying in the UK and travelling to more than 70 countries, Ben was raised opposite shiraz vines in a restored 1890s butter factory, now the Neville family home. He knows the region's highlights, side roads and most memorable characters just as surely as he knows how to pilot a four-wheel drive up and down the treacherously steep hills of Onkaparinga River National Park.

It's our first port of call after being picked up in downtown Adelaide, and Ben's got exclusive rights to operate recreational vehicle tours within the park. We spot Western grey kangaroos and dip down into an ancient canyon alongside the second-longest river in the state. It's morning-tea time, so out comes the bubbly, alongside biodynamic double brie, fresh bread and fruit from local producers, all served on a red chequered tablecloth. Surrounded by eucalypts, it's a scene that provides nourishment for the mind and belly.

Ben explains how McLaren Vale has the most detailed geological map of any wine region in the world, which gives growers and winemakers incredible flexibility to produce sub-flavours and outstanding product. With hot, dry summers, varied soils and the influence of coastal winds blowing off the Great Southern Ocean, the region is home to more than eighty wineries known for their bold dry reds, especially shiraz, grenache and cabernet. It's not quite as globally famous as the Barossa, but then Barossa wineries aren't a stone's throw from a magnificent coastline,

nor do they boast a catapult that shoots watermelons.

'Greg Trott was definitely one of the great eccentrics,' explains Simon Burley, the marketing manager at Wirra Wirra. A legend within the Australian wine community, Trott founded the Wirra Wirra winery, raised the profile of the region's food and wine industry, and mobilised growers to build McLaren Vale's reputation. He was also known for wild ideas – an impressive 'woodhenge' of threaded redgums; a wooden catapult to shoot watermelons at barrels – and frequent disappearances. In the private tasting room, Simon elaborates

over a quaffable glass of Church Block, Wirra Wirra's award-winning blend of cab-sav, shiraz and merlot. 'Greg went into town one day and disappeared. He turned up watching a cricket game . . . in England. This was the days before smartphones and email, mind you. Which is why we named our sauvignon blanc 'Hiding Champion'.' Trott passed away in 2005 but his humour, vision and great wine lives on.

We hop into the four-wheel drive and Ben navigates along unsigned gravel roads that slice through vineyards bursting with shiraz ready for harvest. He points out various spots of interest, including an Aboriginal burial ground, and describes his upbringing in the region with the sort of enthusiasm that can only make you jealous. Especially when he pulls the car into a field, rolls down his window and plucks a juicy fig and a crunchy pear right off the trees, without shifting from his driver's seat. Ten minutes later, we're seated at an outdoor wooden table beneath a Bramley apple tree. Sandwiched between rows of grapevines and the Neville homestead, it's an impossibly picturesque spot, the kind of place you only see in tourist brochures. Lorraine, Ben's mum, brings out fresh salads and olives, and I instantly feel at home.

I personally believe that wine owes as much to the atmosphere in which it is consumed as it does to oak barrels, ageing and grape quality. In this setting, my glass of shiraz never tasted better.

Ben continues his day tour with a drive directly onto the six-kilometre-long Silver Sands Beach, which is buttressed by cliffs and turquoise seas calmed by Kangaroo Island offshore. He puts on some music and, as we skirt the lapping waves, I gaze at the horizon while having an undeniably bucket list moment. It's

been a day of fine and unpretentious wine, fine and unpretentious dining, and fine and unpretentious people. Exploring the Fleurieu is a gourmet experience that perfectly showcases the underrated and undeniably good life on offer in South Australia.

START HERE:
aussiebucketlist.com/fleurieu

Life is Like a Box of Chocolates

The feasting is exceptional in South Australia, and pretty sweet too. Adelaide's Haigh's is the oldest family-owned chocolate maker in the country, known worldwide for crafting exceptional treats. Pop in to their factory on Greenhill Road for a free tour of the facility, samples of the many varieties of chocs, and discounted 'seconds' that taste great but never made the chocolate box.

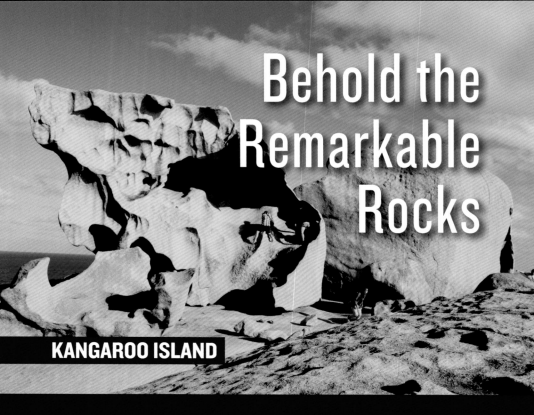

Behold the Remarkable Rocks

KANGAROO ISLAND

There's no shortage of reasons to visit Australia's third-largest island. Kangaroo Island has a postcard-ready, rugged coastline, white sandy beaches, national parks, caves and abundant wildlife encounters. None of this is particularly unique but – as it's all contained within a manageable chunk of land 55 kilometres wide and 155 kilometres long – KI is nothing less than a greatest hits package of Australian travel, with a few distinctly bucket list experiences all its own.

We begin our journey with a scenic ninety-minute drive from Adelaide to Cape Jervis, where the daily Sea-Link ferries depart for KI. Expect twisty roads through leafy country towns, sparkling views of the Mount Lofty Ranges and the calm St Vincent Gulf. A forty-five-minute ferry crossing is required to reach the small town of Penneshaw, and suddenly you're on an island that looks . . . very similar to the mainland. Except KI had no human habitation for thousands of years and dozens of plants evolved slightly differently. Despite the rolling farmland, it feels wilder, justifiably more remote. The island is bigger than the nations of Samoa, Mauritius, Barbados, Luxembourg and Singapore but, with only 4400 permanent residents, it has about one person per square kilometre. As for the influx of tourists, ferry traffic beelines for the island's most popular attractions, starting with the Clifford Honey Farm. KI's isolation ensures it holds the last remaining population of pure-bred Ligurian bees in the world, a docile swarm originally from Italy and prized for their honey. Once you visit a honey farm and learn about the process of honey production, it's difficult to view the gloopy golden goodness in quite the same way again.

Our next stop is the Island Pure Sheep Dairy, where we learn that sheep milk contains twice the calcium of cow's milk, makes sharp and tasty cheese, and is suitable for people who are allergic to dairy. More importantly, we discover that placing impossibly cute lambs up front to play with all but guarantees a memorable experience. A sheep's hop away is the international-award-winning distillery Kangaroo Island Spirits. The gin garden is feeling festive

this afternoon as co-founder Sarah Lark pours a couple of samples for tasting. If the surname sounds familiar, it's because her brother-in-law is the Tasmanian whisky legend Bill Lark (see page 170). Clearly, theirs is a family with a knack for crafting outstanding spirits. The distillery's O'Gin is infused with the island's native coastal daisy, while its old-school Whiskey Barrel Gin and Old Tom Gin have swept awards around the world. All provide a great excuse to sit in the garden, chat with locals and visitors and play with the Lark family's friendly dogs. The only downside is someone else will have to take the wheel. The roads of Kangaroo Island are intoxicating on their own – curvy and smooth,

they meander through epic tree tunnels and slice across dense bushland. Boxer Drive in Flinders Chase National Park has to be one of the most gorgeous strips of coastal road anywhere in the world, although we'll drive to that later. In

the meantime, it's off to the Cape Willoughby Lighthouse to spend a night in one of three lighthouse keepers' heritage accommodation options on the island. Crashing waves and strong wind, as well as a deep sense of mid-19th-century shipping history, combine to provide me with a surprisingly cosy and peaceful night's sleep.

KI's star attraction is the 800 endangered Australian sea lions that live in Seal Bay, the third-largest colony in the country. Almost hunted to extinction, these sea lions see a steady stream of daily visitors, who observe their behaviour from an 900-metre-long boardwalk or on the beach with a guided tour. Having encountered sea lions in numerous places around the world, I was a little dismayed at the guide's constant safety warnings – she gave us the impression that a sea lion was going to attack us at any moment. Seal Bay is marketed as some sort of Galapagos, that bucket list archipelago where seals, marine iguanas, turtles and penguins literally run about your feet. But it's not Galapagos and you should keep your expectations in check.

When I pull into the Kelly Hill Caves, I confess my own

expectations are a little low. Having already visited the country's best show caves in South and Western Australia, how impressive could these bushland caverns be? If you choose the daily Adventure Caving option the answer is: totally bucket list.

'You're going to scramble about a bit in the dust,' says the impressively bearded park guide Nick, in what is probably the biggest understatement in this book. He leads me beyond the modest show cave section into the old parts of the cave. Soon I'm doing the army crawl and clambering up, down and over limestone formations, ducking stalactites and sliding down flow rock. Wearing a headlamp and helmet, I push on through this hands-on and challenging two-hour tour, the air thick with humidity and dust. We find the old bones of a small emu that once lived on the island but was quickly hunted to extinction. Bones of kangaroos, possums and snakes. We squeeze through cracks, roll in dust and give names to formations – *phallactites*, anyone? Nick has been guiding here for well over a decade and he loves his job, so I hope he appreciates it when I say that Kelly Hill is the best adventure cave experience I've done anywhere – Hungary, Slovenia, South Africa, Cook Islands, New Zealand and, yes, Australia too. However, our defining bucket list experience on KI is reserved for the Remarkable Rocks. I arrive at these large, coastal granite structures in the late afternoon, as the orange lichen contrasts spectacularly with the azure ocean. Shaped and battered by the elements for more than 500 million years, the boulders look like nothing else on the planet. Some are hollowed out into echo chambers, others are perfect to climb up, through and over. Standing next to them, you can't help but feel you are somewhere distinct, exhilarating, original and – yes – truly remarkable. Spend a few days exploring Kangaroo Island and it's a feeling that will probably become very familiar indeed.

START HERE:
aussiebucketlist.com/
kangarooisland

Drive on the Beach

If you're self-driving to Kangaroo Island from Adelaide, make sure you budget a couple hours on the way to the ferry terminal to drive your vehicle onto the sweeping white coastline of Silver Sands, Sellicks or Aldinga Beach. There are not many places in the country where beach driving is so accessible, or as spectacular. Calm waves lap up to your wheels, the Mount Lofty Ranges look airbrushed in the distance and, with the windows rolled down and some good music cranked up, you can expect to coast along for kilometres with a big smile on your face.

Look a Great White in the Eye

PORT LINCOLN

O n a beach vacation during my sixth year on Planet Earth, my parents went out for dinner, leaving me to find the movie channel on the hotel television. That night, I watched two films I wish I'd never seen. One had giant spiders eating people, and the name of the movie has been long buried in the roots of my arachnophobia. The second film was *Jaws*. From that point on, every time I went near the sea, or a lake, or even a swimming pool, I'd feel the ominous presence of a massive, intelligent, child-eating great white shark. *Jaws* had given me a full-blown shark phobia – an irrational fear that pink-gummed, sharp-toothed death waited just beneath the water. It is a fear that many of us share. In Port Lincoln, it's time to face the cello music, stare horror in the eye and dispel the damage of Hollywood.

To prepare myself, I read up on sharks and quickly realised just how misunderstood these creatures are, how important they are for our oceans, and how disgusting the shark-fin industry is. Meanwhile, shark attacks are shockingly rare, with most victims returning to the sea and some even campaigning for shark conservation. As the ocean's apex predator, if sharks *really* wanted to eat humans, there would be hundreds of attacks every day. Instead, sharks are content to eat small fish and marine mammals, which is why diving with them is a highlight for many scuba divers. As for cage diving with great whites, it is far more accessible and somewhat controversial. Some marine biologists believe it will to lead to more attacks, as the sharks might associate humans with the food used to draw them for encounters. Others believe that the positive interaction increases our appreciation and understanding of the sharks, thereby aiding conservation and education. Certainly my own experience leans towards the latter.

The Neptune Islands are located 40 nautical miles, or about three hours by boat, from the coast of Port Lincoln. The islands are a hotspot for great whites due to the tens of thousands of long-nosed fur seals that live here. It's one of a handful of places globally that allows bucket listers with no diving experience to hop into a cage and have eye-to-eye contact with this fierce ocean predator. Clad in a wetsuit and breathing through hookah-like regulators, you'll only be about a metre or two below the surface, so you don't have to worry about decompression or altitude. In fact, kids as young as eight can participate, and sometimes even younger if the captain gives the go-ahead. Every care is taken to ensure the safety of the divers *and* the safety of the sharks. Cages

are rounded to ensure they don't hurt the shark if contact is made. Berley, a natural fish product, is used sparingly to attract the sharks, along with a tethered line with tuna gut. The whole operation is watched over by the Department of Environment, Water and Natural Resources. While some operators offer day trips, Rodney Fox Shark Expeditions takes you on a multi-day excursion and lets guests experience the sharks from both surface and ocean floor cages.

What do I feel like before hopping into a cage right near a living, breathing, jagged-toothed phobia? Apprehension, excitement, anxiety – all the feelings that make me feel alive. The cage is roped to the port side, with thick bars and internal handles to keep hands safe. Sharks might come at you head-on, turning just before their head smashes the cage. It's a rousing moment, too vivid to terrify, although it's accompanied by the inevitable scary thought of what would happen if I was on the wrong side of the bars.

The first time I hopped in a cage, a scarred monster of a beast seemed to be waiting for me. I will never forget that moment, coming face-to-face with a dread that had been with me much of my life. There was no menace or anger in the shark's cold, dead stare. Trying to bargain with it would be like trying to bargain with a speeding freight train. The moment lasted just a few seconds before more people jumped into the cage, causing Scarface to swim off gracefully beneath our feet.

Since that moment, I've never had a problem with ocean swimming. In fact, once I got my scuba certification, I actively pursued shark diving in places like the Philippines, Hawaii and Papua New Guinea. The fear of sharks is actually quite irrational, the result of horror movies exploiting our perceived vulnerability in an ecosystem we don't really understand. You are thirty times more likely to be killed by lightning than by a shark. Bees, wasps and falling vending machines kill more people each year. Thousands more people are killed driving to the beach, swimming or just sunbathing, than by sharks. With shark finning now out of control, up to seventy million sharks are massacred every year for an expensive soup considered a delicacy in parts of Asia. One third of all shark species are threatened with extinction, with some populations declining by 98 per cent. The good news is that education campaigns and conservation efforts appear to be working. The great white shark is a protected species worldwide, and there's hope that their numbers will rebound. Good news for the sharks, and also for bucket lists that help us beat our fears.

START HERE:
aussiebucketlist.com/sharks

It all Started with a Shark Attack

In 1963, a great white shark attacked a South Australian spearfishing champ named Rodney Fox. He escaped with his life, broken ribs, a punctured lung and wounds requiring more than 500 stitches. Inspired by a visit to see lions at the Adelaide Zoo, Rodney pioneered a cage contraption that allowed him to return to the seas and become the first person to safely observe great whites underwater. Very quickly, he realised that great whites are deeply misunderstood, and their annihilation was senseless. After initially working with researchers and filmmakers, he launched Rodney Fox Shark Expeditions to the public in 1976, and continues to this day. Incidentally, the inspiration for Rodney's shark cage experience has come full circle, with the Lions 360 experience at Monarto Zoo (see page 44) modelled on his shark dives.

Balloon over the Murray River

BAROSSA VALLEY

If there's one thing you can always guarantee when you travel, it is that there *will* be weather – good, bad, ugly and sometimes extraordinary. All you can do is go along for Mother Nature's ride . . . unless we're talking about hot air ballooning, in which case bad weather stops the ride entirely. This proved to be the case with my aborted flights in Marlborough, New Zealand, and the Maasai Mara in Kenya. It proved to be the case in Victoria's Yarra Valley, and it's looking likely this morning in the beautiful Barossa Valley.

It's too early, too dark and too ominous as my wife and I drive from Adelaide to one of the world's greatest wine regions. Rain is spitting on our windscreen and Ana has resigned herself for yet another missed ballooning opportunity. As she's always keen to remind me, her great-grandfather was an avid balloonist and an early sponsor of the famed Brazilian aviation pioneer Alberto Santos-Dumont. Her great-grandfather also died as a result of injuries sustained in a ballooning accident, but I'm not going to mention that this morning.

We arrive at the modern HQ of Balloon Adventures in Nuriootpa to meet Justin and John Stein, the region's premier balloon operators, in business since 1986. Justin has won ballooning championships

while his dad John is in Australia's Ballooning Federation Hall of Fame. Ballooning accidents are tremendously rare, and there's a common misconception that the activity is dangerous. When you're in experienced, safe hands, there's far more danger driving to the meet-up point. We transfer to Balloon Adventures' four-wheel drive bus, which pulls a trailer with a wicker basket, and head to a local launch site. Justin explains that the increased number of vineyards in the region has made his job more difficult. Since we're completely at the mercy of the winds, landing somewhere clear can be tricky. Other than the ability to increase altitude with hot blasts of air, we will go where the wind takes us. Or not.

'Sorry guys, it's far too turbulent for us to fly here,' says Justin, after testing the conditions by carefully monitoring the path of a small, helium-filled balloon. I clench my fists at the weather gods. My bucket

list goal of gently soaring over neat rows of vines bursting with purple fruit at sunrise – is it to be denied me yet again?

Adds Justin: 'We do have a backup site, though, along the Murray River, so let's go check that out as conditions can be quite different over there.'

Hang on. I can soar over grapevines in the Yarra and the Hunter valleys, but here's an opportunity to drift with the cool morning winds just metres above the mightiest river in the nation! Yes, please.

We drive half an hour along the A20 towards Blanchetown, pulling up into an open field alongside a vineyard. As early morning god-rays pierce through the cloud, we anxiously gaze at another helium balloon Justin releases into the air.

'See that, how the wind took it one way, and then completely changed its direction?,' remarks Justin. I don't know if that's a good thing or a bad thing but – given my track record – I'm not feeling confident.

'All right, let's do it!' Justin adds. I can hardly believe it's actually happening.

John enlists us to help unroll the large, brightly coloured fabric

Best Places to Balloon in Australia

- Barossa Valley, SA
- Alice Springs, NT
- Port Douglas, QLD
- Yarra Valley, VIC
- Canberra, ACT
- Hunter Valley, NSW
- Melbourne, VIC
- Gold Coast, QLD

balloon, called the envelope. A powerful fan blows in cold air and slowly it starts to take shape. He connects the ropes to the ten-passenger wicker basket, which sits below formidable propane burners. When these babies fire, it's like a fighter jet taking off. After a safety briefing, we climb aboard, feel the burners blast hot air into the envelope and gently begin our hour-long flight. Ballooning is soft and placid – nobody's going to get airsick and even people who are

Behold the Mighty Murray

At 2520 kilometres long, the Murray River is Australia's longest single river, and the third longest navigable river in the world. For more than 1800 kilometres it forms the border between New South Wales and Victoria. Only 4 per cent of the water that falls into the Murray-Darling Basin – home to more than two million people – will flow to the sea; the rest evaporates or is diverted for irrigation.

afraid of heights often find the fresh air and natural flow more manageable. It's also hot, with intense heat from the constant burner blasts, and wearing a hat is advisable. We soar over farmland, the little known Roonka Conservation Park, and finally over the mighty Murray, framed by a low-lying canyon and wild, black and grey eucalypts. Cormorants fly beneath us as a flock of sulphur-crested cockatoos screech with curiosity. Ballooning is the only form of flight that won't so much cause a ripple in the waters beneath you. The surrounding South Australian landscape reminds me of the wild African bush, with a pair of kangaroos substituting for a few thousand wildebeest. We land

gracefully, help deflate and pack up the balloon, and drive back to HQ for a fresh champagne breakfast. I toast Santa-Dumont and all the 'balloonatics' of the world. In the end, it doesn't really matter if you balloon in the Barossa, the Yarra Valley, Byron Bay or Alice Springs. Each flight will be different and equally magical – providing, of course, the weather cooperates.

**START HERE:
aussiebucketlist.com/
barossaballoon**

Hand-feed a Southern Bluefin Tuna

VICTOR HARBOR

Dozens of dark shadows slice through the turquoise waters of a holding pen located off the coast of Granite Island. They're as big as sharks, but swim faster and with more deliberation, fading from vision before I can compute that I've seen them at all. These are southern bluefin tuna, weighing up to 200 kilograms in the wild and travelling at speeds of up to 70 kilometres per hour. I'm on a 40-metre-wide in-sea aquarium called the Oceanic Victor, putting on a wetsuit for one of the more unique experiences you'll find in a book *all about* unique experiences. I'm hopping into the water with snorkel and mask, plenty of sardines, and a bucket list swim with the Ferrari of the oceans.

Oceanic Victor was founded as a nature-based tourism and educational facility to provide visitors – and children in particular – the opportunity to interact with marine life. It's the brainchild of Mike Dyer and Yasmin Stehr, whose father achieved international acclaim for pioneering the propagation of prized southern bluefin tuna. A sought-after fish that sells for thousands of dollars each in fish markets around the world, southern bluefin tuna has been overfished to the point of extinction. Ranching them into pools is nothing new, but the ability to breed the fish – and the introduction of strict quotas – has created a hugely successful sustainable tuna industry in Port Lincoln. When Yasmin noticed how positively her kids and their friends reacted to the tuna being studied in the holding pens, she was inspired to bring this experience to the masses. So began a long process of permits and protests, of consultation with top conservationists and marine biologists, to create a hands-on tuna encounter. The netted enclosure was procured in Port Lincoln, and while it is identical to the large pens that sit off the coast of Port Lincoln, it contains a fraction of the biomass. Now located in Victor

Harbor, it holds various species of fish, a couple of Port Jackson sharks, and eighty tuna that have won the bluefin lottery. Each day they are fed and monitored by

marine scientists, and will see out their estimated twenty-year lifespan perfectly safe from the world's sushi markets.

As I hop into the water the crew are tossing in sardines, and I suddenly see a creature that resembles a razor blade with saucer-eyes screaming towards me. It snatches the fish faster than a blink and is gone. This is followed by a series of splashes as different tuna pluck sardines all around me. They're everywhere and nowhere at once, and I find myself spinning around in my buoyant wetsuit trying to grasp the moment. It takes me a few minutes to settle and just let the spectacle unfold before my eyes. Tuna snatch sardines that float inches away from my nose with an uncanny and thrilling precision. It's like being inside a shooting range with bullets designed to *just miss* me. I'm told it's safe to hold out a sardine and let the tuna snatch it directly from my hand. Watching a child-sized bluefin approach you head-on with its mouth open is terrifying. I flinch at the last moment and let go, but the friendly crew are happy to provide as many sardines as I like. Eventually I succeed and, not for the first time on this Aussie adventure, I'm left with the burning question: *How is this a thing?*

Around me are people of all ages sharing a similar experience; indeed, the Oceanic Victor has been designed to inspire and enthral the whole family. If you don't want to get wet, you can pop into an underwater observatory to see the tuna from below, and younger kids will love the on-board touch pool of starfish, mussels, fish and other marine creatures. The crew, which includes marine biologists, help my four-year-old daughter attach sardines to a pole, and she's bursting with joy each time a tuna snatches it from her. As for me, the experience of hand-feeding schools of fish is eclipsed when a crew member brings over

Port Lincoln's Tunarama

Tunarama kicked off in the early 1960s to celebrate the people and traditions of Australia's largest fishery. Held each year over the Australia Day long weekend, it's the biggest bash of the year in the 'Seafood Capital of Australia', with dozens of individual competitions, including prawn peeling, prawn tossing, salmon tossing and watermelon eating. The big daddy is the World Championship Tuna Toss – inspired by the very physical manner of unloading fish at port – with the record more than 37 metres. Fake rubber tuna are used in the trials, with real tuna (unusable by-catch later returned to the ocean) used in the finals.

one of the puppies – a speckled
Port Jackson shark – and invites
me to give it a cuddle and join it for
a swim. With its Miss Piggy lips,
rough skin and big eyes, the shark
is totally at ease with me, leading
me around the six-metre-deep
enclosure so I can wave to my
delighted kids checking out the
action from the observatory. All
under the watchful eye of a scientist
who treats the sharks as you would
your own pet.

This is a book about unique
Australian activities and destinations and it is a book about magical
moments. Within the space of
half an hour I'd swum in the blue

waters of Encounter Bay, hand-fed
magnificent tuna, swum with a
shark, waved to my enraptured kids
underwater, and developed a deep
and lasting respect for one of the
ocean's most incredible fish. The
kind of experience, then, that ticks
all the boxes.

START HERE:
aussiebucketlist.com/
swimwithtuna

Sample some Bush Tucker

After many months of research, I can categorically confirm that Australia boasts some of the finest damn food on the planet. Visit any food market around the country and it's easy to understand why. Aided by an amazing climate, committed producers create a *feed*back loop with educated consumers who won't just settle for any old mango. Still, the experience of walking through a market, sampling plump fruits, smelly cheeses and rich, baked treats is one that can be replicated around the world. So when Cheryl Turner brings out a smorgasbord of bush meats and foraged tucker, it's a pretty clear indicator that Adelaide Central Market is in a field all its own.

Since its humble beginnings in 1869, it is now one of the largest covered markets in the southern hemisphere, attracting more than eight million visitors a year. Stall offerings are strictly controlled so it doesn't become over-commercialised and, for one of the city's biggest tourist attractions, it feels refreshingly local. Of course, it helps to have a guide like Cheryl to show you around. She works for Food Tours Australia, the brainchild of a former stall owner who wants to help visitors experience the market's highlights, efficiently and according to their interests. Since I'm obsessed with unique experiences, Cheryl leads me directly to Stall 55, home to Something Wild, Australia's first national Indigenous native greens and game wholesaler. In the display case are cuts of fresh kangaroo, camel, crocodile, emu, open-range boar, magpie goose and venison. Heck, there's even a sampler kebab with all of the above for sale, and duck thrown in for good measure. Something Wild is owned by former AFL star Daniel Motlop, and prides itself on working with and providing opportunities for rural Indigenous communities.

'The only farmed product on this platter is the smoked crocodile,' explains Cheryl. Of course the croc tastes like chicken, since these crocs are fed chicken and everyone knows you are what you eat. Next to it is a bowl of muntries – a sweet and sharp-tasting pea-sized berry also known as bush apple or muntaberry. It grows on shrubs on the south coast, and has one of the longest histories of any of Australia's bush foods. Next I pop a quandong in my mouth; this blood-red species of wild peach is packed with vitamin C. It's tart and sweet and reminds me of Amazonian camu camu. Karkalla, also known as a beach banana, is a green succulent foraged on the coast and prized for its salty, puckering flavour. The redgum-smoked kangaroo is lean and tender, while the emu mettwurst sausage is spiced with aptly named pepper berry.

There are two questions that never fail to amuse me on my travels. Question one is: 'Do you want to see what this baby can do?' – typically followed by the sudden rapid movement of a plane-glider-car-animal that causes my stomach to migrate to my throat.

Questions two is: 'Guess what you're eating?' – and my stomach usually does the same thing.

Australia's Bucket List Food Markets

....

- Adelaide Central Market, Adelaide
- Queen Victoria Market, Melbourne
- Farm Gate Market, Hobart
- Carriageworks Farmers Market, Sydney
- Fremantle Market, Perth

Cheryl has just teaspooned what appears to be chopped garlic, mint and herbs onto my hand. I lick it with my tongue and my tastebuds embark on a rollercoaster of unusual citrusy and occasionally shocking flavours. Cheryl then drops question number two. Turns out I'm eating raw *oecophylla smaragdina* – biting green ants commonly found in the northern Australian bush. Their green abdomens pack intense lemony flavour and, like most insects, they are full of protein. Green ants are harvested up north and add distinct punch to cheese and ice-cream. They do not taste anything like the nutty termites I've sampled in South American jungles, or even chicken, for that matter.

Suitably inspired by the unique tastes of the outback,

I continue onwards to sample creamy cheeses, truffle-infused mushrooms, ripe fruit, hot breads and local condiments that belong in every fridge door. The market is perfectly sized, neither overwhelming nor overly crowded.

'South Australia uses minimal pesticides or herbicides,' explains Cheryl, as she hands me a bunch of local red grapes that taste like lychees. I ask Food Tour Australia's founder, Mark Gleeson, what makes the Adelaide Central Market so popular with visitors and locals alike.

'When you visit, you're looking straight into the heart of Adelaide itself – our lifestyle, community, family and food, that all gathers together like ingredients in a great meal,' he says. That nails it perfectly: a bucket list foodie experience with a sprinkle of green ants for the memories.

START HERE:
aussiebucketlist.com/
centralmarket

See Giant Marsupials in Ancient Caves

There you are, an everyday *Diprotodon optatum*, ambling your two-and-a-half ton body around on a pleasant afternoon when, suddenly, the ground gives way and . . . *whoopsies.* You've fallen into one of a series of caves formed over half a million years ago, as changing sea levels and a corrosive water table carved into the malleable limestone. If you were human, you might have climbed out of this pickle. But as a two-metre-high, three-metre-long wombat, spelunking is not your strong suit. So you settle down to expire, graciously leaving your fossil for future paleontologists. Hundreds of other animals have been trapped too. Together, your remains will encourage the excavation of two dozen caves, allow South Australia to claim its only UNESCO World Heritage site, inspire animatronic artists and bring visitors from around the world. Who would have thought that your fateful day would create such a positive ripple through time?

The thermometer is edging over 40 degrees when I drive into Naracoorte Caves National Park,

located about a three-and-a-half-hour drive from Adelaide. I can't think of a better afternoon to explore cool, dark, subterranean caverns. Twenty-eight caves are located within the park's three square kilometres, with most visitors touring one or more of the highlight caves. The Victoria Fossil Cave is the most scientifically significant, revealed in 1969 to contain one of the richest collections of Pleistocene fossils yet discovered. It turns out that ninety-three different species of mammals, reptiles and birds shared the fate of our large furry friend, giving us a fascinating insight into

More of Australia's Bucket List Showcaves

- Newdegate Cave in the Hastings Cave State Reserve, TAS
- Jenolan Caves in the Blue Mountains, NSW
- Cutta Cutta Caves Nature Park near Katherine, NT
- Chillagoe-Mungana Caves National Park, QLD
- Byaduk Caves, near Hamilton, VIC
- Jewel Cave, near Margaret River, WA

the lives of Australia's now-extinct megafauna.

Australia has always been the realm of the marsupial, only the animals back then were much larger. There were rhino-sized wombats, giant-limbed, short-faced kangaroos, and one very nasty marsupial lion, the apex predator. Of course there were also oversized lizards, birds, tortoises and snakes, all of whom went the way of the dodo when modern humans arrived in Australia. Inside the Wonambi Fossil Centre, some of these bizarre animals have been recreated with animatronics, giving us a glimpse of what it would have been like to stumble across them 200,000 years ago. Across the parking lot is the Stick-Tomato Cave, which contains some pretty stalactites and stalagmites and is also used to introduce adventurous visitors to the joys of spelunking – helmets, headlamps and all. The Alexandra Cave, discovered in 1908, is a showstopper. Leading us deep into the large cavern, our guide Tom explains how water created the columns, flowstones, helictites and exceedingly fragile soda straws. From what I can gather, the most stunning feature is actually an

artificial installation created by the cave's modern discoverer, William Reddan, a showman who developed the caves as a tourist attraction. His mirror-glass reflecting pool sits beneath a delicate limestone formation, and looks deceptively natural, so kudos to Bill. 'One film crew waited hours for a single drop to create a ripple,' says Tom. Just

then, a drop falls and with that singular ripple I can see what the camera crew were after. So still is the water, it looks like a special effect, the drop creating a ripple in the space-time continuum.

Visitors have been enjoying these caves for centuries. In fact the Blanche Cave, once known as the Big Cave, was used by townsfolk for parties, community events and (I guess) wild Victorian-era discos. There was a lot of damage. Fragile ecosystems take millennia

to form and need a far more respectful, gentle touch. With its showcaves and interpretive walks, evening tours and enthusiastic guides, Naracoorte Caves' remarkable history, stories, fauna and formations will continue to inspire bucket listers well into the future. Rest easy, Mr Diprotodon. You deserve it.

START HERE:
aussiebucketlist.com/naracoorte

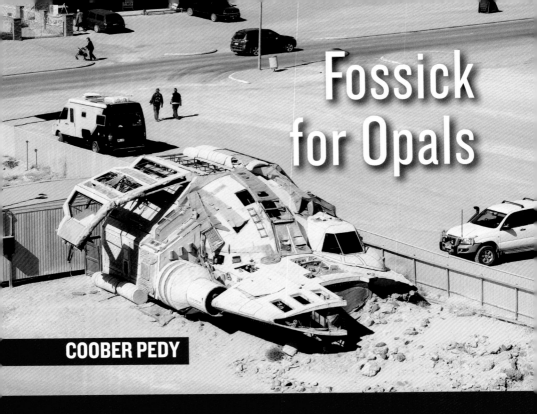

Fossick for Opals

COOBER PEDY

Triangular mounds of dry, outback desert dirt are the first indicators you're no longer in Kansas. Then you see the old trucks beneath strange elevated barrels. Finally, you notice the facades of underground homes, the kind of thing you'd expect to see in a post-apocalyptic sci-fi movie. Hang on a moment, is that a grounded spaceship? Welcome to the opal capital of the world. There's nowhere else on the planet quite like it.

In 1915, a teenage boy accidentally discovered a different treasure on a gold prospecting trip with his father. Scouting within a moonscape halfway between Alice Springs and Adelaide, they didn't know a former inland sea had drained water and minerals through the silica, creating the ideal conditions to produce this particularly valuable gemstone. Rainbow-coloured opal has been prized for millennia, an alluring gem renowned for its beauty and rarity. Within months of the first discovery, hundreds of prospectors had arrived to stake their claim and, more than a century later, Coober Pedy continues to produce around 70 per cent of the world's opal. While the price of Australia's national gemstone has dropped, opal mining still generates tens of millions of dollars each year. Coober Pedy attracts outback road-trippers and Ghan passengers with its miner-owned opal shops, an opal museum, and the opportunity to sleep in an underground hotel. According to the local council, 50 per cent of the population live underground in roomy 'dugouts', which provide shelter from the heat, wind and evening cold. A constant and comfortable interior temperature also means no energy bills and an added opportunity to strike it rich during household

renovations. 'The town prohibits any mining within its borders, but if you're expanding your dugout and hit opal, well, it's yours to keep.' My guide in the museum was born and raised in Coober Pedy, and it doesn't strike her the least bit odd that people would choose to live in dark and windowless caves. 'Hang on a second, doesn't that make you troglodytes?' I ask, inadvertently causing offence. 'We are *not* living in caves, we are living in *dugouts*,' she responds. Caves don't have satellite television, modern bathrooms and kitchens. Some of these hillside dugouts are *mansion*-sized, linked by tunnels and large enough to

be hotels. Interior walls might be painted but typically maintain their sandstone patina, finished with wood glue to stop the dust.

On the museum tour, I learn that water is piped in from artesian wells via a desalination plant 24 kilometres away, and that the town is off-grid, with 70 per cent of its energy needs met by solar and wind power and the rest by battery. I discover that there is a hefty price difference between solid, doublet and triplet opals, with black opal being the most expensive. Meanwhile, those strange trucks with the barrels are called blowers, and they remove sand excavated by explosives and tunnelling machines. Gone are the days when miners would fossick with a chisel and hammer, although visitors can still give it a go at an area called the Jewel Box on the edge of town. There, it's finders keepers, and I'm told stories of tourists chiselling out opals worth thousands of dollars. 'It's very much a game of luck,' regales an old Greek miner shortly before a fabulous lunch of grilled lamb and herbed chicken kebabs in an underground restaurant. Inches of dirt might separate a rich vein of black opal from bare dirt, and don't be fooled by the sparkling 'potch' – worthless and colourless opal that nevertheless makes up to 95 per cent of the opal found. Miners are not required to clear away their failed dig, which explains the mounds of dirt surrounding the town, some of which date back over a century.

I climb a hill to get a better view of the dugouts and immediately spot a spaceship in need of repair. Turns out it's a prop from the Vin Diesel movie *Pitch Black*. *Mad Max Beyond Thunderdome* and *Red Planet* were also filmed here – it's the perfect alien planet movie location. Being in a remote desert also means expensive props

Breakaway to the Dog Fence

A short drive out of Coober Pedy along the Stuart Highway lie the Breakaways, geological relics of the vast inland sea that covered the area around 70 million years ago. Deeply significant for the local Indigenous people, the mesas and distinctly coloured hills appear to have broken off the escarpment. Not far away is one of the longest structures in the world, the 5300-kilometre-plus Dog Fence (also known as the Dingo Fence). It was erected in 1885 to prevent dingoes from the north attacking sheep in the south and continues to save farmers millions of dollars in lost livestock.

and equipment can be discarded. There's rusted gear everywhere you look, the legacy of those who busted out, or the roughly 10 per cent who made it big. You'll quickly discover that Coober Pedy (a name that loosely translates from an Aboriginal term for 'man in a hole') has no shortage of big personalities. Across from the museum I'm drawn to a shop with a big sign out front promising Waffles & Gems. Here I meet a large man in a kilt named Jimmy, who arrived from Edinburgh to find his fortune forty years ago. He's still an active miner and his opal jewellery is priced, as he points out, better than anything we'll find across the street. Unfortunately, I didn't have time to taste the waffles.

I drive past the town's working drive-in that apparently still runs an original clip asking the audience not to light dynamite while the picture is playing. Visitors also pop in to the Serbian Orthodox Church, an impressive cavern with intricate statues carved into the solid rock walls. There's a dusty 18-hole golf course, where players carry their own artificial turf with them for tee-offs. Remarkably, it shares a reciprocal membership agreement with St Andrews in Scotland. A strange and eccentric world unto itself, Coober Pedy is remote and fascinating, a rough gem well worth polishing on our Great Australian Bucket List.

START HERE:
aussiebucketlist.com/cooberpedy

NEW SOUTH WALES

AUSTRALIAN CAPITAL TERRITORY

Canberra

■ *Tidbinbilla*

VICTORIA

AUSTRALIAN CAPITAL TERRITORY

Tasman Sea

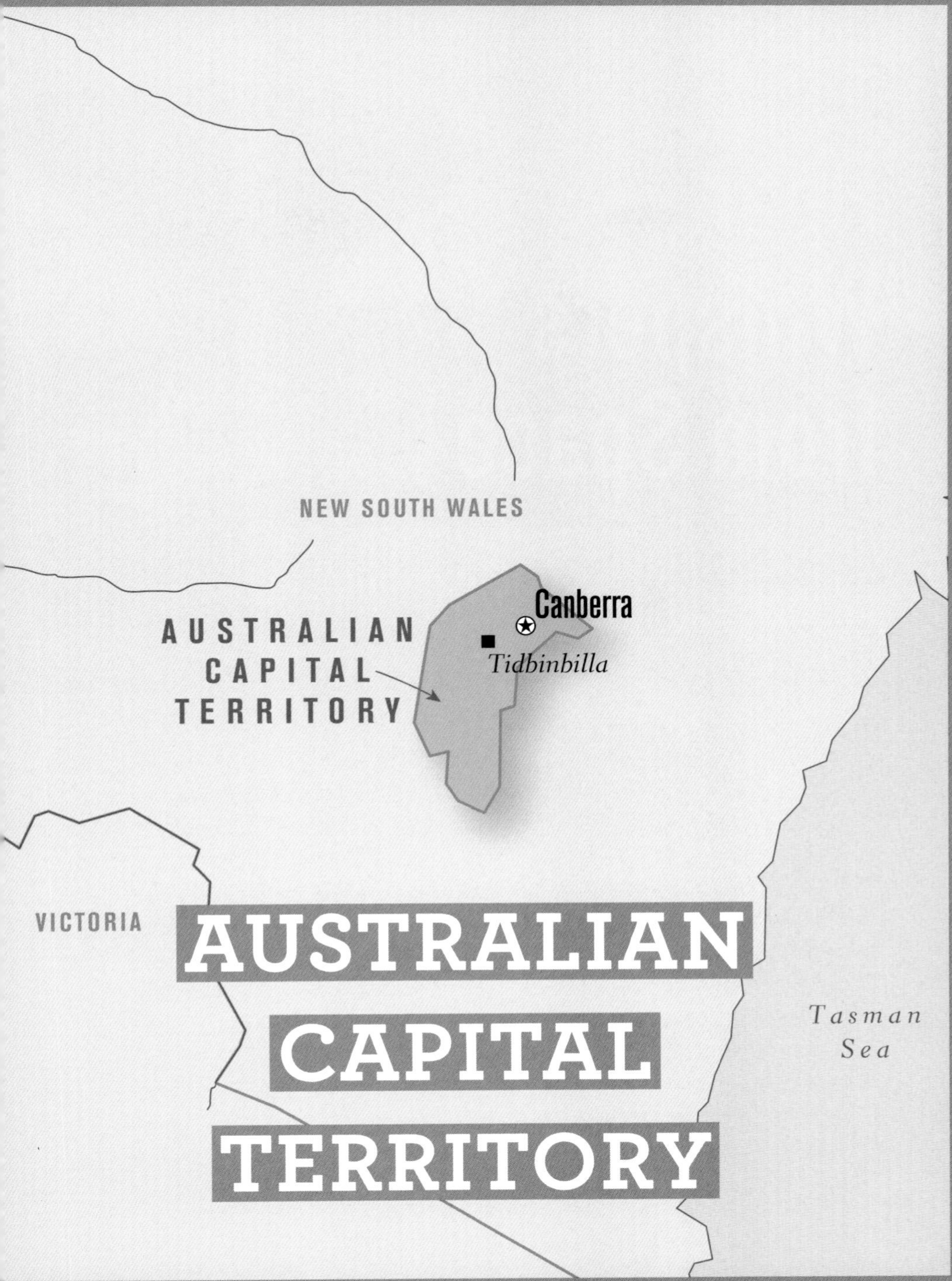

Hear Whispers from Space

TIDBINBILLA

Twenty-four hours a day, seven days a week, the unsung heroes of modern space exploration gaze into the heavens. They are responsible for nearly every picture we have of the celestial bodies in our solar system and beyond; every new announcement about galaxies and planets, black holes and distant stars; every new mission that takes humanity beyond the moon. NASA, SpaceX and launch pads like Cape Canaveral are well known to most Earthlings, especially those of us with our heads in the stars. It's time, therefore, to pay tribute – and make a bucket list visit – to Australia's low-key yet essential contribution to the past, present and future of deep space exploration. It's just a 45-minute drive from Canberra, so you don't even have to go to the end of the universe.

In the early 1960s, NASA developed the Deep Space Network to ensure that satellites exploring the depths of space would remain in constant communication. It would require the construction, management and maintenance of enormous antennas strategically located around the planet. California's Mojave Desert got one, the other is near Madrid, and the southern hemisphere's complex is in Tidbinbilla, ACT. The location was chosen because of wide-open valleys, good weather, stable granite geography, proximity to a major city and lack of radio interference.

Funded entirely by NASA, the Canberra Deep Space Communication Complex uses a mix of 70-metre and 34-metre dishes to track and provide two-way radio transmissions with dozens of spacecraft scouring the solar system and beyond. Raw information is received as either analogue (for older satellites like *Voyager I* and *Voyager II*) or binary data. It is then filtered for background radio static and sent off, in real time, to NASA scientists. Outbound transmissions last only seconds and are measured in the tens of kilowatts, while incoming signals come from many millions or billions of kilometres away and are *billions* of times weaker than those from a tiny watch battery. Consider the *Voyager I*, which was launched in 1977 and is the most distant man-made object in space. It's still communicating with the Deep Space Network, providing just the faintest of whispers that nevertheless contain crucial information for scientists around the world. This is why Tidbinbilla needs very big antennas, and why a sign advises all visitors to switch off their mobile phones. Nobody wants radio interference from your latest Facebook post to obscure the first signs of intelligent extraterrestrial life.

Having watched too many bad science fiction movies, I expected an Area 51 level of security. Instead, everyone is invited to visit the facility, order a flat white from the cafe and learn all about modern space research. The biggest dish of the four located here is Deep Space Station 43 (DSS-43), towering 22 storeys high, with a base structure weighing more than 8000 tons. The largest steerable parabolic dish in the southern hemisphere, DSS-43's sheer size and high-tech wizardry contrast sharply with the scenic farmland that surrounds it. Maintained by an all-Australian team of engineers, programmers and troubleshooters, DSS-43 commenced operations in 1973 to support the Apollo 17 moon mission. Unlike that famous scene in the Aussie film *The Dish*, nobody plays cricket in it, as even a tiny dent will interfere with radio signals. It was Tidbinbilla's 26-metre dish DSS-46 – then located at a different facility near Canberra – that brought back the first images of Neil Armstrong stepping onto the moon in July 1969. (The film features the 64-metre dish located in Parkes, New South Wales, which picked up television signals eight minutes later.) For

certain, Neil Armstrong *did* land on the moon. Among the quirky and interesting wall displays in the visitor centre is a panel dismissing conspiracy theories.

'Beyond the fact that the data was gathered *right here*, the Russians would have blown the lid on any announcement that wasn't scientifically legitimate, explains NASA Operations Support Officer Glen Nagle. He tells me how the fascinating yet modest visitor centre had even more modest origins: curious people would simply show up and yell at workers to explain how the dishes worked. Now expanded to include a life-size replica of the Mars Rover, donated space paraphernalia, food kits, scale models, a theatre, on-site café and live data tracking of transmissions on a large TV panel, it remains a small visitor centre with a big heart that inspires awe, curiosity and wonder. My daughter is glued to a display holding a small, fist-sized chunk of moon rock, sparkling with silica and one of the largest pieces of moon rock on display anywhere in the world. Moon rock would be considered invaluable – if a US judge hadn't valuated it after an attempted theft at a NASA facility in the US. Explains Glen: 'The rock is priceless, of course, but if you had to mount your own mission to the moon to get a piece this size, get ready to spend about $1.3 billion in replacement value.'

This is fun stuff, but the work of the four antennas is a serious endeavour. As scientists continue to unlock the secrets of the universe, each step takes us closer to becoming an interplanetary species. Dozens of missions from 27 countries rely on Canberra, which works with its two sister complexes as air traffic control for deep space. There is no military role, no barbed wire or intrigue. Information collected is publicly available through online science projects and free software that allows anyone to study black holes, count craters on Mars and help classify distant planets. As yet, no intelligent form of extraterrestrial life has been in contact, but it's tempting and reassuring to think the first words they might hear back are: 'G'day mate!'

START HERE:
**aussiebucketlist/
canberradeepspace**

Spot a Platypus in Tidbinbilla

Bring your gaze back down to earth at the Tidbinbilla Nature Reserve, located just down the road from the Deep Space Centre. Spanning more than 50 square kilometres, the reserve lets you take a bushwalk on one of the 22 marked trails in search of a who's who of Australian wildlife. Don't miss the stunning Sanctuary – fenced off from predators – which provides an accessible pathway through a large wetland ecosystem. Keep an eye out for birdlife, reptiles and a creature so weird it must surely have come from outer space – the platypus.

Honour the Past

CANBERRA

Warrant officer George Thomas McBryde is just one name engraved on a bronze panel on the walls of a long hallway. His name is etched here along with more than 102,000 members of the Australian armed forces – young men and women who sacrificed their lives in the name of duty, from the earliest international conflict in 1885 in Sudan to the present day. The panels and hallways are brightened by the addition of thousands of plastic red poppies, a spontaneous gesture from the many, many people who have paid their respects. Each name in the Commemorative Area is a tragedy, and it's difficult not to feel emotionally hollowed out. So many lives lost, so many families devastated, so many painful stories.

The Australian War Memorial in Canberra was conceived in 1916 by Charles Bean, the country's official World War I historian, to honour the dead, create an archive of remembrance, give the public some understanding of the war experience, and provide a place for families to grieve. By the time the building was opened on November 11, 1941, the nation was once again at war. The horrific 'War to End All Wars' had proved to be just an opening act, and tens of thousands of young Australian soldiers would soon be fighting for their lives, King and country, in North Africa, Europe and Asia. The memorial serves as a museum, shrine, gallery and research facility.

As our volunteer guide Richard explains during a highlights tour, the memorial tells the story of Australia's role in international conflict from a uniquely and unapologetically Australian perspective: a young nation that has repeatedly fought on the side of its allies, and paid a tremendously heavy price. Historical exhibits are immaculately presented, from weaponry, planes and equipment to documents, imagery and uniforms. Richard points out the mud-caked tunic of Private G.J. Giles, personally gathered by

Charles Bean in France in 1918. 'It has never been washed. That's real World War I battlefield mud,' explains Richard. A huge hall holds a massive Lancaster Bomber, the reconstructed wrecks of the midget-class Japanese submarines that attacked Sydney Harbour, naval guns and various WWI-era planes. History and military enthusiasts can spend several days exploring the various galleries, which include huge sections about post-1945 conflicts, modern peacekeeping efforts and special exhibitions. The dioramas in the First World War gallery are particularly mesmerising. Created in the 1920s – long before, as Richard says, 'there were GoPros and YouTube' – the three-dimensional artist renditions of battle scenes have a jarring attention to detail. The brutal Somme Winter, a rare victory at Lone Pine, the horrific Battle of Pozières, the trenches at Bullecourt, the moonscape of Ypres – the dioramas provide visitors with a shockingly lifelike glimpse into the atrocious conditions and unimaginable violence. In the Second World War gallery, I stand in a vibrating bomber simulation during a fateful mission. The bridge

Visiting Gallipoli

It may be halfway around the world, but a visit to the site of the nation's most infamous battle is on many an Australian's bucket list. The Gallipoli peninsula is located about four hours' drive from Istanbul and features three main battlefields and several iconic memorials, most notably the Canakkale Martyrs Memorial, the British Memorial at Cape Helles, the Lone Pine Australian Memorial and Anzac Cove. The Gallipoli Simulation Centre is a good place to start, as it's not far from the cliffs of Anzac Cove where the battle commenced. Various cemeteries nearby are testament to the bloodshed on both sides. Up the hill and on the other side of the Simulation Centre is Lone Pine, the Nek (where the Light Brigade were ordered to charge into heavy gunfire), and Chunuk Bair, with its New Zealand memorial and cemetery and statue of Atatürk, founder of modern Turkey. Each Anzac Day, Gallipoli attracts many thousands of visitors, who pay their respects and honour the past. Lest we forget.

of the HMAS Brisbane warship has been faithfully recreated, while excellent sound and light shows include *Lord of the Rings* director Peter Jackson's stunning *Over the Front* documentary repeating every hour in the ANZAC Hall.

The Australian casualties of World War I are beyond comprehension – 416,809 men enlisted, with more than 216,000 injured and more than 62,000 dead. This occurred in a nation of less than five million people at that time, with women picking up the slack back home (and, as the memorial reminds us, in active service too). These 62,000 names are found on the bronze panels to the left of the Hall of Memory. To the right are the nearly 40,000 names from World War II. Then Korea (340), Vietnam (521) and more recent conflicts like Afghanistan (at the time of writing, 42). Visitors will leave the Australian War Memorial stirred by many sombre emotions. In the face of so many tragic stories and so many names, hope is in short supply. Sacrifices continue to be made and many brave men and women continue to put their lives on the line. Yet the decreasing number of names on those bronze

plates is surely a sign that the worst is behind us.

It is just shy of 5pm, and warrant officer George Thomas McBryde is about to be properly remembered. Since 2013, the daily Last Post Ceremony has honoured the life of one name on the Roll of Honour. Today, it's the turn of the 21-year-old from Rockhampton, Queensland. A small crowd gathers as the late afternoon sun reflects off the narrow memorial pool housing an eternal flame. Next to several fresh wreaths is a picture of George's white headstone, located in an English cemetery. The national anthem is sung; a piper plays a haunting tune. We hear how the young man trained as a gunner in England and Canada, transferring to the elite RAF 460 Squadron in the last few months of World War II. After conducting a successful raid in Germany, George and the rest of his six-man bomber crew were killed in a plane crash not far from their base near Cambridge. He had joined the squadron just two weeks before his death. George Thomas McBryde did not win a Victoria Cross or survive any great battles. He was just a lad doing what he felt he must, a boy thrust into a monstrous war that consumed innocence on an industrial scale. The words carved into the Tomb of the Unknown Australian Soldier tell it straight: *He is all of them, and he is one of us.*

As the short story of George's life concludes in front of a crowd of respectful visitors, I turn around and see Parliament House on Capital Hill in direct line of sight. I wonder if cooler heads prevail in today's great game of geo-politics. With any luck, we might prevent any more names appearing on the wall. In the meantime, even if the Australian armed forces miraculously avoid any future casualties, the Last Post Ceremony could continue to honour one name on the Roll of Honour, every day, until the year 2295.

START HERE:
aussiebucketlist.com/ warmemorial

Watch Question Time

CANBERRA

The seat of government says much about the nation in which it resides. Old-world clock towers and gargoyles in Westminster and Ottawa, the imposing white dome of Washington's Capitol Hill, France's opulent Palais Bourbon. The largest administrative building in the world is the Palace of the Parliament in Bucharest, a colossal monument to a corrupt dictator. Israel has its stern Knesset, New Zealand its quirky Beehive, Germany its imposing Reichstag, Hungary its Neo-Gothic fairytale castle. Most parliaments offer daily tours to explore inside the buildings. On a cool, misty autumn morning, I find myself drifting over Parliament House in Canberra, gazing down from the basket of a hot air balloon. 'Bet you can't do this in Washington,' says our pilot Gary from Balloon Aloft.

I bet there are lots of things you can do in – and above – Parliament House in Canberra that you can't do on Capitol Hill. Like showing up and wandering about this enormous building by yourself, discovering art, history and your own political curiosity.

Completed in 1988 at a cost of $1.1 billion, Parliament House is the most recognisable and striking landmark in Canberra. It was originally expected to cost $220 million, but this *is* a government building after all. An 81-metre, 250-ton flagpole sits atop the building, which was inspired by the shape of two boomerangs. The entire complex is located on a hill, and from above looks like a particularly vulnerable fortress. Besides a couple guards out the front carrying intimidating machine guns (and some crash barriers to prevent suspicious vehicles getting too close), the building is noticeably approachable. At the entrance, I am quickly screened through security and find myself in the cavernous main foyer where I am surprised by its white walls and distinct sense of minimalism. Although it has 4500 rooms, the building's absence of pomp, glitz and kitschy hallmarks of power

reinforces the notion that Australia is a new world. Not that it is all barren and bare – Parliament House has more than 6000 works of art, from statues and portraits to the massive tapestry that hangs in the impressive Great Hall (available, at a steep cost, for weddings, embassy parties, conference events and bar mitzvahs). The large portraits of past prime ministers are particularly fascinating, as they provide a glimpse into the face of political power. Former PM John Gorton is the only one casually dressed, Paul Keating looks like he's sulking, Malcolm Fraser looks smug, the veins in John Howard's hands are problematically realistic, and Gough Whitlam's portrait (by the late Clifton Pugh) is a little abstract, seemingly the only departure from a traditional style. It was the 1970s, and things were groovier back then – although it didn't turn out too groovy for Whitlam, but that's another story.

After checking out some of the other exhibits – including the original Yirrkala bark petition for Aboriginal land rights, a rare copy of the Magna Carta and displays about the history and mechanisms of Australian parliament – I join a free forty-minute tour to visit the House of Representatives and the Senate. Unfortunately, it's not a sitting day, which means I won't be able to take one of the 388 seats in the public gallery and observe Question Time, undoubtedly the most popular time to visit and typically what makes up all of the parliamentary footage on the news.

'Question Time is only about 5 per cent of what politicians do here,' explains our guide Scott. 'In fact, 86 per cent of the time, both parties vote together and actually get stuff done.'

We're seated in the House of Representatives, which looks bigger than it does on TV. Scott explains how the 2700 clocks around the building announce when a vote is to occur, and that representatives have just four minutes to make it into the House before the doors are locked. He points out the press gallery and the importance of the media in holding members and their party to account. Above the public benches is a soundproof room where the 130,000 school kids that visit Parliament each year can watch without disrupting proceedings. In keeping with

Balloon over the Capital

You won't see hot air balloons floating over the White House or Westminster. The Canberra Balloon Spectacular takes place every March and is one of the top ballooning events in the world. Dozens of hot air balloons in all shapes and sizes take off daily from the lawns of Old Parliament House. Sign up for incredible sunrise views over the capital and Parliament House, or simply enjoy the spectacle from below.

British tradition, the House of Representatives is coloured green, albeit a eucalyptus shade more suited to the nation. Scott's explanations are refreshingly candid, especially when we cross over to the red-hued Senate. As we sit in the public viewing gallery looking at a slightly different bench configuration, he acknowledges the controversial aspects of the Senate and explains how

Australia's political system – a hybrid of the British and American systems colloquially referred to as Washminster – maintains healthy checks and balances and gives each state an equal voice in government. Some of the Australian members of our group murmur in dis/agreement, while the Swedes, Americans, Chinese and I merely find it interesting. It would have been more so if Question Time was in session, so we could see desk-thumping debates and barbed zingers as political leaders thrashed out legislation and the issues of the day. Regardless, just like every Australian is legally obliged to vote – a vital component of democracy that is absent in the USA, UK and Canada – it should be mandatory to visit Australia's hallways of power and educate yourself about how that vote is used.

START HERE:
aussiebucketlist/parliamenthouse

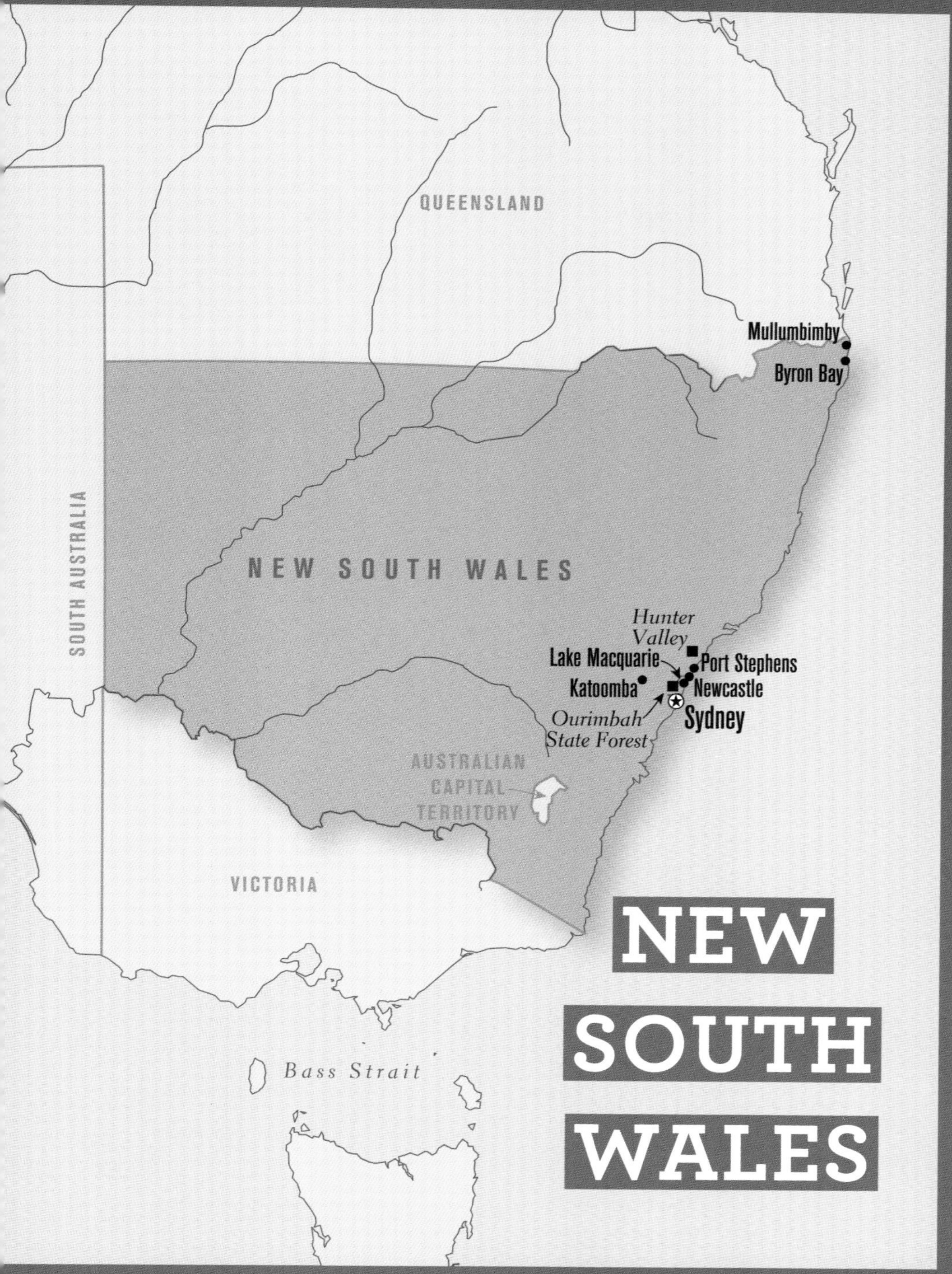

QUEENSLAND

Mullumbimby

Byron Bay

SOUTH AUSTRALIA

NEW SOUTH WALES

Hunter
Valley

Lake Macquarie · Port Stephens

Katoomba · Newcastle

Ourimbah
State Forest

Sydney

AUSTRALIAN
CAPITAL
TERRITORY

VICTORIA

Bass Strait

NEW
SOUTH
WALES

Swoop through the Forest

L et us honour the passionate few committed to the creation of something new. Those inspired to imagine, invent, innovate and, ultimately, produce a fresh experience for everyone's benefit – be it light bulbs, gadgets, or (my personal favourite) bucket list adventures. Folks like A.J. Hackett, who pioneered bungy jumping, or Paul Cave, who founded Sydney Bridgelimb, or Frederic Galimard, who envisioned something quite extraordinary in the forests of the New South Wales Central Coast.

Ziplines and flying foxes are fun because you soar through or above the trees – at great heights or speed – from one point to the next. Frederic imagined a contraption that would let us do more than that; one that would spiral and zigzag, dip and curl in one seamless motion from start to finish. It only took *five thousand* hours of construction and testing for TreeTops Adventures to unveil their Xtreme TreeTop Crazy Rider. Skirting trees on a kilometre-long track through Ourimbah State Forest? It takes me less than five minutes to decide it's a worthy addition to our bucket list.

Located about ninety minutes' drive north of Sydney, TreeTops' Central Coast adventure park features a ropes course for adults and kids, various vertical climbing challenges and the revolutionary Crazy Rider. Eco-friendly and built with the support of the Forestry Corporation of NSW, the ride is located within a stand of trees where the birds sing brightly and the air is fresh. Greeted by friendly staff, I'm run through the safety precautions, slipped into a helmet and harness, and handed a pulley attachment for a short walk through the forest to the pioneer launch

Xtreme platform. Along the way, interpretative boards tell me about the forest birds and bush and, with a recent sprinkling of rain, there's an earthy fragrance in the air. A guide quickly and safely attaches me to the steel pipe system, and away I go. Immediately it feels like I'm going to crash into trees up ahead but, even with my legs straight out, I'm perfectly safe in all directions (and getting a total kick out of the unpredictable turns). A sudden dip boosts my speed and along comes the first of four 360-degree tree loops, clocking in with an impressive 2G of force that I feel in the pit of my stomach. It's a unique thrill worthy of a *whoop;* the forest bird calls are joined by my

spot. This is a shorter, 330-metre-long rollercoaster zipline, with little G-force, so it's best suited to those who want to nibble on the experience, as opposed to tuck in.

Straight away I'm impressed by how comfortable I am. Frederic's engineering team devised a pulley system that lets riders comfortably sit back without a harness pulling down on the waist. Holding onto the pulley system with my legs facing forward, I'm guided by gravity between trunks and branches that seem close enough to touch but are safely out of harm's way. At under a minute in ride time, it's over too soon, so I'm excited to walk back through the forest to the

Australian Zipline Adventures

- Jungle Surfing Canopy Tours, Cape Tribulation, QLD (see page 229)
- Treetop Challenge, Tamborine Mountain, QLD
- Otway Fly Treetop Adventures, Beech Forest, VIC
- Hollybank Treetops Adventures, Launceston, TAS
- Forest Adventures South West, Busselton, WA

screams and laughter, especially when I swirl around the highlight 540-degree loop.

It is neither a rollercoaster, toboggan nor zipline, and yet it is somehow more fun than all three. Rollercoasters don't immerse you in nature, toboggans don't elevate you mid-air up to six storeys high and ziplines don't allow you to dip, spiral and spin around the forest. My ride lasts about three and half minutes, although heavier riders will go quicker, and lighter riders a little slower. You do have to weigh between 40 and 120 kilograms to participate, but the experience is proudly accessible for those in wheelchairs. At the time of writing,

Ourimbah hosts the fastest and longest tree-top rollercoaster in the world, although Frederic's success has him designing similar rides in Australia and beyond. With an experience this remarkable, who can blame him? So here's to the designers and builders, the dreamers and doers, the ambitious folk who are devoted to new experiences. Some people truly can see the forest for the trees.

START HERE:
aussiebucketlist.com/
treetoprollercoaster

Cook Something Fishy and Fabulous

Everyone in the exhausting world of dating knows there are plenty of fish in the sea. In fact, fifty tonnes of fresh seafood are traded at the nation's largest seafood market *every day*. Salmon, barramundi and tuna, sure, but also trumpetfish and stargazers, cobblers, pike eel, eastern pigfish and, occasionally, blob fish, too. Ten percent of all the marine creatures we eat are found in Australian waters, and, while it might not compete with massive fish markets Asia in terms of volume, Sydney Fish Market is the largest of its kind in the southern hemisphere and the third-largest in the world by variety.

Starting at 5.30am each weekday, up to two hundred buyers gather on the market's auction-room floor to size up the daily haul of fish, crabs, rock lobster, prawns and shellfish. What follows is an auction designed to ensure that 99 per cent of the roughly 2700 crates on offer are sold within a few short hours. Later that day, you might find the same seafood on your dinner plate.

'There are too many miscon-ceptions about seafood and we depend too much on the same four fish varieties,' says Alex Stollznow, the market's enthusiastic and refreshingly honest guide. Picking up a palm-sized triangle dart fish, he wonders why we're intimidated by small fish with bones, but will happily eat chicken wings. There are around six thousand commer-cial species of fish in Australia, comprising about two-thirds of everything that swims. I get the impression Alex has tried them all, and would bring a few surprises to a summer BBQ. 'Only a few blob fish find their way to the market every year, and I typically snap them up because they're delicious,' he says, leading us to the floor.

Every day, a Fish Market tour kicks off at 6.45am, when the auction is in full swing and the floor is swimming with action. Three large screens face tier-seated buyers, who carefully monitor a countdown of prices on giant digital clocks. Since the floor is not refrigerated, every hour counts in terms of keeping the product fresh for consumers and the prices stable for buyer, seller and market middleman alike. A reverse auction sets the price above market value and it slowly drops one dollar per revolution until buyers stop the clock. It's a system that was developed by the Dutch during the tulip fever craze of the 1600s, and it motivates a purchase much faster than a traditional auction. Screens display the type of fish, whether it is wild caught or aquaculture, and the origin. Buyers represent retailers,

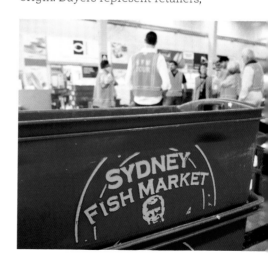

wholesalers, seafood restaurants and international consortiums, which ship prized Australian product directly to Asian markets where it is sold at a considerable markup.

'This is a bailer shell, which used to cost next to nothing. Then Noma (voted the world's best restaurant) showed up and used it in a dish, and now it's $17 a kilogram. You only use 5 per cent of the meat, but it still tastes like the best scallop you've ever had.' Alex is a trove of information about the market, the industry and eating seafood. I learn that looking at the mouth of the fish will tell you its diet, and its diet will tell you its flavour. Yes, movie director James Cameron did base those *Aliens* monster facehuggers on the

Balmain bug and – if you can get beyond that image – bugs have delicious tails comparable in flavour to much pricier rock lobsters. Yellowfin tuna is graded on the quality of its flesh, and local fishermen use the Japanese sashimi method to haul in, bleed, strip, ice and hang each fish in less than two minutes.

'Don't worry, it's not alive,' deadpans Alex, as he demonstrates some of this technique over a crate holding expensive Yellowfin tuna. We look at mixed crates and bycatch and learn that, for all this abundance of seafood, Sydney Fish Market and the Australian fishing industry is deeply committed to sustainable practices. Species are carefully monitored to ensure stocks

Seafood in Australia

Although Australia possesses the third-largest fishing zone in the world, the country imports far more seafood than it exports, with local production only meeting 30 per cent of domestic demand. More than half the seafood Australia imports comes from Thailand, China and Vietnam, countries that rank relatively low on the UN Code of Conduct for Responsible Fisheries (Australia ranks fourth). The average Australian eats about 25 kilograms of seafood per year, but dietary health guide-lines recommend increasing our fish and seafood intake by as much as 40 per cent. The Sustainable Seafood Guide is available as a free app to help find the right kind of seafood from the right kind of fisheries and producers, ensuring plenty of fish remain in the sea for future generations.

shops, we meet a guy who shucks three thousand oysters a day, eating dozens of discards along the way. Lee is in his fifties, but he has the complexion of a toddler. Next, Alex pulls out a massive Tasmanian king crab, which is armed with a massive – albeit useless – pincer. The market retailers display their daily catch on ice, and as I wander around I realise my seafood diet is shockingly limited. Wondering how I might cook some of this stuff, I head upstairs to the Sydney Seafood School, which is perfectly positioned to answer that very question.

Founded in 1989, Sydney Seafood School hosts more than 12,000 guests a year and offers dozens of cooking classes, from guest-chef sessions to today's 'Fast and Fabulous' lunchtime class. I'm seated with two dozen other students in a modern auditorium as Fiona Baxter teaches us how to prepare crab cakes with horseradish dressing, smoked trout with risoni salad, and stir-fried prawns with asparagus and sugar snap peas. These are three amazing seafood recipes for budding, not-quite-ambitious chefs. With bird's-eye cameras capturing her hands at work, Fiona drops useful kitchen tips such as how

are healthy, so that Australia's oceans can continue to provide for generations to come. Outside the auction room at one of the retail

to prepare garlic and ginger, peel prawns, preserve lemons, debone a smoked trout and efficiently use chopping boards. Since I do most of the cooking at home, I immediately scribble a note on the recipe booklet: *Take more cooking classes!* We divide into groups and head into the adjacent cooking stations; they are spotless, modern and fully equipped with everything we need to prepare our dishes. Gordon Ramsay would stomp all over Team Bucket List, as our small group proves that cooking is never *quite* as easy as it looks. That being said, we follow the recipes, do our best, and all three dishes emerge brilliantly, tasting just as good as they look.

Downstairs, we pick up a tray of a dozen freshly shucked Sydney rock oysters for under $20 and head home to continue the feast. Bucket lists inspire us to do remarkable things, but they can also teach us about the world we live in, and even the food we put in our mouths. A visit to Sydney Fish Market leaves me deeply impressed with Australia's seafood bounty and the fascinating industry that brings it to our dinner tables.

START HERE:
aussiebucketlist.com/
sydneyfishmarket

Spend a Night at the Opera

SYDNEY

Every day – and on the hour – visitors from Australia and around the world sign up for tours of the Sydney Opera House. There's the entry level tour, the early morning behind-the-scenes backstage tour, tours in Mandarin and Spanish, Korean, German, French and Japanese. With no disrespect, most of the 200,000 people who take these tours each year have never been to the opera, would fall asleep if they did and probably aren't the most ardent theatre-lovers. But it doesn't matter because something else has completely stolen the show. Ladies and gentlemen, please give a standing ovation for . . . the building itself. The Sydney Opera House always gives an award-winning performance. Drama, intrigue, passion, politics and genius are infused within the tiles of those instantly recognisable and iconic white sails. It's a tale best revealed in three acts.

ACT ONE: On the Nature of Foundation

It's the early 1950s, and the population of Australia is exploding. The director of the NSW Conservatorium of Music, Eugene Goossens, believes Sydney is ready for a world-class theatre. An ambitious state premier, Joseph Cahill, embraces the idea to cement his cultural and political legacy. They announce an international design competition, and receive 233 entries from 32 countries. Cue drama and intrigue until the winning proposal is announced: an outlandish design rescued from the contest's reject pile. The architect is a 34-year-old Dane by the name of Jørn Utzon, and the design is inspired by the natural world and Mayan pyramids. His sketches depict a remarkable structure unlike anything the world has ever seen. Judges declare it 'genius'. With political and financial support waning, the project is quickly greenlit and construction at a former tram depot on Bennelong Point commences in 1959. Nobody stops to consider that Utzon never consulted engineers when designing his proposal and had no idea how to physically construct his dramatic vision. The estimated budget is $7 million

More Facts about the Sydney Opera House

- The roof is covered with more than one million Swedish-made tiles, covering 1.62 hectares.
- Thirty-five kilometres of pipes move cool seawater pumped from the harbour around the building, maintaining the temperature.
- The Concert Hall must be kept at 22.5 degrees to ensure orchestra instruments remain in tune.
- The Grand Organ in the Concert Hall is the world's largest mechanical organ, with more than ten thousand pipes.
- If laid end-to-end, the tension cable used during construction would reach Canberra.
- The highest roof shell towers 67 metres above sea level, the equivalent of a twenty-two-storey building.
- Two million people watch a performance at the Sydney Opera House each year, and two hundred thousand take a guided tour.

and construction is expected to take three years. Before this act concludes, a side plot develops that involves Goossens, the dark arts, erotica and a supposed witch in Kings Cross. It doesn't have much to do with our story, but it is saucy. While Goossens returns to his native England in disgrace, the show must go on.

ACT TWO: On the Nature of Dreams, and the Nightmare of Reality

Within two years of breaking ground, construction is forty-seven weeks behind schedule. Engineers still have no idea how to build Utzon's iconic freestanding shells with any structural integrity. Over a dozen ideas fail the test until, finally, eureka! The shells will be constructed as weather-resistant segments from a single sphere, much like pieces of an orange. Construction continues slowly, and by 1966 taxpayers have forked out almost $30 million with the exteriors still incomplete. At this point, New South Wales sees a change in government, the entire project becomes an off-white elephant (if the tiles were white, the sun's reflection would blind anyone who looked at the building) and Utzon is forced to resign. He returns to Denmark in disgust and will never visit Sydney again. Under the leadership of Peter Hall, a team of architects and engineers recalibrate and re-visualise the interiors, dramatically altering Utzon's vision. Construction begins anew and in 1973 Queen Elizabeth formerly opens the Sydney Opera House for business, $95 million over budget and ten years behind schedule. Despite all the controversies, there is no denying it: a new world landmark had been created, and a soprano had yet to unleash a single note.

ACT THREE: On the Nature of Redemption

Up to fifteen hundred performances a year attended by an audience of 2 million; eight million site visitors a year; a UNESCO World Heritage Site; and without doubt the most iconic and recognisable landmark in Australia – clearly, the Sydney Opera House is *not* just another building. Although its history is modern, it nevertheless is part of the global cultural fabric and stands tall with icons like the Eiffel Tower, the Statue of Liberty and Big Ben. Other cities have attempted to mimic its striking design and location – see Vancouver's Canada Place or Dubai Opera – but Sydney's jewel continues to stand alone, unique and majestic. On the daily tour, you learn about the innovative solutions to the challenging design, such as heat-reflective glass to keep the interior cool, or double-baked tiles so the shells are cleaned with every raindrop. You hear how modern renovations brought light into the foyer 'dungeon' and how nets above the orchestra pit in the Joan Sutherland Theatre have stopped chickens falling on the heads of musicians. You'll visit the grand Concert Hall, and the flexible Studio space, and pose on the royal purple staircase. Beyond the history, you'll also learn that Utzon's contribution was formerly recognised with a flurry of awards in his later life, although the great architect refused to revisit Australia and died in 2008 without ever seeing the masterpiece that built his career.

There's enough drama in the story of the Sydney Opera House to fill several operas, and this chapter offers just the briefest of a synopsis. The daily tours are interesting – especially for those of limited time or budget – but our bucket list insists you buy a ticket, take your seat, enjoy a show and give a standing ovation. Bravo, bravo!

START HERE:
**aussiebucketlist.com/
sydneyoperahouse**

Learn about Country on a Sand Dune Adventure

Thumb on the throttle, I'm ripping a quad bike through the largest coastal dune system in the southern hemisphere. With the Pacific Ocean visible from the tallest dunes, the landscape is far from a lifeless sandy desert. The Worimi Conservation Lands are alive with history, people, stories and culture, and embody one of the more important adventures on our national bucket list. For this is not just a chapter about the exhilaration of conquering 30-metre-high dunes on a 400cc quad bike. It is the story of an Aboriginal community proudly embracing their history and identity, while building and sustaining a successful future. It is a story of how different cultures can connect through adventure, and a story that Australia needs.

This book is not the forum to delve into the tragedy that befell the nation's Indigenous people. Growing up in South Africa and living in Canada, I'm fully aware that centuries of entrenched, government-sanctioned racism has scarred generations – or wiped them out entirely – in a manner non-Indigenous people can never understand. As a result, pain, distrust and bitterness are infused into the fabric of Aboriginal life. In the world of tourism, it is too easy to overlook the reality of injustice. From the Americas to Asia, some tourism organisations have deliberately steered me away from Indigenous stories, or channelled me towards glossy cultural shows that pay lip service to a culture through clichés and stereotypes. I've asked hundreds of people on my Australian journey what inspires them to travel, and one of the most common answers is 'to experience different cultures.' Travellers want to connect and understand; to learn, discuss and participate in a meaningful interaction that benefits all parties around the campfire.

In 2007, almost 11,000 acres of land along the New South Wales coast was granted to the Worimi Local Aboriginal Land Council. Most of it was leased back to the NSW National Parks and Wildlife Service, with key

Leading a group of tourists from around the world, Andrew pauses our quad-bike adventure on the top of a dune, from which we can see the blue ocean sparkling in the distance. 'Our company is owned and operated 100 per cent by the Worimi LALC Aboriginal community,' he continues. 'Aboriginal culture means that we are part of the land, not owners of it. It is who we are, it's not mine, it's me.'

He explains how unused ordinance was dumped on the coast during World War II, how the land was used as bombing range, and the beach strung with razor wire to avert a Japanese invasion. Much later, the dunes were invaded by campers and four-wheel drive enthusiasts, who paid little respect to the land or its cultural significance.

'*Midden* is a Scottish word for a rubbish heap of human waste, but our sites are not rubbish heaps. These are our stories, our history and we call them *Ngurras* (ancient campsites). A majority of the *Ngurras* found in the dunes are burial grounds that date back many generations,' says Andrew.

He discusses the geological formation of the dunes, the

parcels retained by the council for business ventures to generate income. With kilometres of unspoilt coastal dunes, the opportunity for epic quad biking was recognised, coupled with an idea to promote and celebrate Worimi culture and heritage. Daily quad-bike tours are viewed through a cultural lens, connecting this striking landscape with a people that have always inhabited it.

'I often say to people: "Don't just pick up a book and read about Aboriginal people, come and share in our culture and speak to the people the book is written about!",' explains the CEO of Sand Dune Adventures, Andrew Smith.

shipwrecks that have littered the coast, and how coastal winds are constantly reshaping the dunes, covering up evidence while revealing more history. We hop back on our bikes and blitz through more spectacular dunes with a deeper understanding of this remarkable environment. We stop to toboggan down a particularly steep hill on thin plastic boards, an activity which elicits wild giggles from the Japanese girls in my group. Another Worimi guide, Jim Lawrence, asks us to follow him on our bikes to a nearby cultural site. He demonstrates how rubbing wattle leaves creates a fragrant soap, how you can crush lemon myrtle leaves to relieve a sore throat, and how a banksia flower can be lit and used as a torch.

I imagine what it must have been like living amongst these dunes for many thousands of years, thriving in an area that stretched nearly 4000 square kilometres. I wonder what the Worimi must have thought of the arrival of European settlers, and how they endured it. This included timber speculators who, according to 19th-century British company agent Robert Dawson, shot the Worimi on sight.

'Jim, can I ask you a question?'
'Go ahead, Robin.'
'Can we talk about the Aboriginal experience in Australia?'

Jim is honest and forthright, and answers my many questions under the baking mid-morning sun. We discuss my First Nation experiences in Canada, the similarities that exist

Cuddle a Stingray

Sharks and stingrays get a bad wrap. Although horses and kangaroos kill far more people than sharks each year, the ocean's apex predator gets ravaged in the press. And then there's the Steve Irwin tragedy – killed by a stingray. Husband and wife team Ryan and Lia Pereira are working hard to change perceptions. They took over a hands-on shark and ray aquarium in Port Stephens and turned it into Irukandji Shark and Ray Encounters, a business devoted to busting harmful myths and educating visitors about marine conservation. Visitors can slip on a wetsuit and get into a series of pools with more than 200 creatures, including curious southern eagle rays, friendly Port Jackson sharks, cuddly blue spotted mask rays, massive smooth rays and 3-metre-long tawny nurse sharks. The facility is a little rough around the edges but Ryan and Lia's devotion to and passion for their animals is inspiring, and the lessons they impart to visitors of all ages is vital. In the words of David Attenborough: 'No one will protect what they don't care about; and no one will care about what they have never experienced.'

with some tribal bands mired in social troubles and unable to move forward, and others working hard towards a brighter future.

'It's all about education, education, education. We have to learn to work within the system, while always being true to our culture and identity,' says Jim. There is pain and frustration and outrage in his comments, but also hope and humour and generosity.

Sand Dune Adventures is a not-for-profit enterprise that employs more than forty people, while providing opportunities and scholarships for members of the Worimi community. The company is driven by a vision to sustain, respect and protect its heritage, and authentically connect with people who visit from around Australia and abroad. Quad biking the massive coastal dunes in Worimi Country is a thrilling bucket list adventure. The fact that it provides an opportunity for dialogue with just one of the many diverse Aboriginal communities of Australia makes it utterly essential.

START HERE:
**aussiebucketlist.com/
sandduneadventure**

Learn to Surf

BONDI BEACH / BYRON BAY

'**G**reat wave, man!'
I've just fallen off my foam learner board in the shallow waters of Byron Bay, and some guy is giving the international hand signal for 'well done!'. It was my first proper wave, barely, and I must have looked as graceful as a flying emu. So I look around to see who caught the great wave in question, but there's nobody behind me. And then I know, at that moment, that I had indeed got up, stayed up, and flown along the break. It crystalised for me why people of all ages and abilities are obsessed with surfing, and why Bondi Beach and Byron Bay are the two best places in the country to learn how to do it.

'I've never met anyone who's felt worse when they get out of the ocean, than before they got in it,' explains Brenda Miley outside her shop on Bondi Beach. Let's Go Surfing started out the back of Brenda's Kombi van in 1995, when she combined her passion for surfing (and especially encouraging girls into the sport) with a love of teaching. Her company now has offices in Bondi, Byron and Maroubra, and has introduced tens of thousands of students to the sport. Today, Brenda will be taking my wife and me into the rolling swells of Australia's most famous beach. The turquoise waters, soft

Best Places to Learn to Surf in NSW

- Byron Bay
- Bondi Beach
- Maroubra
- Yamba
- Manly Beach
- Crescent Head
- The Farm, Killalea State Park
- Jetty Beach, Coffs Harbour

sand and hard bodies of Bondi never cease to amaze me. In a major world city, beaches just shouldn't look *this* good (and, of course, they only get better as you move up and down the

coast). Sydney is Australia's gateway city, and the 1-kilometre-long Bondi crescent sees more traffic than any other beach in the country. With an exposed beach break and reliably good conditions, Bondi has more and more tourists wanting to try surfing, and locals too.

'About 50 per cent of our business is tourists, 50 per cent locals. We have programs for mums, programs for kids, after school programs. Having someone hold your hand when you go out there is a big thing,' explains Brenda. Learning to surf is not easy, and the curve is steep, but nobody ever forgets his or her first wave. Today, the waves are a little big and the current is a little strong. Experienced surfers are gathered as usual at the north end of the beach

but, despite Brenda's patience and supreme effort, I'm struggling to stay up. On the other hand, my wife is standing up straight away. She's Brazilian, so I'm surprised she doesn't break out into a samba. If you've ever wondered why surfers look so tanned and fit, it's because they're paddling hard and spend a lot of time in the sun, waiting for that perfect wave. Sitting upright on my board, lifted by the swells, I'm coached by Brenda to let go of expectations, stop worrying about standing up, and just enjoy the ocean. Each wave is different, a

natural wonder, and it reminds us to slow down. Out here, nobody is looking at smartphones, worrying about work, stewing in Sydney's awful traffic.

'I'm suuuuuurrrffffing!' squeals one of the students, a young English guy on his first wave, having a major life moment. Bondi won't present *my* moment today, but what's the rush?

'If there's one thing surfing has taught me more than anything, it's patience.' Blake Whittaker, a senior instructor at Let's Go Surfing in Byron Bay, is pointing out the peeling point break of the Pass. He'd given me the choice of surfing the Wreck or Main Beach,

ideal spots to learn, with consistent north-facing waves.

'But if you're ready for it, my goal is to give you the best wave of your life, which we'll find at the Pass,' he says. My brain wants to practice standing up but my heart wants the best wave of my life – and this book, as you've probably noticed, is all about following your heart.

Renowned as one of the best surf breaks in the country, the Pass serves up rolling waves you can ride and ride and ride. What's more, we don't have to paddle but can simply walk out, hop on our boards, and Blake can launch us on the wave. I'm immediately struck not

only by the scenic beauty of Byron Bay, but also by the sheer diversity of people surfing. There are long-haired surfer dudes, mums and dads, backpackers, babes and business types. People on foamy blue boards, long boards and shredders. Surfing is a great democratiser, because in the ocean nobody cares who you are, what you own, how good you are, or where you come from. Like life itself, everyone is on their own wave, and every wave is guaranteed to be different.

On my board, hands close to my ribs, looking straight ahead, I manage to stand pretty quickly with some help from Blake. A few waves in, I get up and stay up, and the wave just keeps going and going. Gravity seems to disappear as the soothing whoosh of water and the warm wind embrace me. It's just me, the ocean, and a most *awesome* wave. Blake says that most people only need about five lessons before they're rocking the bigger waves, gaining confidence in their balance, paddling, and ability to read the ocean. And it only gets better from there. For every wave promises a different ride, and so does every beach in the country. Surfers know exactly what I'm talking about. If you've never hopped on a board, don't worry, you're in the finest of hands with a quality surf school. And in Bondi Beach and Byron Bay, the very finest of locations.

START HERE:
aussiebucketlist.com/learntosurf

Bucket List Places to Surf in Australia

- [x] Byron Bay and Lennox Head, NSW
- [ ] Margaret River, WA
- [ ] Torquay, VIC
- [ ] Noosa, QLD
- [ ] Victor Harbor, SA
- [ ] Bicheno, TAS
- [ ] Snapper Rocks, QLD

Feel the Energy of Crystal Castle

Throughout human history, different cultures around the world have treasured crystals. Formed over millions of years, crystals are believed to generate, store, regulate, transmit and transform energy. This makes them particularly valuable and alluring to those of a new age and alternative bent, and simply gorgeous to look at for the rest of us. This is the story of a local crystal wholesaler who dreamt of creating a subtropical rainforest garden bejewelled with the world's largest crystals. Seduced by the promise of owning an unusual home built on clear-cut land about twenty minutes from Byron Bay, Naren King battled to raise financing and took on many risks. But you can't fault the man's intuition – the risks paid off.

The hippies and the dippies that the Byron Bay area is known for began to show up to absorb the energy from Naren's growing crystal collection. How could you not provide organic tea, a retail store selling crystals, and labyrinths to help visitors 'find' themselves? Sure, it's not like the Macadamia Castle down the road, another tourist attraction that *actually* looks like a castle. But Naren believed that if you build it, they will come. Thirty years later, he continues to be proven right.

There is nowhere on the planet quite like Crystal Castle and the Shambhala Gardens. Driving in on a scenic country road, I'm welcomed by flapping Tibetan prayer flags that wave at me like colourful hands. Though inspired by Eastern spiritual traditions, the Castle is not a religious place, and nobody is pushing anything other than harmony, beauty and balance – and perhaps the products and services that might help you get there. The Kalachakra World Peace Stupa is a striking monument built by Tibetan Buddhists, filled with sacred objects, and blessed by a representative of the Dalai Lama. One of only seven such

structures in the world, and the only one in the southern hemisphere, the stupa is a site of pilgrimage and reflection. Behind it, I remove my shoes for a reflexology walk, stepping on smooth pebbles that surround a four-tonne chunk of

rose quartz. Nearby is a tree with thousands of notes tied to it, each note bearing a wish or vow from a visitor. The Damanhur spiral is an energy link connecting to the Sacred Woods in Italy, and there are various rules to follow to keep the link charged. It's getting a bit out there for me, but those into this kind of thing will enjoy it (just don't deactivate the Stargate by crossing the stone lines). A small cement labyrinth reminds us that mazes were built for us to get lost in, but ancient labyrinths were spaces for meditative enquiry. Behind closed curtains is the Enchanted Cave – if

it doesn't take your breath away, check your pulse. Five-and-a-half metres wide and weighing 20 tons, it is the largest amethyst geode in the world, a massive, hollow, egg-shaped rock lined with sparkling purple stardust. Peeking inside, it's as if I've immersed myself in one of those Hubble Telescope photos of a distant galaxy, with surreal, yet strangely organic light and colour. Naren had to re-mortgage his property to procure and ship the cave from its discovery site in remote northern Uruguay. Visitors can pay extra to meditate within the cave itself;

the energy within it is almost tangible. Revisiting it several times throughout the morning, I noticed how not a single visitor entered the small, dark room without saying 'Wow!'

Steps away is the Fountain of Peace, where a 310-kilogram polished orb of rose quartz set atop a block of dark granite spins on millimetres of water. Adjacent is a painted mural inspired by the temples of Angkor Wat, with an archway framed by a 3.4-metre-tall amethyst geode. Inspired visitors are now led into a meditation room, the vegetarian cafe and a retail space, where all manner of crystal geodes, jewellery, books, semi-precious stones, candles and other new age knick-knacks are sold. You can also pay to have your tarot read and your aura photographed. No doubt there will be some visitors not quite aligned to the energy of the place, and they might wonder if the entire experience is a cleverly masked and expensive retail excursion. It's certainly a business, but one devoted to the healing and transformative powers of crystals and meditation, and one that has donated tens of thousands of dollars to worthy charities in Nepal. It has also restored a clear-cut landscape into incredible gardens and regenerated rare subtropical rainforest.

I wander along the Buddha Walk, where visitors donate coins on the statues of deities like Ganesh, Lakshmi, and Avalokiteshvara (all money collected is donated to charities). Some take a seat on the

Crystal Clear about Geodes

Geodes are spherical rocks with hollow cavities that contain crystals. In volcanic rock, they are formed when bubbles within lava slowly cools. Over millions of years, groundwater leeches into the cavity through cracks, depositing various minerals. When silicon and oxygen combine, it creates quartz. Structures in the crystal atoms reflect various light waves, resulting in different colours. You won't know what the geode will look like until you crack it open. Every geode is unique, with amethyst crystals particularly prized for their appearance and energy.

ancient petrified rock logs from Madagascar, or cool off beneath the shade of a creaking bamboo forest. Perhaps now you are ready to participate in one of the daily experiences, like a calming meditation or puja ritual. Perhaps now you're ready to recharge between the Crystal Guardians. Split in two, the world's tallest quartz geode towers five-and-a-half metres high, casting a shadow over the beautiful valley. Made of smoky quartz sprinkled with shimmering amethyst and calcite crystal flowers, the pair face each other like two hands gently cupping anyone who stands between them,

which is precisely what you're invited to do. Weighing 20 tons and also discovered in Uruguay, these magnificent crystal sentinels transcend words. If you close your eyes, take a deep breath and place a hand on each stone, the crystals might just flood you with a deep sense of harmony. Whether you choose to believe in the power of crystal energy or not, there's no denying the unique beauty of these magical stones, waiting for you in a place that is just as unique, beautiful and magical, too.

START HERE:
aussiebucketlist.com/
crystalgardens

Freefall over Lake Macquarie

For a pivotal scene in the movie *The Bucket List*, special effects were used to superimpose the faces of Jack Nicholson and Morgan Freeman onto stunt doubles enjoying a tandem skydive. Come on, Jack! Really, Morgan? One of the tandem pilots at Skydive Newcastle tells me his oldest clients were well over ninety, but it really shouldn't matter how old you are. Having tried just about everything else in the world of commercial adventure, I think there is simply no bigger rush than falling out of a plane from 4500 metres. It's a relatively safe adventure that I believe *anyone* can — and should — do before they die.

Yes, safe. Safety procedures and innovative mechanisms have all but eliminated accidents (although in the rare tragic cases when one does happen, you will *definitely* hear about it on the news). There's more chance you'll get stung to death by honeybees, killed by a champagne cork, get your ticket punched by a cow or be struck by lightning than die on a commercial tandem skydive. My tandem instructor Dave shows me a sensor that will deploy the parachute automatically, and patiently explains the workings of his dual-chute the way a parent might convince a toddler that a new pair of shoes are the perfect fit.

Tandem jumps let experienced professionals take care of everything, while you merely enjoy the ride – no training required, no experience necessary. Skydive Australia, a publicly traded company, hosts hundreds of jumpers *every day* in eighteen drop zones around the country. I'm hoping this paragraph has reassured you about the risk, because I'd like to move on to what it feels like to edge your way along a bench towards an open door on a small plane high above the largest coastal seawater lake in Australia.

There is no bad place to tandem skydive. Each drop zone will have its own charm and unique features. I chose Lake Macquarie because of its stunning water features: the Pacific Ocean, long sandy beaches and a channel feeding a sparkling gem-blue lake streaked with sand banks. I couldn't have asked for a more friendly, reassuring and calming tandem instructor than Dave, a man with the demeanour of someone who clearly enjoys his job. And after several days of wet autumn weather, I also couldn't have asked for a sunnier and clear day. I pull on some blue overalls, slip into a harness and listen to Dave explaining the simple

landing procedure. Unfortunately, there's too much wind today to land on the beach, but the good news is there's another adventure lined up at the airport when we get back. (See page 140).

We climb into the plane and begin our ascent. This is a part of the world that truly needs to be seen from above.

'We're attached, so if you go anywhere, I'm coming with you,' says Dave, after checking and rechecking the various clips and attachments.

'That's only because I think we've got a real connection,' I reply.

The altimeter on his wrist ticks higher and higher and a red-orange-green light at the back of the plane tells us we're getting close.

'Any butterflies, Robin?' Dave asks.

'Just one really big one, with spikes on the tips of its wings,' I answer back.

I know that, statistically, driving to the airport from my room at the Oaks Cypress Lakes Resort in the Hunter Valley was way more dangerous than tandem skydiving. Yet every cell in my body is screaming: 'What the hell are you doing, you idiot? Do you think you have wings? Does having a bird name make you a bird? Eagles may soar but chickens don't get sucked into jet engines. Tell Dave you'll land with the pilot and go back to the hotel for a nice shiraz and wedge of roasted Camembert.'

My cells, as you can tell, are particularly obnoxious, and really like their cheese and wine. Point being, being petrified is part of the experience, and a personal challenge each rookie jumper needs to overcome. Like so many experiences in this book, it's not the danger or risk that's holding you back – it's fear. Nelson Mandela said that 'courage is not the absence of fear, but the triumph over it.' And Michael Jordan: 'Limits, like fear, are often an illusion.' Franklin D. Roosevelt, Mark Twain, Plato, heck even Taylor Swift have great quotes about fear. There's healthy fear: the thought of jumping out of a plane without a parachute. There is also an unhealthy fear: the thought that prevents you from jumping out of a plane with a parachute and someone else to operate it. The

fear that holds us back from life experiences that are impossible to replicate, impossible to forget and almost impossible to describe.

Holding my harness, head tucked back into Dave's chest, we scoot over to the edge and drop. The first few seconds are disorientating, because plummeting is not a sensation non-skydivers are familiar with. We quickly stabilise, Dave's hand appears with a thumbs-up, and my wits have returned sufficiently to return the gesture. If the rush of terminal velocity wasn't forcing a smile from ear to ear, I would be doing it anyway. Just a few seconds into the 40-second freefall, I look

around, spin 360 degrees, and feel the forces of gravity massaging every inch of my body. Unlike in the movies, there's way too much wind to communicate verbally until the parachute deploys and, suddenly, we're floating gently under its canopy. Dave lets me take the steering lines and, enjoying the sensation of control, I spin us around to take in the enormity of Lake Macquarie's magical view. It doesn't take long before he gives me the signal to tuck my legs up for the landing, and we slide softly on the grass just metres from the tarmac where we boarded the plane. I'm pickled with adrenalin and busting with exuberance. This moment is waiting for you on the New South Wales coast, and all around the country, too. It's never too late to put your own face in the picture, and live your own life to the fullest. No stunt doubles or special effects necessary.

START HERE:
aussiebucketlist.com/
skydivenewcastle

Scenic Flights in Microlights

Bundle your skydive with a bucket list flight of a lifetime. Also located at Lake Macquarie Airport, Airborne is an Australian manufacturer of world-class microlights that also offers pilot training and scenic flights in microlights, gyrocopters and hang gliders. Rory Duncan, an Australian hang-gliding champion and the third generation in his pioneering family-run business, takes me for an introductory flight in one of their new M3 Sport microlights. Comfortably seated and strapped in, he fires up the Rotax four-stroke engine and within seconds we're flying like birds above the spectacular coastline, with Rory steering the wing as he would a hang-glider. Communicating via headset, he points out Caves Beach, Catherine Hill Bay, and a spot where sharks are known to gather at the mouth of the Swansea Channel. It's unnervingly liberating to be so exposed this high up, yet even if the engine was to fail, microlights can glide to safety. With skydives and Airborne flights available in discounted packages, you should seriously consider booking yourself in for a double-whammy bucket list morning over Lake Macquarie.

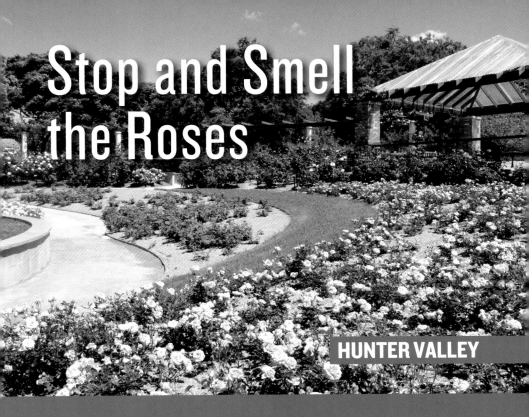

Stop and Smell the Roses

HUNTER VALLEY

Around 35,000 rose bushes, representing 150 different varieties, are spread across 12 hectares in Australia's largest show gardens. How could our bucket list not stop for a sniff? The creation of entrepreneurs Bill and Imelda Roche, the Hunter Valley Gardens are just one of the many petals that make up the Hunter Valley, a region well known for its blossoming lifestyle. Two hours' drive from Sydney, it is Australia's oldest wine region, home to more than 150 vineyards and all the other attractions that fine wine brings: restaurants, hotels, golf courses, festivals, markets and shopping. Rolling hills lined with vines and the distant Great Dividing Range certainly paint a fetching view.

With its proximity to Australia's biggest city, the Hunter Valley sees millions of visitors every year, including a steady stream of bridal parties and plenty of interest from the business and political elite. This perhaps explains why the Roche Group also owns a hotel, vineyard, restaurant and shopping village, located close to their lovely gardens in Pokolbin. There are ten themed gardens and more than 8 kilometres of pathways, all built over four years by a team of forty landscape architects and gardeners. Hopping on board a 35-minute introductory train ride, I learn how landscapers are assigned a particular garden for two years and then rotate. How the famous Butchart Gardens on Vancouver Island inspired the Sunken Garden. How Bill bought the naming rights to the Imelda rose as an anniversary present for his wife, and the variety can only be found here. We see the Moon Gate in the Chinese Garden that wards off bad spirits, the two-storey Japanese pagoda overlooking a pond of curious koi, the French and English-inspired Formal Garden, the cascading geraniums and pelargoniums in the Italian Grotto. Antique gates that are 160 years old lead us into the Indian Garden, which has impressive mosaics,

hedges and the distinct fragrance of curry plants permeating the air.

Open during events, there's a towering 25-metre ferris wheel, flying swing chair, 35-metre-long superslide, and lovely Venetian carousel for the kids. For families visiting outside of special events – including Snow Time, Springtime in the Gardens, Rose Spectacular or Christmas Lights – the Storybook Garden delights kids with life-size recreations of Alice in Wonderland, Hansel and Gretel (the house of candy cleverly doubles as toilets for over-excited toddlers), Humpty Dumpty, Hey Diddle Diddle and Jack and Jill. As I wander along the pathways, it's hard not to admire the vision and hard work that goes into the place; the 100 kilometres of irrigation that recycles water through the gardens, the 250,000 annuals, 6000 trees, 500,000-plus shrubs and over a million ground covers. Maintaining all this without public funding is not cheap, and some might find the entrance fee a little hefty, especially considering that the

Royal Botanic Garden in Sydney, the Blue Mountains Botanic Garden and the Australian Botanic Garden in Mount Annan are all free, and closer to the city. Still, the rich and royal have historically locked up their manicured garden estates, and the Roches have made theirs public – at a price – providing a location for the 150 to 200 weddings the gardens host each year. Any rosy excuse that will get us into the lovely Hunter Valley is well worth stopping for.

START HERE:
**aussiebucketlist.com/
huntervalley**

Australia's Bucket List Gardens

☐ Australian National Botanic Gardens, Canberra, ACT

☐ The Australian Garden, Cranbourne, VIC

☑ Kings Park and Botanical Garden, Perth, WA

☐ Royal Tasmanian Botanical Gardens, Hobart, TAS

☐ Maleny Botanic Gardens, QLD

☐ Alice Springs Desert Park, NT

☐ Adelaide Botanic Garden, SA

Marvel at the Blue Mountains

There's a scene in the movie *Superman III* when our hero flies to a coal mine with comedy legend Richard Pryor. Superman picks up a piece of coal, squeezes it with his super strong strength and, voila, he is holding a large sparkling diamond. Harry Hammon and his sister Isobel did one better. It's 1945, and tourists are driving up from Sydney to the Blue Mountains to ride a steeply inclined coal mine railway. Although built to haul coal and shale up a cliff from the mine to the town of Katoomba, the train also ferried passengers, who would pay a sixpence on weekends and holidays to experience the railway's thrilling 52-degree incline. When the mine lost its major contract, the siblings bought the property to focus on tourism. Today, Scenic World is a third-generation, family-run business, and Australia's most visited privately owned attraction.

The modest 12-seater wooden coal skip has made way for a modern 84-passenger train, and the world's steepest passenger railway is now accompanied by the glass-bottomed Skyway and enormous Cableway.

'Where are the mountains?' asks my daughter as we drive into the foothills of the Blue Mountains. In Western Canada, where we live, we're accustomed to seeing peaks towering above us, but here the road has meandered off the highway through a series of small towns, and the mountains are nowhere to be seen. Soon we arrive in the main centre of Katoomba, where the abundance of restaurants and coffee shops are testament to the region's popularity. The town sits on an escarpment that gazes across an expansive valley, part of the 10,000 square-kilometre Greater Blue Mountains World Heritage Area. The viewing area at Echo Point, about 2 kilometres from town, is one of the most visited spots in Australia. Here you can see the Three Sisters rock formation, the dense forest of the Jamison Valley, and a distinctly blue-ish haze on the horizon.

'The reason you can't see the mountains is because we're right at the top of one of them,' I explain to my daughter. 'Don't worry, we've come to the right place to change that.' First we hop on board Scenic World's Skyway, which carries visitors 270 metres above the ravine floor and over the lovely Katoomba waterfall. It opened in 1958 as the country's first cable car, and Skyway's latest carriage features a glass-bottomed area so you can enjoy looking down as well as out. It's the best ride to see the Three Sisters, as they gaze over a vista

so vast and untamed it's jarring to think we're just ninety minutes from Sydney's gridlock. Some passengers will use the Skyway as a means to access the 140 kilometres of trails inside Blue Mountains National Park, but most will return across the ravine, grab a bite to eat and head to the Cableway. It's the steepest and largest aerial cable car in the southern hemisphere, with a multi-tiered floor so everyone gets a grand view as we descend 510 metres into the valley.

The plateau has created unusual atmospheric conditions, giving rise to more than forty endemic species of plants, many dating back to the Jurassic era. It is also home to ninety species of eucalypts, which release fine particles of oil into the atmosphere, scattering light rays and causing the namesake blue haze. When we disembark, we follow a 2.4-kilometre wooden boardwalk on a loop alongside sassafras and lilli pilli trees, ancient ferns and apple gums. And while it's unlikely you'll spot a quoll, koala or sooty owl, you might hear a phone ring that's actually a birdcall. The superb lyrebird is capable of mimicking many different sounds, including ringtones and chainsaws.

The Giant Stairway

For those with more time and stamina, consider a historic trail that takes you from Echo Point down more than eight hundred steps into the valley. The steps were originally cut in 1909, and the Three Sisters tower above you as you hike 4.7 kilometres one-way along Federation Pass to Katoomba Falls. Here, you can either climb up the gruelling 2.4 kilometre Furber Steps to the top or, better yet, hop on board the Scenic Railway for a very steep ride of a lifetime.

The path leads us to the original coal mine entrance, which has information boards about the arduous history of late 19th-century mining. Nearby is the steep railway car that kick-started tourism here. It was originally powered by coal, and when I stand at the bottom of the 310-metre-track, I realise they must have needed a lot of it to get up this hill. Today everything is electric, with swishy automatic doors, smiling operators and a button that automatically adjusts the incline of your forward-facing chair for comfort and thrills. It doesn't take very long to get to the top but it is plenty long enough to make you hold tight, brace your knees against the cushioned support bar and wonder – as I have many times on this journey – how is this a thing?

It's a question Harry Hammon probably asked himself when American servicemen showed up during the war, looking for the legendary steep railway car. It's a thing because the location is extraordinary, the views are staggering and there's nowhere else in the world where you can ride anything like it. With all due respect to Superman, the Scenic Railway even won the Best Use of Steel Award from Master Builders Australia. Forget super strength – it took vision, financial risk and hard work for the Hammons to transform a failed coal mine into a diamond attraction on our Great Australian Bucket List.

START HERE:
aussiebucketlist.com/scenicworld

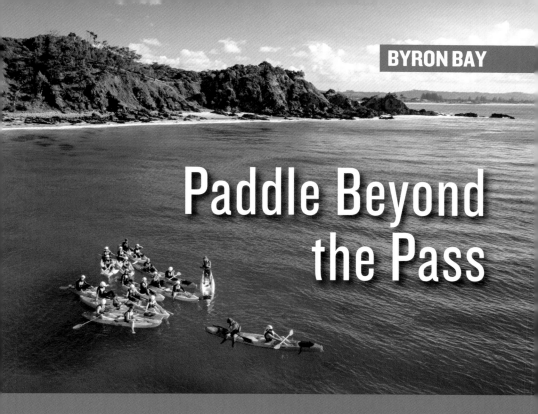

Paddle Beyond the Pass

'Forget Byron the *town*, this is Byron *Bay!*' It is Sunday morning and Dougie Meagher and his crew have somehow managed to get thirty tourists on sea kayaks beyond the crashing waves and big swells rolling into Clarkes Beach. A small crowd has gathered to watch this superhuman effort. Go Sea Kayaks' owner, Kurt Tutt, steers, pushes and paddles out a kayak with two women on it, hands over the paddle, dives into the water, swims 50 metres back to shore and repeats it all over again. A three-time world title surf lifesaving medallist, Kurt makes it look easy, although just watching him makes my biceps shudder. The waves are choppier than usual this morning, and it's a busy long weekend. Despite a few challenges, everyone is eventually over the break and paddling towards Cape Byron Lighthouse. With Dougie around, it's easy to enjoy our accomplishment.

'Happy, happy, joy, joy, love, peace and good vibes!' he tells us. 'What a great day! Look how clear this water is! Soak your feet in our soothing Byron salts!' Everything Dougie says demands an exclamation mark, and he's totally right.

Before Byron Bay became Australia's hotspot for surfing, yoga, beach life, celebrities and backpacking, it was and remains a gorgeous inlet on the most easterly tip of the country. The Arakwal people called it Cavvanbah, a meeting place, although Captain James Cook had other ideas. He named it Byron Bay after a fellow sailor and the early days of European settlement belie the peaceful, new-age cosmic energy that permeates the place today. Humpback whales were once herded and slaughtered right on Main Beach, painting the sands

in blood. There was wholesale timber forestry, pig, beef and dairy farming, sand mining, meat processing – all of which is increasingly hard to imagine given the region's reputation as a granola tourist mecca, and a protected natural paradise. The reinvention and rehabilitation since the 1960s is so remarkable it's no wonder Dougie is upbeat.

'Did you see that turtle? Who here saw a turtle? Wasn't he great? Over there's the Pass, that's one of the best surf spots in the country!'

A boat departs from the beach with divers on their way to the renowned Julian Rocks, while dozens of surfers gather close to the rocks to catch the incoming waves.

'See those millionaires on the hill?' says Dougie, pointing out large mansions that sit above the Pass. 'They pay a lot of money so they can look at us kayakers having a great time!'

Our three-person kayaks are sturdy and stable, and Go Sea Kayaks' adventures are family friendly. Today, the big swells are proving to be a little challenging even for the adults. Rolling with the waves, I start to feel a bit seasick. Dougie suggests that I dip my cap

into the water to remind my head that I'm basically swimming.

'It's a better cure for seasickness than any pill!'

I follow his advice and, sure enough, the queasiness eases. We're paddling out this morning in the hope of encountering the bay's 100-strong resident bottle-nose dolphins. If it were June to November, we'd be on the lookout for humpback whales returning from Antarctica, safe from whalers but certainly in the sights of excited locals and visitors. Kayaking among dolphins and whales is magical, and crowds also gather at the 19th-century Cape Byron

Lighthouse for sweeping ocean views and wildlife spotting.

'Yesterday I saw the dolphins from the lighthouse,' says Roni, a fellow kayaker. Dougie is standing on his kayak looking for dorsal fins.

'I'm also seeing those dorsal fin . . . *waves*! They're everywhere this morning! When we get lifted by a beautiful Byron wave, it's like being on the top of a mountain, so keep a lookout!'

In fact, your chances of seeing dolphins are so good Go Sea Kayak guarantee it, and will take you out again for free if you miss them. I once went on a whale-watching excursion in Canada's Bay of Fundy with a supposed 99 per cent chance of seeing whales – and we didn't see any whales. Call me a jinx. I have had incredible dolphin and whale encounters over the years, although they generally occur when I'm in the water not looking for dolphins and whales. Despite Dougie's enthusiasm and the strong odds, the local dolphins decide to avoid the kayaks this morning.

'That's Mother Nature! We get what we're given, but don't worry, we'll take you out again for another opportunity! Hasn't it been fun this morning? It's sure been an adventure!'

Hopping off the kayak, we soak in the turquoise bay with water clear enough to see the shallow ocean floor. It *has* been fun, and it has been an adventure. Especially when we kayak on the crests of waves back to shore. You'll never forget the first time you surfed on a sea kayak. Some days the wildlife come out to play, and some days they don't. Don't fret. The opportunity to paddle into Australia's most famous bay, soak up inspiring natural beauty and meet local characters happens daily – bucket list guaranteed!

START HERE:
aussiebucketlist.com/ seakayakbyronbay

The Sun from Cape Byron

There weren't nearly as many people packed into Shark Bay, Western Australia, to see the last sunset in the country – but this *is* Byron Bay. Every morning, crowds hike up Lighthouse Road to catch the sun breaking like a yolk across Australia's most easterly horizon. There is parking at the top but it's very limited and fills up fast. Make a morning of it and continue onto the 4-kilometre loop of the Cape Byron Walking Track, taking in views of the Pass, Wategos Beach and the brightest lighthouse of its kind in the southern hemisphere.

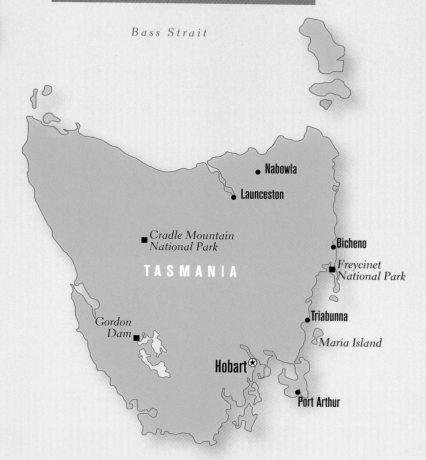

VICTORIA

TASMANIA

Bass Strait

- Nabowla
- Launceston

■ Cradle Mountain
National Park

TASMANIA

- Bicheno

*Freycinet
National Park*

- Triabunna

Maria Island

Hobart ⋆

Gordon
Dam ■

- Port Arthur

INDIAN OCEAN

Cycle, Kayak And Walk

TASMANIA'S EAST COAST

With deep respect for those bucket listers who choose to cycle or hike their way across the nation, I — like many readers — lack the fitness, time or energy to even attempt such an endeavour. Tasmania's east coast is rich with incredible nature experiences in relatively close proximity, making it the perfect location to attempt an active multi-day outdoor excursion. How to do this without the full physical slog, the equipment expenses, or the logistical headaches? Consider Tasmanian Expeditions' Cycle, Kayak and Walk Tasmania trip — a six-day, once-in-a-lifetime adventure that ticks all the bucket list boxes.

Joining me are a dozen travellers from the USA, England and Australia, ranging in age and physical ability, but blessed with a spirit of discovery. Gathered by our two guides in Launceston, we kick things off with a drive to Fingal, towing bikes and gear on a trailer. Ahead is an introductory 43-kilometre ride through rolling hills and pure pastoral bliss. I've never ridden anywhere near that sort of distance before, but the hills are kind, the weather fine, the camaraderie already in place, and the support van trailing behind us reassuring. Everyone pedals at their own pace, and nobody is particularly perturbed when I *moo* to the cows, *baa-baa* to the sheep, or urge myself

on with song. We gear down for the day's highlight, a 7-kilometre blitz down the steep St Mary's Pass for our first glimpse of the Tasman Sea. Cruising along a final coastal stretch rewards us with cold pints from the Ironhouse Brewery, a refreshing conclusion to our first day in the saddle. While our guides Maddy and Belle prepare the first of many fine dinners, I explore the coastal rocks of Bicheno in search of fairy penguins. Instead I find a good show watching tourists get soaked by the aptly named Blow Hole. Sunset casts a lovely glow across the sky, as my tired muscles tingle with the buzz of accomplishment.

The trick of multi-day adventures is to deny your body an

opportunity to stiffen up. Constant exercise quashes muscular rebellions. After a wholesome breakfast, we're back in the saddle for the morning's 42-kilometre ride to Tasmania's most popular outdoor destination, Freycinet National Park. With some tips from the group's more seasoned riders, I adjust my gears (*thumb it to the summit!*) and settle into the rhythm of undulating hills, challenging myself with each one and pushing myself further outside my comfort zone. Cycling is travel with your five senses turned up and tuned in. Feeling the wind, tasting the breeze, smelling the eucalypts (and the occasional tang of Tasmania's inescapable road kill). As my eyes

take it all in, I hear the leaves rustle and my pedals churn. It becomes meditative, with wheels spinning

How Wineglass Bay Got its Name

Sure, you can choose to believe the bay looks like a wine glass. More likely, Wineglass Bay got its name from the sheer volume of whales slaughtered and processed here in the 1800s, right on the beach. Migrating north from Antarctica, humpbacks and southern right whales – named because they were the *right* kind of whale to kill – were harpooned in such numbers that the crystal clear waters of the bay were said to turn cabernet with blood, and were polluted with rotting whale blubber. Eventually, the whales died out, the whalers moved on, and the stain of violence faded.

in my head just as surely as they do on the bike itself. I settle towards the back of the group and make a resolution to get in better shape, inspired by the strong pace set by fellow riders in their late fifties and sixties. Especially since this afternoon's activity is a hilly 6-kilometre hike to the azure jewel of Freycinet, and one of the world's best beaches.

I was fortunate to visit Wineglass Bay as a backpacker a dozen years ago. As the sand squeaked beneath my feet, I recall wondering: 'This spot is magic, but where are all the people?' It was peak summer and our small group seemed to have the state's oldest national park all to ourselves. The years since have seen tourism explode in Tasmania, as word got out that Tassie is Australia's best-kept secret. Today, the parking lot is full of tour buses, and the short hike up the saddle to the viewpoint over Wineglass Bay is packed with tourists. Fortunately, most don't continue down the steep steps to the white-sand beach itself, which remains just as empty – and as stunning – as I remember it. Stripping off my sweaty clothes, I dive headfirst into crisp waves, emerging like a new human being – invigorated, elated, inspired. Gathered that evening

for another fresh-cooked dinner in our cabins in Coles Bay, we toast a day that brought all the physical challenges, and beauty, that such travel affords.

The following morning, over-looked by a range of pink-tinted granite mountains, we kayak along the Coles Bay coastline. Blessed with calm waters, mild sunshine and an affable guide, we paddle for three hours, giving our legs a short break and our arms a taste of the action. Spotting stingrays in the clear turquoise waters beneath us, we stop at a beach to have morning tea, learning about Freycinet's history and many characters. Unfortunately, there are no multi-day kayaking

trips featured in my Australian Bucket List, but this short stint in Freycinet convinced me there should be. After lunch – a daily selection of cold cuts, cheese wraps, salads and condiments – it's back on the bikes for the final stretch of cycling. After 10 kilometres of gorgeous coastline, I tap out while much of the group continues inland. The support van – loaded with a silver bowl of never-ending snacks – picks up riders as they reach their limit. Back at our hotel, our tired muscles are massaged in a powerful hot tub, and our bellies are filled with grilled steak, local wine and fresh veggies in the picnic area outside our rooms.

With our cycles parked on the

trailer, the weather gods unleash powerful winds and heavy rain as we make the half-hour ferry crossing from Triabunna to Darlington, Maria Island's visitor settlement. We spend the next two days camping and hiking amidst wombats and kangaroos, exploring a place so magical it deserves – and gets – its own chapter in this book (see page 190).

I write these words mere hours after bidding farewell to the dozen people who signed up for what *National Geographic Traveler* named one of its '50 Tours of a Lifetime.' Long ago, I learned that the success of any group adventure depends on chemistry, and that the people you meet make or break the

trip. Luckily for me, this tour was blessed with an easy camaraderie. We gather around the picnic table on our final night to reflect on the week's highlights. St Mary's Pass. Wineglass Bay. The abundant wildlife. Maria Island. The food. The rolling country roads.

'For me, the best part of the trip was having everyone's support and friendship,' says Lorraine from Brisbane. Our guide Maddy, who along with Belle displayed remarkable energy and patience, concludes with her favourite moment:

'I'll never forget looking back after that long ride on day three, and seeing everyone just smiling on their bikes.'

Indeed. I freshly recall the challenge of pedalling eastern Tasmania's beautiful countryside, exploring its magnificent coastline, hiking rugged forests and sharing stories with travellers from near and far. These are the moments, and Tasmania is the place, on which such bucket list memories are made.

START HERE:
**aussiebucketlist.com/
cycle-kayak-walk**

Abseil off Gordon Dam

STRATHGORDON

To be honest, it's something I would expect to find in New Zealand. The Kiwis have built a thriving industry around doing something silly with gravity: rolling down a hill in a large plastic ball; canyon swinging; base jumping by wire; swooping; sledging; body flying; and of course bungee jumping – all of which I highly recommend. Still, as I hoist myself onto the edge of an imposing 140-metre-high concrete dam wall that just happens to be holding back thirty-seven times more water than Sydney harbour, I'm grateful that the world's highest commercial abseil is in Australia. In New Zealand, they would make you jump head-first off the damn thing. Abseiling is a far gentler and more enjoyable means of descent. It also allows you to look around and appreciate your surroundings – which is something you should do often in stunning south-western Tasmania.

I'm on an early morning drive from Hobart, the summer sun rising over valleys lush with fruit orchards. The scenery becomes more wild and remote once I enter Gordon River Road outside of Maydena. This early in the morning, it's somewhat perturbing to have to slalom the victims of last night's traffic. I don't know why Tasmanian marsupials are so hell-bent on auto-suicide, but they do an impressive job at it. The forests open up to reveal rugged mountains and sweeping valleys, as Route B61 skirts and occasionally enters Southwest National Park, part of the Tasmanian Wilderness World Heritage Area. One of the best reasons to tick off any bucket list experience is the fact that one has to physically get there. Today, the Gordon River Road easily cruises onto my 'Best Drives in Australia' list; I just wish I had more time for the short walks on the trails that lead off the road. Gordon Dam is well worth the two-and-a-half hour drive from Hobart, whether you decide to abseil off the 198-metre-long dam wall or not.

Completed in 1978, the damming of the Gordon River created the largest supply of fresh water in Australia. An ardent abseil

enthusiast and tour operator named Bill Harris believed the impressive arching dam wall would be a spectacular location to conquer. With the blessing of Hydro Tasmania, Aardvark Adventures have been operating their Gordon Dam abseil for more than twenty years.

'There are three main dangers to be aware of,' explains Macca, in charge on the morning of my visit.

'The drive here, which can be hazardous especially if the roads are wet. Friction in the harness mechanism, and tight bends in the rope.' Given the relative safety of abseiling, the drive is really the only dangerous bit, especially if you're a marsupial. The ropes can support two tons of weight and there are various safety mechanisms to ensure a smooth descent. With abseiling, you set your own pace. By releasing the rope you can fly down to the bottom in seconds, or enjoy several minutes dangling like an ant on a long string of dental floss. You could even do both: Aardvark's ticket includes as many descents as you like, providing you're willing to climb 480 ladder rungs to return topside.

'I'd say most of our customers intend to do it more than once but,

after the ladders, 95 per cent don't,' explains Macca. What goes down, must come up; the steel ladders have platforms for rest breaks, but returning to the top of the wall is still exhausting. Incidentally, the record ascent is five minutes and thirty-five seconds, and that includes the additional 235 steps to get to the road. As he double-checks my harness, Macca tells me the oldest person to abseil the dam wall was 87. This means the oldest person to climb the ladders was 87, so stop whingeing. I hop over the wall, holding on to the steel bars, trying not to notice the nerve-racking drop beneath me. The convex shape of the wall means I'll be lowering

Aussie Rap Jumping

Australian abseiling (a.k.a. rap jumping, angel jumping or deepelling) is just the sort of weird activity the Australian Army would invent. In order to face the enemy and be able to fire a weapon, you abseil off a building or helicopter *face-forward*, while keeping one hand free. It's easy enough to master, but triggers a new level of thrill as you descend looking at the very ground you'd rather not be looking at. Commercialised by a former SAS soldier, rap jumping can be tackled at the Urban Central Backpacker Hostel in Melbourne.

bottom my adrenalin hand-tremble is a whopping 8 out of 10. The dam wall is impressive from above but the experience of standing right at the bottom, by yourself, with so much water on the other side – well, that's unforgettable. I detach from my harness, yell 'clear!' for Macca to pull up the ropes, and begin to gather myself for the next challenge. I think about Jacob's Ladder in Perth (see page 302), the Big Tree climb (see page 252) and anything else to take my mind off the task at hand. In truth, the ladder ascent isn't as bad as it looks – providing you take it slow, get into a rhythm, entertain the birds with songs you'd sing in the shower, and place a bottle of water at the top so you don't have to climb the additional 235 steps to get refreshments from your car. Twenty minutes later, I'm chatting with dam visitors who are wondering if they should strap up. 'Oh it's *definitely* worth doing,' I say. 'The world's highest abseil? We're talking huge points for Australia at the next Bucket List Bledisoe Cup.'

myself down in the fresh Tasmanian air, and won't be using my legs to bounce off the wall like you've seen in the movies. The big test is leaning back for the first time, putting all my weight on the harness.

'Make sure you're comfort-able – you don't want to be halfway down in pain,' advises Macca. I make some adjustments to avoid screaming with a falsetto. The long heavy rope I'll need to descend is tucked into a pink bag hanging off a carabiner between my legs. I push off slowly and my whoops and hollers echo off the concrete, amplified by the pretty creek below. I lower myself down in fits and starts, and by the time I reach the

START HERE:
aussiebucketlist.com/ gordondamabseil

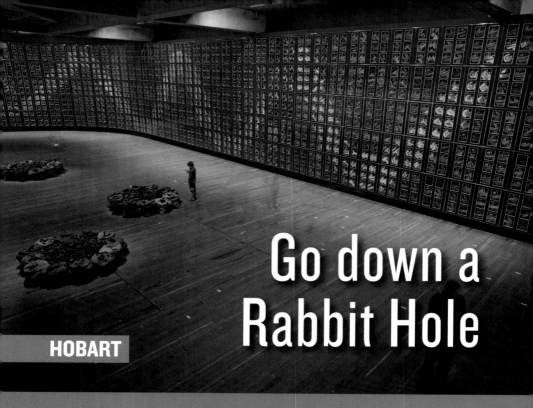

Go down a Rabbit Hole

This is a bold chapter about a very bold personal endeavour, and I'm going to kick it off with a bold claim: The Museum of Old and New Art (MONA) is the world's best contemporary art museum. The brainchild of a local Hobart millionaire named David Walsh, MONA is neither a place nor destination; it is an *experience* that will challenge, inspire, disturb, entertain, nourish and puzzle. Filled with wacky paintings, mind-bending sculptures, quirky contraptions, odd spaces and baffling displays, it takes you down a rabbit hole of creativity like no other art museum I've ever been to. Not the Louvre, Hermitage or Guggenheim. Not the Tate Modern, Centre Pompidou or Met. I will try and likely fail miserably in the following paragraphs to explain the reasons why. Art is funny like that.

Excessive wealth, as most of us hopefully realise, is not always accompanied by excessive happiness. Everything in life tends to be fairly relative. One of the principles of Hinduism is that happiness can only be achieved when you give something back to your community, when you contribute something meaningful above your own needs and ego.

This is why philanthropy is a very big deal for the mega rich, and the not so rich too. Folks like Bill Gates – who doesn't get nearly the amount of credit he deserves – are literally trying to fix the world. And some, like David Walsh, are trying to make us think. Walsh made his considerable fortune with a gambling algorithm and, instead of sailing off into the sunset on a super yacht (here's looking at you, Russian oligarchs), he invested tens of millions of dollars into an art museum to inspire the masses. Bear in mind, this is not New York, Paris, London or Madrid. This is *Hobart*. Hobart, an unassuming yet fetching city of just over 220,000 people, where one can let one's imagination – and art collection – run free.

As MONA is built into the cliffs of the Berriedale Peninsula alongside the River Derwent, most visitors arrive via the museum's catamaran, a twenty-five-minute sail from downtown Hobart. The museum grounds are surrounded by Walsh's vineyard and boast free-roaming chickens and ducks, massive modern sculptures and bewildered cruise ship tourists expecting something a little more grandiose. As I play with my kids outside on a big trampoline (an art piece too), I'm asked several times where the entrance is.

'Well, you see that shiny, un-assuming portal with no signs? Go through there. And get used to the lack of signs.'

While recognising that the artist and their intention is important, it is Walsh's vision to let the art speak for itself. This is why there are no artwork captions, although visitors can collect a small but easy-to-use 'O' device, which senses where you are, identifies the art surrounding you, and explains everything you need to know about it. This includes 'Art Wank' essays for tradi-tionalists, refreshingly candid voice recordings from the curators and

'Gonzo' notes from Walsh himself explaining why he bought the piece and what he gets out of it. The tone is approachable, often humorous, and does not take itself too seri-ously. This alone separates MONA from every other major art museum I've ever been to – Walsh and his crack team of curators sound like the kind of folks you could share a beer with.

I've always believed art comes alive in stories: the stories of the artists, the art itself and those that unfold in our heads when we view it. As you descend deep under-ground via a spiral staircase to the

The Character Hotel

Hobart has a world-class modern art gallery and it also has a world-class luxury boutique hotel. The MACq 01, set on the waterfront, is inspired by local Tasmanian personalities, with every one of its 114 rooms themed after a historical or modern character. Their personal stories are embossed on the door of every room, and are based on five archetypes: The Fighting Believers, The Hearty and Resilient, The Colourful and Quirky, The Grounded Yet Exceptional and the Curious and Creative.

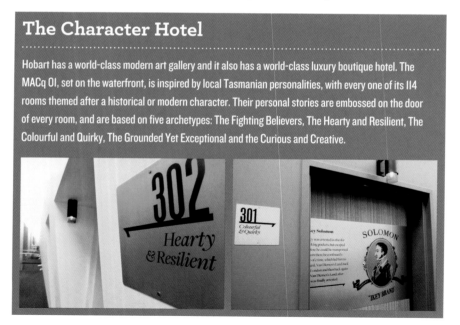

lowest level and slowly make your way through a series of chambers and rooms back towards the light, MONA is packed with stories. Tales of Birth, Death, Systems and Power. Spaces for Love, Sex, Technology and Spirituality. Exhibits that are funny – witness thirty fans singing across different screens in Candice Breitz's *Queen: A Portrait of Madonna*. Exhibits that inspire awe, like Sidney Nolan's massive *Snake*, for which the museum was specifically built. In James Turrell's *Event Horizon*, I stand in a bizarre white room where the lines of reality blur to evoke sensory hallucinations. The *Cloaca Professional*

is a contraption that literally manufactures faeces, while Erwin Wurm's overstuffed *Fat Car* is a stinging representation of consumerism. MONA's architecture often recalls the lair of Dr Evil, with nooks and doorways leading to large chambers, neon-lit tunnel walkways, pockets of decadence, fine dining and weird meditational orbs. I'd go into further detail, but you really need to explore it for yourself, and take away your own opinions of the experience.

With dozens of events held each year – and the hands-on approach of Walsh and his art curator wife Kirsha Kaechele – expect much

more than a museum. There's an on-site boutique hotel, outstanding restaurant, café and wine bar, live concert venue, educational programs, and a subtle yet constant turnover of exhibits. It's all dished up with down-to-earth Tasmanian hospitality, a jarring lack of pretension, and the odd realisation that it has all been financed by a professional gambler.

At the end of the day, processing all that I have seen and learnt, I'm splayed on a pink beanbag watching my wife and daughter dance to a West African band playing on MONA's outdoor stage.

It's a fine life. Sure, money can sit in a bank, trust fund or stock market shares. Walsh has used it to create an imaginative playground for the community (who don't pay entrance fees) and boatloads of visitors (who do). Australia's largest privately funded museum, MONA itself is a work of art. No visit to Tasmania would be complete without jumping headfirst down the rabbit hole, and drawing your own conclusions.

START HERE:
aussiebucketlist.com/mona

Take a Sip of Liquid Gold

My younger brother is a beer and whisky aficionado. One of those chaps who rates his drinks on various apps and participates in late-night tasting sessions that, while limited in budget, are full of enthusiasm. On the day of his wedding he presented us, his groomsmen, with a bottle of the finest Scotch he could muster, a bottle that he'd been saving for years. Only it wasn't Scotch at all. It was a bottle of French Oak single malt whisky from Sullivans Cove in Tasmania. And this is how I come to be standing next to a copper still in a whisky distillery outside of Hobart, lightheaded from the spirits permeating the air.

The distillation of alcohol was a major industry in the early days of Tasmania's colonial and convict history. Living in brutal conditions, drinking oneself blind was a form of pain relief and escapism and, by extension, the cause of illness and violence. By 1838, a governor named John Franklin (the same bloke who would disappear with his ships in search of the Northwest Passage) banned distilleries on the island, a law that remained in effect for more than 150 years. All that changed when Bill Lark, a man they call Australia's 'Godfather of Whisky', decided to create his own distillery in 1990. After successfully petitioning for the law to be overturned, Lark Distilleries opened in 1992, with Sullivans Cove following a couple of years later. Bill Lark was the first to recognise that Tasmania is an ideal location for the production of malt whisky. The air here is so clean, the World Meteorological Organization uses it as a benchmark against which air pollution is measured. This carries over into the exceptionally high quality of rainwater, springs and, ultimately, the golden liquid that finds its way into your whisky glass. Flavourful Tasmanian barley thrives in the island's cooler maritime temperate climate, low humidity, and rich basalt soil. The island's notoriously strict quarantine procedures also protect crops from outside contamination. Bill personally helped set up many of the dozen-plus distilleries in operation today, and is only the seventh person outside of Scotland and Ireland to be inducted into the Whisky Hall of Fame. This is why I'm toasting my brother, Bill Lark and Sullivans Cove master distiller Patrick Maguire when I finally get my hands on a taster of the French Oak single-cask, single malt that put Tasmanian whisky on the global stage.

Producing just twenty thousand bottles a year, Sullivans Cove was selling the French Oak at just $150 a bottle when the World Whiskies Awards proclaimed it the World's Best Single Malt in 2014. Yes, better than anything produced in Scotland or Ireland. The next day it was impossible to find a bottle, and if you're lucky enough to source one on the secondary market, it could cost you upwards of $15,000. Sullivans Cove continues to produce the most awarded whisky in the country, and new batches of the French Oak sell for more than $450 a bottle. Which is why I'm nursing my taster like a glass full of liquid sunshine.

'Our still is shaped like a brandy still as opposed to a whisky still,' explains our guide Cameron, leading a daily tasting tour of the Sullivans Cove distillery. 'Every part of the process impacts the flavour. Unlike the big distilleries, everything happens right here on site with no automation, from the ageing to the bottling.'

Cameron walks us through the process of making fine single-malt whisky. I learn about wash runs and low wine solutions, about copper sulphate, the dangers of methyl alcohol and the vital importance of barrels and ageing. I wonder why they don't use local eucalypts or

pine for their barrels. 'Pine has sap and eucalyptus oil is toxic,' answers Cameron. 'Although there's still experimentation, we can thank the Scottish for figuring out the exact process to make the world's finest whisky.' I taste some of the distilled spirit before it is aged in Oak, and it tastes like vodka. Indeed, Sullivans Cove produce their own vodka and Hobart No 4 Gin, richly flavoured with four Tasmanian botanicals. Like most distilled spirits worldwide, Scotch used to be clear. It was the English taxation system that forced distillers to hide their spirits in wine, port and sherry barrels, where they soon discovered the complex flavours and colours imparted by the wood. Not much has changed in the hundreds of years since. Speaking of which, Sullivans Cove don't list the whisky's age on their bottles.

'Older is not necessarily better. It's just older and more expensive,' remarks Patrick, a local whisky guide. Indeed, the bottle of Sullivans Cove French Oak that conquered the world was aged just eight years and nine months. The distiller decides when the cask is ready, knowing full well that every single barrel of whisky will be different, and that different releases will appeal to different palettes.

After trying the excellent entry level double-cask and fine American Oak single-cask, I swirl my French Oak taster, admiring its winner's trophy colour. Inhaling deeply, I let the Oak, toffee and spice scents fire up my brain. Finally, I take a sip of this extraordinary golden drop. No wonder my brother carried it back to Canada and saved it for his wedding to a bride he had yet to meet. The explosion of fine distilleries on the island has led to the creation of the excellent Tasmanian Whisky Trail touring route. Our bucket list distillery is just one stop on the trail, where you can meet the makers, learn the history, and taste the gold.

START HERE:
aussiebucketlist.com/whisky

The Difference between Whisky, Whiskey, Scotch, Rye and Bourbon

Technically, it's all whisky, which is a type of liquor made from a mash of fermented grain. The name and spelling may differ depending on geography and, in some cases, the grain mash used.

Scotch whisky is always made from malted barley, and is only made in Scotland. It is spelt without an 'e', which the Irish added and took to the United States.

Irish Whiskey is made in Ireland, and tends to have more relaxed rules when it comes to cereal blends.

Bourbon is always made from a grain mixture of at least 51% corn, and is only made in the United States.

Tennessee Whiskey is bourbon made in Tennessee, using charcoaled casks.

Canadian Rye is a whisky (the preferred spelling in Canada, Japan and Australia) that is typically smoother than whiskey, and not necessarily made of rye. In the United States, rye must be distilled from at least 51% rye. On that confusing note, I need a beer.

Plunge into Dove Canyon

CRADLE MOUNTAIN

Is there an experience more exhilarating than jumping feet-first into a pool of crystal clear, waterfall-fed canyon water? Canyoning is a magnificent adventure, but it's *really* difficult to find a location. The pools have to be just the right depth for rock jumping. The canyon walls must be steep, the water should be clean enough to drink, it can't be too dangerous, and, most importantly, the location has to be accessible so you can find it. Combining aspects of climbing, hiking, rock jumping and swimming, canyoning turns nature into a waterpark. You can climb, leap, swim, abseil, splash and slide – only the 'rides' in this waterpark are 400-million-year-old rocks.

Such is the case with Cradle Mountain National Park's Dove Canyon. The South Africans might call it *kloofing*, the Japanese *river tracing*, and Americans *canyoneering*, but there are very few places on Earth where you can show up at a visitor centre, sign a waiver, get fitted out in a wetsuit, and be guided to the water adventure of a lifetime.

Cradle Mountain National Park sees plenty of traffic. It's one of the most beautiful and iconic regions of Tasmania, a hikers paradise. Several years ago, some river kayakers went searching for the first descent of the Dove River. Soon enough, they discovered the river was in fact a canyon and, while the rocky, narrow drops ruled out kayaks, it did look ideal for canyoning. Four years of planning and permits later, Dove Mountain Canyon Tours opened for business.

Ever since I got a taste of canyoning in Costa Rica, I've kept my eyes out for a similar adventure.

Dove Lake Circuit

If you're going to do one easy walk in Cradle Mountain, it's this one. Looping 5.7 kilometres around Dove Lake, this boardwalk stroll brings together the national park's greatest hits: mountain views, magical rainforest, endemic plant life, lake swims, glacial rocks, history and, with a bit of luck, some wildlife too. Photographers the world over come here to capture the dual peaks of Cradle Mountain looming over the fagus, moss-covered myrtle beech trees, emerald King Billy pine and pandani. It feels like fairies should be scooting about the Ballroom Forest, but you're more likely to see a platypus zipping along the creek.

It seemed at once impossibly dangerous – gushing water, rock jumping, abseiling, sliding off steep ravines – and yet, guided by professionals, reassuringly safe. There's no turning back though, and you have to be fit enough to swim, climb and, most importantly, hike. At Cradle Mountain, I pack my wetsuit, booties, life jacket and helmet into a dry bag for the forty-minute hike along the Dove Canyon Trail. Joining a group of three couples, I stroll along a wooden boardwalk over plumes of exotic button grass, a short hike that quickly demonstrates why Cradle Mountain is so revered. Turning into the bush, we traipse along the trail until we find the 'changing rock,' a spot to squeeze into our 5mm wetsuits for the challenge ahead. It doesn't take long before we're sweating in our booties, a hot sun cooking us like sausages in their casings. But this is about to change, fast.

To enter the canyon, our guide Ben invites us one by one to the edge of the ravine. Roped into our harnesses, we begin to lower ourselves awkwardly, looking up at the rock in front. Ben tells us to kick out with our legs and instead of landing on the ground, we unexpectedly plunge into a refreshing canyon pool. The shock and elation is worth the price of admission. Stained with tannins from the surrounding plants, the water is tea-coloured but perfectly safe to drink. Gathered at the bottom, we begin the first of seven challenges. First up is the biggest waterfall jump, Freestyle Falls. With a lower water level than usual, it's a seven-metre jump into a deep pool below, which can be accomplished however we wish. This early on, most people take the leap of faith, although I make a mental note to keep my arms at my sides so I don't slap the water and sting my hands. One guy attempts an ambitious somersault and lands on his face, which sounds terrible, but even he has to laugh at his epic fail.

Ben reveals some of the history of the canyon. The kayakers believed they were the first to discover Dove Canyon, but later learned about a prospector named James Philosopher King, who cut down a stand of King Billy pines and planned to float them downriver to the sea, where he'd collect the valuable wood and make a small fortune. When the wood didn't show up, Jimmy King

hiked to Dove River, discovered the canyon, and saw that his treasure had become stuck at various bottle-necks. Today, a large King Billy pine log still rests in the canyon and is worth tens of thousands of dollars, but is now a protected timber. We stand on another log and execute a 'car seat' jump into a pool, and then gather ourselves at The Pit. Here, the water appears to vanish beneath our feet into a cavern. One at a time, we step up and jump, amazed to be having so much fun in such a seemingly dangerous location. It's as if at any moment an adult will appear and yell at us to stop. Especially since The Pit leads directly into the Laundry Chute, where thousands of years of gushing water has created a rocky slide that fits the human body perfectly. We lean back, straighten up and slide around a large boulder into another pool, swimming underneath a waterfall into a little cavern.

Gathered on a clearing, we eat a packed lunch including the Cradle Mountain Special – a wrap filled with two-thirds peanut butter and one-third Nutella – and continue onwards. The wetsuit is more than sufficient to keep us warm, although my hands are feeling numb from the 16-degree water. After another abseil, Ben urges us to 'jump with style' over Tea Cup Falls, and then we're encouraged to forward flip into Horsey Falls, which everyone manages to do

perfectly. There's one last unnamed rock jump, and then the fun part is over. Now comes the twenty-minute hike up the ravine in our wetsuits, and the forty-minute hike out to the parking lot. It's certainly no walk in the park. This full-day trip is for people fifteen years and up who are physically fit (the company does offer a less challenging experience for younger participants). Cradle Mountain is world-renowned as one of the most unique wilderness destinations on the planet. Combine your visit with an adventure as thrilling as this one, and you've got yourself a wet and wonderful highlight on The Great Australian Bucket List.

START HERE:
aussiebucketlist.com/canyoning

Hear the Devils Grunt

CRADLE MOUNTAIN

onsider the tasselled wobbegong, the spiny lumpsucker, the satanic leaf gecko, the tufted titmouse and a giant Caribbean frog known as the Mountain Chicken. You probably haven't because, despite their somewhat fascinating natural history, they just don't match up to a panther, a piranha, a marlin, a falcon, an orca or rhino. These are animals that sound sharp, fast and powerful, animals that scream 'badass!'. I'm carrying my daughter into the Devils @ Cradle breeding facility and she asks me, as only a four-year-old can: 'What's so special about Tasmanian devils?'

As we'll soon learn, the largest marsupial carnivore in the country is not even Australia's apex native predator (that honour goes to quolls, but more on that later). It is, however, a remarkable creature – a cartoon celebrity, a reminder of the fierce marsupials that have passed, and the centre of a conservation program to save the species from a devastating facial tumour disease. It also has one of the most snarling and snappy monikers in the entire animal kingdom.

Most of us *have* considered the Tasmanian devil. Possessing a notoriously fierce demeanour, the Tassie devil is the size of a small dog, black furred and distinctly pungent. Despite what foreigners might think, devils do not move around at the centre of a whirlwind. A solitary creature that mostly scavenges its meals, devils have a bite that's said to be among the most powerful of all land predators. Although they are only found in the wild in Tasmania (and in just about every Australian zoo and wildlife park elsewhere), devils did once live on the mainland. Along with thylacines, aka the Tasmanian

tiger, devils are thought to have disappeared from the mainland thousands of years ago when dingoes first found their way to the continent from Asia. Since the feral dogs never made it to Tasmania, marsupial carnivores continued to thrive until the arrival of European colonists, hunters, road vehicles, and a nasty face cancer. The last remaining thylacine died in 1936 at the Hobart Zoo, and conservation facilities like Devils @ Cradle are doing their utmost to ensure the devil does not meet a similar fate.

I arrive for the 5.30pm devil feeding session and the little monsters are getting excited. Located within Cradle Mountain National Park, the sanctuary is part of the nationwide Captive Breeding Program, established to create an 'insurance population' of devils. For all is not well with our grunting, snorting marsupial. Beside loss of habitat and road deaths, a contagious facial tumour disease has all but wiped out the wild eastern population, with no cure in sight. Once contracted, the disease causes lesions to appear on the mouth and within three to five months the whirlwind tragically stops spinning. Devils @ Cradle also operate a Field Monitoring and Orphan Rehabilitation program for the devils as well as two species of quoll, another marsupial carnivore found in Tasmania but in serious decline on the mainland (see Text Box).

It's the loud, hissing, throat-clearing, chalkboard-scratching sounds of the devil that gave *Sarcophilus harrisii* its notorious name. Although shy and hard to spot, the devil's hellish sounds were heard by early settlers in the bush and the name stuck. I'm learning these and other devil facts from a guide as she begins throwing chunks of meat into the enclosures. Devils will eat until they explode, so the food is measured and consists of local wildlife. The faculty

Forget Drop Bears, it's Drop Quolls

Like the devil, the spotted-tail quoll is also a carnivorous marsupial. Unlike the devil, it's a fierce and deadly hunter that stalks from the trees and pounces on prey from above, crushing victims' necks with its powerful jaws. Solitary and ruthless, quolls are still found on the mainland as the apex native predator. Unfortunately, their numbers have seriously declined due to the impact of cane toads, feral cats and habitat loss.

would love to use roadkill, but quarantine restrictions rule it out. It's every devil for him or herself at mealtimes; as they engage in a tug-of-war with the meat, battles ensue and distinct hierarchies are established. I learn that females give birth to between 20 and 40 offspring, but these tiny critters will battle to the death so that only four will be able to feed off the available teats. I learn that once devils are grown, they will turn on their own mothers – and each other – and go off on their solitary ways. Seventy-five per cent of young devils die before they reach 12 to 14 months of age, the victims of dogs, cars, owls and quolls (the true badass on the island). Their white markings are as individual as fingerprints, they're great swimmers, and they are no threat to humans – although I wouldn't want to be on the wrong side of a devil bite.

You can encounter captive devils around the country, but they're Tasmanian creatures, and Devils @ Cradle is the best place to see and learn about them (and quolls, too). With its mythical status, ferocious attitude, and badass moniker, the Tasmanian devil is a uniquely Australian creature that snarls its way onto our Australian bucket list.

START HERE:
aussiebucketlist.com/devil

Listen for Ghosts

PORT ARTHUR

According to the Mayan Dreamspell calendar, the date of my birth signals that I am 'guided by death'. This might explain why I ended up writing books about things to do before you die, and why I seem to spend an inordinate amount of time taking ghost tours. Port Arthur is one of the eleven locations around the country that make up Australia's UNESCO World Heritage Convict Sites listing. The spirits of the afterlife are particularly restless in Tasmania's most popular tourist attraction.

Port Arthur is notorious because it is where repeat offenders and other *really* bad apples were imprisoned, and subjected to a new penal system designed to 'grind men honest'. It is also notorious because it is the site of Australia's most horrific and deadly modern mass shooting. Giving that event any more coverage only plays into the hands of the lunatic who perpetrated it, and so I will respectfully decline to say anything further. Besides, there's plenty of colonial-era lunacy to focus on instead, like the Separate Prison System, which used solitary confinement and isolation to theoretically inspire morality, but which in reality drove prisoners insane. Prisoners were confined in solitary quarters with no human contact and in deathly silence. Once a week they could attend church, but they were hooded in transit and placed within small boxes that removed any human contact. Subsequently, many found themselves in the mental asylum built adjacent to the prison, or joining the roughly 1400 dead convicts buried on the Isle of the Dead. Point being: for forty-four years, Port Arthur was a very nasty place, populated by very nasty people, who had done, were doing and were destined to do very nasty things. During the 20th century, the historic ruins of the prison and its prime location on the lovely Tasman Peninsula began attracting tourists, and today it sees many thousands of visitors each year. This is why half a dozen ninety-minute Ghost Tours leave the Visitor Centre every evening, guided by storytellers armed with chilling tales of ethereal mysteries, all set within the ominous atmosphere of Port Arthur itself.

Holding a candle-lit lantern, our guide Carl explains the five types of supernatural experiences visitors report at Port Arthur: apparitions, bad smells, hearing things,

emotional hauntings and physical sensations of being touched or grabbed.

'Personally, I don't know why you're on this tour,' he jokes.

It's getting dark as we set off for the ruins of the multi-denominational church. Clouds cast shadows beneath an almost full moon as Carl reveals the two murders that took place during construction, and the hauntings visitors have reported since.

'One night, guests saw a dark shadow move across the walls . . . but it was only a wallaby.'

Ghost tour visitors want their money's worth, so they'd probably prefer the above story to contain a real-life ghoul, if only to justify the ticket price. Our next stop is the Parsonage, reputedly one of the most haunted houses in the country. Carl instructs two young Israeli girls to knock on the door and place their lantern in the first room. It is now very dark, the shadows are long, and the leaves are rustling in the wind. Stories of apparitions, footsteps and phantoms have them well spooked. Carl does a great job ensuring nobody in their right mind would spend more than a few minutes in the

Parsonage at night. Less spooky is the surgeon's basement dissection room, where sordid tales of grave robbery are shared around the same slab on which they worked. Neck hairs grow rigid again in the Separate Prison, which has a particularly nasty atmosphere by lantern light. Now we learn about the heavy footsteps that chased a late-night guide out of the building. We learn of two female visitors being pulled towards the cells. We learn that our imaginations are far more terrifying than anything we might encounter in the real world. I want to hang back and look into the cells but Carl looks uneasy and I feel a little queasy, so we head outside, look at the stars and conclude the tour in peace.

Van Diemen's Land was renamed Tasmania in 1856 to dispense with its reputation for

A Foxy Tasmanian Scandal

In 2001, the Federal and Tasmanian governments embarked on an aggressive program to eradicate the red fox in Tasmania, as it was seen as a threat to native wildlife. The program ran for thirteen years and cost $50 million. And then . . . the fox hunt turned fishy. In 2014, an independent study found that the evidence for foxes existing on the island was bogus: the scats discovered had come from interstate, as had a solitary dead fox. Personally, I think the fox hunt categorically proves Tasmanian tigers are truly extinct. If they weren't extinct before, the fox eradication program probably took care of them. Perhaps the money might have been better spent proving the existence of ghosts in Port Arthur.

being the home of bad apples. Ironically, the island is now known for growing rather excellent apples. The Isle of the Dead, the Point Puer Boy's Prison . . . whatever tour you choose, there's plenty to learn about Port Arthur's legacy, its unsettling history, bad science and unholy spirits.

START HERE:
ausssiebucketlist.com/portarthur

Cycle Down a Mountain

KUNANYI/MOUNT WELLINGTON

While it's certainly not the only bicycle experience to tick off in Tasmania, or even in this book, this ride does have a crucial element we can all appreciate: *down*. Bike rides are great but, unless you're into pain and muscular glory, they're even more fun when all you have to do is hang on, apply the brakes and let gravity do the rest. Add spectacular views over one of Australia's most beautiful cities – or the chance to rip through some local trails – and this bucket list experience all but pedals itself.

The peak called kunanyi/ Mount Wellington (a dual name that respects the mountain's Indigenous heritage) towers 1271 metres over Hobart. It features the Jurassic dolerite 'organ pipe' cliffs that I've seen on mountains in Argentina, South Africa and Antarctica, geological reminders of the days when all three were linked as the Gondwana supercontinent.

More importantly for local residents, the imposing mountain creates a rain shadow, allowing Hobart to be the second driest capital in the nation, even though it is located in a rather wet state.

Often capped with snow year-round, the summit lookout has significantly lower temperatures than downtown Hobart. You can also expect blustery winds, a sensational view and a dozen people wearing fluorescent vests standing next to mountain bikes. Under Down Under Tours run two to three descents of the mountain every day during summer, providing transfers, bikes, guides and a support vehicle. On the drive up, passing the remains of hardwood trees destroyed in a huge mountain fire in 1967, our guide points out hazards to watch for.

'We'll be going down 21 kilometres. Don't worry, I've rarely seen anyone break out in a sweat,' he says, reassuringly.

Certainly, the weather is cooperating a lot better than my first descent a dozen years ago. I still remember the wind chill blowing through my bones, and

More Bucket List Mountain Bike Rides in Australia

- Mount Buller, VIC
- Thredbo, NSW
- Stromlo Forest Park, ACT
- Derby, TAS
- Bright, VIC
- Falls Creek, VIC
- Ourimbah State Forest, NSW
- Maydena Bike Park, TAS
- Arthur's Seat, VIC
- Kalamunda, WA

the disappointing view of mist from the lookout point. Today I see Greater Hobart and its surrounds in all its glory – the city, hills, islands, ocean and Derwent River. I also see people arriving at the summit having pedalled up by bicycle, which must be spectacular fitness training and/or a horrendous form of physical torture. We hop on our bikes and begin the first descent to a spot where we can regroup, take some photos and adjust our seats for comfort. Two kilometres pass very quickly when you're rocketing down a steep hill surrounded by alpine forest. We're advised to keep left as we're sharing the road with cars, and without lines in the road vehicles tend to gravitate towards the centre. We're merely cruising down, taking corners as fast as our nerves can handle, with our support vehicle bringing up the rear. At our next meeting spot, our guide Lainie points out an optical illusion. In the distance below is the gentle arc of the Tasman Bridge linking Hobart to the eastern suburbs. 'If you stand the Tasman Bridge on its end, it would be taller than Mount Wellington,' she muses, which seems illogical from way up here, but since the bridge is 1.4 kilometres

long, it makes perfect sense.

As we continue onwards, the flora changes to reflect the altitude, although I'm too busy looking ahead and smiling with the exhilaration of speed. Bikers can opt for an off-road section next, which everyone in my group agrees would be a fine idea. Although there will be some peddling and tricky navigation over loose gravel, it's an opportunity to experience the unspoiled natural environment off the paved road. Biking on forest trails, we reconnect with the road and continue into the suburbs that have been cut into the foothills. We stop at the Cascade Brewery to admire the old convict-cut stones, and pedal past the historic Female Factory (where thousands of convict women and children were imprisoned) before joining city traffic. Snaking through various neighbourhoods, we conclude the ride at our departure point on Elizabeth Street. All in, it's a two-and-a-half-hour round trip, although without the stops to regroup and chat, you could shave much of that time off. As a tour, it's a fine way to orientate yourself around Hobart, and easily one of the world's best commercial biking descents.

Our short stint in the forest leaves me hungry for more. With its hilly surrounds, fresh air and great views, Tasmania offers some of the best mountain biking in the country. That same afternoon, Harry Nichols – local hero, up-and-coming Enduro World Series competitor and Discovery Parks brand ambassador – agrees to take me into the Meehan Range bike park in Clarence. It's a popular playground of marked trails, tracks and jumps, although this time I have to pedal up to enjoy the down. Harry blitzes on runs named Corkscrew, Cliff Top and Smooth as Butter, and I do an awful job trying to keep up.

I do, however, execute a couple of awkward wipeouts.

'Please don't do as I do. Just go where I go,' I tell Harry.

Harry tells me about the Maydena Bike Park, the country's biggest gravity-based bike path, which opened up about ninety minutes outside the city. Tasmania has a welcoming community of mountain bikers, volunteers, bike shops and trail keepers; it's the kind of destination that belongs on any enthusiastic mountain biker's bucket list. As for the rest of us, all we have to do is sit in the saddle and start at the top of a mountain.

START HERE:
aussiebucketlist.com/

Marvel at the Painted Cliffs

MARIA ISLAND

Tasmania is a stunning island full of natural and historical wonders that sits off the coast of mainland Australia. Maria Island – pronounced by the locals as *Ma-rye-ah* – is a stunning island full of natural and historical wonders that sits off the coast of mainland Tasmania. Maria Island is like Tasmania concentrate.

Looking for history? The legacy of the Oyster Bay Aboriginal community can still be found on the island. It also boasts one of the eleven spots nationwide that make up Australia's UNESCO World Heritage Convict Sites listing. Visitors can spend the night in the original penitentiary from the island's first convict era in the 1820s, and explore interactive exhibits from the island's subsequent use as a probation station, farm, cement factory and national park. Looking for wildlife? Don't trip over the bare-nosed wombats that gather in the grazed, fairway-like fields each evening, and keep an eye out for Forester (Eastern grey) kangaroos, pademelons, Cape Barren geese, possums, echidnas and the disease-free Tasmanian devils that have been successfully introduced on the island. Indeed, I saw all of these creatures within a few short hours, often at the same time.

As for geological wonders, take a short and scenic coastal hike to the Fossil Cliffs, where the quarried limestone is embedded with the ancient fossils of shells – although good luck tearing your eyeballs away from the huge swells smashing into the sheer cliff-face. Or hike in the opposite direction across a field and along a white sandy beach to the Painted Cliffs, an overhang of stained sandstone that transforms in sunlight into a surreal geological masterpiece. Carved

by wind and wave, it's one of my favourite spots in the whole country. Bring or rent a bike to pedal alongside massive trees in pristine forest, feeling strong breezes from the Mercury Passage whip your hair and invigorate the soul. Snorkel off the beaches to explore marine life in a protected habitat that includes kelp forests and rock lobsters. Choose from a number of day hikes, including a solid walk up to the 620-metre granite summit of twin peaks Bishop and Clerk. Scramble to the top of the rocks for an ocean and island view that goes on forever, but make sure you've got three points of contact and a hat that won't blow off in a strong wind. Sit around the large fireplaces with travellers from the world over,

dining on campground tucker, playing table tennis, debating the past and future. Everything you bring in must be taken out, and make sure you keep those food bins locked up, as some of the possums could crack a bank safe.

Yes, Tasmania offers similar experiences across the state, but the fact that all this is condensed into such a small area – all located within a short distance of the Darlington Probation Station – makes Maria Island a must-visit on any Australian bucket list. Spend at least one night, dress warmly and play nice with the wombats.

START HERE:
aussiebucketlist.com/mariaisland

See Lavender Fields Forever

NABOWLA

For thousands of years, lavender has bequeathed many benefits to the human race. Part of the mint family, the most popular species of the genus, *lavandula angustifolia*, has been cultivated for fragrance, medicinal properties, flavour, and use in spiritual offerings. Traditionally, lavender has been used to relieve stress, prevent infections, promote sleep, improve mood, aid digestion, repel insects, reduce inflammation and enhance skin and hair. It can also be used to make teas, sweets and cakes. Knowing all this, it's easy to appreciate the world's largest private lavender farm, especially in December and January, when the picturesque, curved rows of lavender are in bloom.

The Bridestowe Lavender Estate was founded in 1922 by an English perfumer named C.K. Denny, who arrived in Australia with a bag of seeds and the firm belief that Tasmania's climate and soil would produce the world's finest lavender. Two decades later, his son Tim identified the farm's best lavender plants for producing essential oils, and used five clones to expand into a larger farm near Nabowla (about 50 kilometres west of Launceston). Renowned for its quality, Bridestowe became a top supplier of lavender to perfumeries worldwide and by the 1980s produced 15 per cent of the world's finest lavender oil. The Denny family retired, watched their farm flail through a series of corporate owners, and finally took over again in 2007 to restore Bridestowe to its former glory. They soon realised that 120 acres of blooming lavender contours surrounded by native bush is an attraction unto itself.

Today, tens of thousands of visitors flock to the farm to experience the stunning view, learn about lavender production and indulge in lavender-infused ice cream, fudge, teas and other treats. And then there's Bobbie the Bear.

As part of their product range, Bridestowe created a plush purple teddy bear stuffed with lavender that could be warmed up and used as a soothing heat pack. In 2014, a famous Chinese model shared her love for Bobbie on social media. Suddenly, millions of young Chinese women became convinced they needed a Bobbie too. Next thing you know, 65,000 Chinese tourists are visiting the farm, Chinese President Xi Jinping is gifted a Bobbie on a Tasmanian visit, Bobbie gets a TV show and fake Bobbies contaminated with weevils lead to a blanket ban on lavender bears in China. The estate says demand for Bobbie the Bear outstrips supply 'ten to one'; each Bobbie is handmade on the farm and they simply can't keep

TASMANIA

Tasmazia and the Village of Lower Crackpot

Another lavender farm worth visiting in northern Tasmania is a zany maze complex and model village called Tasmazia. The laird of the miniature Village of Lower Crackpot is the eccentric and often boiler-suited Brian Inder, a self-described 'Sydney refugee' who moved to the island and brought to life his passion for mazes and model architecture. Tasmazia features famous and bizarre buildings meticulously modelled at 1:5 scale, some of the world's largest mazes (including one with 3.5 kilometres of pathways), hilarious signs and quirks like the Monument to Whistleblowers. The lavender blooms in January.

up. A luxury hotel development is now underway to appeal to the increasing number of visitors, 60 per cent of whom arrive from China. The estate, and Tasmanian tourism in general, will just have to grin and bear it. In the meantime,

any visitor to Bridestowe will notice how the lavender has infused the atmosphere with a soothing, therapeutic sense of calm.

A self-guided tour leads you from the Woodcroft Cafe to the silver tanks of the oil distillery, where you learn how 180,000 kilograms of cut flowers are processed each season, how 100 kilograms of flowers produce one kilogram of essential oil, along with an infused water solution used in room and linen fresheners. You'll learn how to apply a few lavender drops to a bath to aid mild skin conditions or assist in the healing of minor burns. How a few neat drops alleviate insect bites and stings, and how the aroma of lavender can relieve headaches, stress, tension or restless sleep. Exit through the gift shop, where dozens of products are available to purchase. Of course, you can get lavender products elsewhere, but as for the unforgettable sight of the world's finest lavender stretching on forever? That experience is strictly reserved for Tasmania.

START HERE:
aussiebucketlist.com/ bridestowelavender

Polish Jewellery in the Sand

THE WHITSUNDAYS

There are many superlatives to describe the colour of the sea and sands of the Whitsundays. An archipelago of seventy-four islands and sections of the Great Barrier Reef, the Whitsundays are one of the world's great boating destinations. Among the many unforgettable experiences in the region, two are of immediate interest for our bucket list. One is Reefsleep (see page 203), and the other is in this chapter, where we want nothing more than to kick back on Whitehaven Beach and enjoy its crystal blue-green water, talcum-powder-soft sand and paradise-infused colours.

A friend with a boat once told me that BOAT is actually an acronym for "burn another thousand." Like the vast majority of people on Earth, I'm assuming you're not *boat* rich (as opposed to just plain rich). But if you *are* boat rich, your boat might not be in the Whitsundays – and if it is, that's incredible, thanks for the invite! In the meantime, Cruise Whitsundays gives us all the opportunity to sail among the islands in their fleet of modern catamarans, which ferry passengers from Airlie Beach to Hamilton Island (the main hub of the Whitsundays) and beyond. Hamilton is a resort island with all the trimmings: there are high-end luxury hotels, budget accommodations and everything in-between; there are jet boat safaris, overnight sailing trips, shopping villages, wildlife parks and long sandy beaches. Located on the east coast of Whitsunday Island (not to be confused with the archipelago), Whitehaven Bay is widely touted as one of the world's great beaches, and is a popular day trip from Airlie Beach or Hamilton Island. The beauty of any beach is in the eye of the beholder, but Whitehaven certainly provides a bucket lister with a great excuse to hop on board a boat, motor through the islands,

and find out what all the fuss is about. Which is exactly what I did.

'Look at the colour of that water!' says every first-time passenger on the Cruise Whitsundays Orca. Turquoise laced with the rich hue of a glass avocado? Emerald diffused with toothpaste-gel aquamarine? Polished jade with a dash of ANZ Bank-blue? Over the intercom, the captain points out Long Island, Hook Island and the appropriately named Daydream Island. We learn that the Ngaro people lived here long before Captain Cook sailed through the islands on June 3, 1770, giving them the name we know today. Fishing, logging and farming brought settlers to the area, but increased transportation costs eventually put a lid on timber and agriculture, replacing it with tourism, which today is the region's biggest industry. More than 96 per cent of the Whitsundays is protected and managed by Queensland's Parks and Wildlife Service, and the Great Barrier Reef itself is, of course, under the safeguard of World Heritage listing. This explains the pristine condition of the environment, the incredible colours, and the fact that you can use the 98 per cent quartz sand of Whitehaven Beach to polish jewellery and manufacture fine optical lenses.

The Orca pulls into Whitehaven Bay, where 7 kilometres of crescent beach awaits us. All guests are encouraged to go barefoot, the better to leave only footprints behind. A chalkboard lists the day's activities: feeding dart fish, beach cricket, volleyball, a bushwalk, a sandcastle competition. Cruise Whitsundays provides beach toys and pop-up shade tents, refreshments and, heck, even a masseuse for beach massage. While the boat was full of people, there's

Australia's Best Beaches

Ask ten Australians what their favourite beach is and you'll get fourteen answers. In a country with more than 50,000 kilometres of coastline and 10,000-plus beaches, here are the beaches that stand out for me:

- [ ] Whitehaven Beach, QLD – For the sand, colour and remoteness

- [x] Cape Hillsborough, QLD – For the kangaroos and wallabies at sunrise
- [ ] Main Beach, Noosa, QLD – For the safe and gentle family-friendly surf
- [ ] Burleigh Heads, QLD – For the *real* Surfers Paradise
- [ ] Bondi Beach, Sydney, NSW – For the urban beach experience
- [ ] Hyams Beach, Jervis Bay, NSW – For the white sand
- [ ] The Pass and Main Beach, Byron Bay, NSW – For the surfing and beach bods
- [ ] Selicks Beach and Silver Sands, SA – For the driving
- [ ] Little Beach, Two Peoples Bay Nature Reserve, WA – For the rock pools
- [ ] Shell Beach, WA – For the endless cockleshells
- [ ] Cable Beach, WA – For the camels, of course
- [ ] Squeaky Beach, Wilsons Promontory, VIC – For the squeak
- [ ] Wineglass Bay, TAS – For the sand, the sea and the view

no shortage of beach to find a secluded spot with unspoilt views of the envy-green, glacier-coloured blue waters lapping at the shore. The only sore spot, literally, is the risk of nasty box jellyfish and irukandji stingers in the northern Queensland seas from October to May. Passengers are advised to wear the supplied protective stinger suits, which some do and some don't. I ask the crew about the risks and learn that sometimes you can see the jellies, and other times the risk is very low. 'Look, even if the stingers are as rare as unicorns, it's still a unicorn that can really ruin your holiday,' says a boatie named Brent. So, despite the warm sea temperature and sunny weather, nobody is spending too much time in the water, but the beach itself makes up for it.

On squeaky-footed romantic walks you might spot white-bellied sea eagles, iguanas and monitor lizards, and fish darting in the clear waters. Other bays on the island offer world-class snorkelling, bush hikes, fishing and sea kayaking. Whitehaven is just one of the reasons why more than eight million people visit the Whitsundays every year. We return home for a memorable sunset at sea, the peach-fuzz sky requiring its own catalogue of creative descriptions. Whichever way you want to approach the Whitsundays, there's a bucket list berth with your name on it.

START HERE:
aussiebucketlist.com/whitehaven

Sleep on the Reef

THE WHITSUNDAYS

En route to the Cruise Whitsundays pontoon anchored off Hardy Reef, the captain of the Sea Flight informs passengers that four hours on the Great Barrier Reef might seem long, but it's actually not much time at all. There are opportunities for snorkelling or guided snorkel safaris; scuba diving; scenic helicopter tours; short trips in a semi-submersible with viewing windows; an underwater observation deck; and rides on a jet-propelled Seabob. What draws my attention, however, is an excursion promising a 'Bucket List Night Out'. For when the wave-piercing catamaran departs with hundreds of day-trippers later that afternoon, Reefsleep guests stay behind — 40 nautical miles off shore, alone with the world's biggest natural wonder.

We are now just twenty guests, two hosts, and three crew members. We have hot showers, flushing toilets and all the gear we need; the 45-metre-long pontoon will be ours until 11am the next morning. I watch the tide roll back to reveal the reef, a living landscape rising in the middle of the Whitsundays-clear water, alive with countless marine life feeding on the reef's nutrients. Blessed with a clear and calm sunny day in late April, our snorkelling is nothing short of divine. Among our group of Germans, Kiwis,

Chinese and Australians are snorkellers discovering the ocean's wonders for the first time. We see rainbow-coloured parrotfish, shimmering schools of yellowtail fusiliers and huge schools of baitfish gathered together for the benefit of patrolling great trevally. There are blue sergeant majors and lemon damsels, butterflyfish, bannerfish, angelfish, tuskfish, rabbitfish, and toothy triggerfish. Rays of sunshine illuminate the purple lips of giant clams, the blue tips of staghorn, the orange wisps of soft spaghetti

coral, sea whips, plate corals and the purple contours of brain coral. A green turtle makes an appearance, as does Maggie, a huge Maori wrasse that the crew treat like a lovable pet. In the water we wear stinger suits and remain under the watchful eye of a crew member at all times, and as the afternoon sun approaches the horizon we return to the pontoon to freshen up. Appetisers are brought out, cold beers are cracked and glass flutes are filled with chilled bubbly. After weeks of pre-season sketchy weather, we could not have asked for a smoother day, or a clearer sky. For this is the promise of Reefsleep: a sky of full of stars for dinner, and the Milky Way for dessert.

'Sous vide?' I ask our host Natalie, who is preparing our meal in the galley.

'Yes, not many people would know what that is.'

The bags contain beef steak and lamb shanks that are slowly boiled according to the principles of a high-tech culinary trend. The results are melt-in-the-mouth dishes you typically only find in expensive restaurants. The Germans pre-ordered the seafood platter, which has oysters, crab, Moreton Bay bug, prawns and calamari. With rich desserts of cheesecake, lemon tart and a dense chocolate torte, nobody is going to bed hungry.

We are all abuzz from one

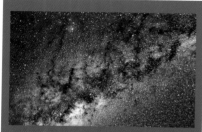

Be the Stargazing Know-it-All

As the stars explode overhead, impress your fellow Reefsleepers with your knowledge of the Australian night sky.

- The Southern Cross (or Crux) is the smallest of the 88 constellations, and its five stars are thought to be between 10 and 20 million years old.

- Stars don't twinkle; starlight hits turbulence in the Earth's atmosphere, bouncing about to give us the impression they're twinkling.

- The brightest star, Sirius, is 20 times brighter than our sun.

- Without binoculars, you're only going to see up to 2500 stars at best, a *tiny* fraction of the estimated 400 billion stars in our galaxy.

- The sun is a very small star compared to others in the galaxy, it's just the closest star to us (149.6 miilion kilometres away).

- Shooting stars are actually small rocks or space dust burning up in our atmosphere, more accurately called meteors.

- The four constellations most visible from Australia are Carina, Crux, Vela and Centaurus.

of those sunsets you never forget – when the sky's colours are unusually crisp and the ocean transitions from bright blue to mercury and deepest purple. Thousands of seasonal white-headed noddies gather on the pontoon railings to keep us company. A visit to the underwater observatory, the waters lit by a spotlight, reveal the giant trevally vigorously feasting on the schools of baitfish 'born into anxiety', as one crew member puts it. Above deck, the half-moon casts a glow that is almost bright enough to read by, perhaps robbing us of the full stargazing experience, although nobody is complaining. Our accommodation for the night is the pontoon's exposed top deck, which holds one- and two-person canvas swags, each containing pillows, sheets and a folded towel. The swag design allows us to lie back and gaze at the night sky and – with no mosquitoes, flies or bugs to worry about – I keep my attention fixed directly above me, hoping to spot a shooting star or satellite.

After a full day enjoying the reef and a terrific meal washed down with a few beers, sleeping under the stars proves to be as good as a sleeping tablet. I wake from my

slumber just after four o'clock in the morning, emerging to see the golden moon on our eastern horizon and a pre-dawn sky bathing in magnificent starlight. At 6.30am, an egg-yolk sun cracks the horizon. Breakfast is served, and we have the Hardy Reef to ourselves for a few hours before the Seaflight catamaran arrives with eager day-trippers and tonight's group of Reefsleepers. In just twenty-four hours, it feels like we've joined an exclusive club with privileged access to an experience that is more affordable than you would think. We've been blessed with the opportunity to own a piece of the Great Barrier Reef, if only for one magical night.

START HERE:
aussiebucketlist.com/reefsleep

Eat Your Heart Out

BRISBANE

'There is nothing like Eat Street anywhere in the world.' It's the first sentence you'll read on the Eat Street Northshore website and, for a book about unique Australian experiences, it's a tasty statement to investigate. Which is how I come to be chatting with a woman named Peter Hackworth – yes, Peter – in a vertical hydroponic shipping container bursting with kale leaves. An octogenarian with sixty years' experience in Brisbane's food and music scene, Peter is one of four market partners who passionately believe in bringing amazing food and lots of fun to everyone, including dogs.

'We had to fight for it, but why shouldn't you be able to go out with your family and your dog,' says Peter. 'We love dogs!'

She's leading me around Eat Street on an overcast Friday afternoon, shortly before the market opens for the weekend. Imagine 180 colourful shipping containers arranged into a neighbourhood of restaurants, bars, stores and stages. The boulevards are purposely wide enough to accommodate large crowds, there are whole sections dedicated to regional cuisines, as well as desserts and quirky retail offerings. All meals are deliberately priced under $15 to make it affordable, and the entry fee is nominal. Given there's live music on three stages, performance artists and plenty of free parking, it's a stark contrast to the high prices that generally accompany top Australian attractions.

'It's expensive to eat out these days, with mortgages, bills . . .' explains Peter. 'We wanted to create a place where the whole family can have a great night out, and everyone can eat whatever they want.'

Open Friday to Sunday all year round, Eat Street is located right on the river on Brisbane's North Shore, and resembles no other

market I've visited. There are no chains or franchises, with each vendor hand-picked by Peter and her team. There's French, Peruvian, Hungarian, Chinese, Mexican and Turkish stalls (to name but a few of the many cuisines represented here), a guy who makes the world's best ginger beer, as well as grilled meats, fresh seafood and Samba, the amazing chef from Brazil. Sushi, pizza, burgers and oysters are also on the menu. In the bustle to open for business in an hour, everyone still greets Peter warmly and stops for a chat as they walk past. She

asks them about their kids, cracks a joke and discusses the weather forecast. 'We're all a family here,' she explains. If good food is always cooked with love, it might explain why Eat Street is so popular. There are plenty of seating areas, and Peter points out the containers that have been refurbished to accommodate private parties, events and even weddings. Peter's idea to use shipping containers turned out to be brilliant: they're perfectly sized for small kitchens, easy to arrange and stand up well to the elements. One of the Eat Street partners, television personality Jacki MacDonald, insists we head upstairs to check out a different sort of container. The Modular Farms Co. uses vertical hydroponics to grow leafy vegetables and herbs in a fully enclosed and sustainable environment. Just one container can grow salad leaves for the entire market. It's innovative and different and the kind of thinking that has allowed Eat Street to transcend being any old city market. It has become an experience.

A few hours later, the market is bursting at the seams. A nine-piece band is performing popular jazz tunes on the stage in the Main Deck, while two virtuoso guitarists are enthralling diners in the graffiti-lined Laneway. Kids are running amok under the stars beneath the silent film at the OpenSky Theatre. Neon signs and tens of thousands of LED lights make the market sparkle; the atmosphere is fun, festive and distinctly local. I sample a melt-in-your-mouth brisket from a container called Rogue Spice, while my daughter beelines it for the decadent sweets in Kombi Alley. As well as young families, I spy dozens of dates, a glitzy party in the Riverdeck function space,

Night Kayak on Moreton Island

Located 35 kilometres off the coast and a 75-minute ferry ride from Brisbane, Moreton Island is the world's third largest sand island and is well worth a visit. It offers various adventures within its pristine environment – boating, stand-up paddle boarding, snorkelling, surfing, beach biking, fishing and more. Climb up Mount Tempest which, at 285 metres, is one of the world's highest coastal dunes. The Tangalooma Island Resort is famous for its Wild Dolphin Feeding Experience, and their Transparent Night Kayak Tour is definitely worth looking into. On it, you'll encounter abundant marine life gathered each evening around fifteen sunken shipwrecks.

teenagers, and parents happy to let the kids explore on their own. There's a lineup for fresh mocktails, while the Swedish Candy Bar and the oyster shucker are in high demand. As the night progresses, a hilarious musical trio from New Zealand belt out popular hits and a young hip-hop boy band crew wow everyone with their flashy dance moves. With my delighted kids fully entertained (and a little wired courtesy of a stall called Professor Fairy Floss), it all adds up to one of the best nights out I've enjoyed in any Australian city. I found East Street to be unpretentious, warm-hearted, accessible and dedicated to the community. After visiting South Bank and the Queen Street pedestrian mall, I've come to think this is representative of Brisbane itself.

'We're the first of its kind in Australia, and Brisbane is *never* the first in Australia,' says Peter with a smile. Named for the son she was supposed to be, Peter's drive, dedication and long history as a Queensland food maven has led to the creation of a market that's truly worthy of its claim: There is nothing like Eat Street anywhere in the world.

START HERE:
aussiebucketlist.com/eatstreet

Walk in an Ancient Rainforest

MOSSMAN GORGE

'Well, this has been one of the more fascinating hours of my life,' proclaims a tourist from Colorado, and I'm inclined to agree. Mossman Gorge, located about twenty minutes' drive from Port Douglas, sits at the southern end of Daintree National Park attracting visitors with stunning rainforest trails and some of the purest waters on the planet. Operating out of the visitor centre and supporting the local Kuku Yalanji Indigenous community, Ngadiku Dreamtime Walks take you along private tracks deeper into the world's oldest rainforest, learning about culture, flora and fauna you won't find anywhere else. Our guide this morning is Mooks, who has many unique stories to tell, the least of which is his own.

One of ten children, Mooks was chosen by his grandfather to inherit the healing traditions of his ancestors. He was raised off-grid in the bush, living off and learning all about the rainforest. Although never formally educated, he is fluent in ten Indigenous languages and is an encyclopedia of wisdom. Ten different Indigenous communities once inhabited these rainforests, but centuries of European settlement literally decimated them. Mooks is the last existing traditional healer in the rainforest of Northern Queensland, although he didn't tell us that, it's something I uncovered later. 'My grandfather was a black tracker, a bounty hunter. We were warned authorities were coming, and I was saved twice from being stolen away. My grandmother once disguised me with charcoal. Another time I hid in a mail bag until the people left. I wouldn't be here today if they stole me,' Mooks says.

It's been my experience that Indigenous experiences can sometimes feel a little manicured, a little too glossy. Yet sometimes, like today, there are personalities and an atmosphere that feels unmistakably authentic, resulting in the kind of interaction that makes cultures want to connect in the first place. We take the Mossman Gorge shuttle from the visitor centre, passing the rainforest circuit drop-off and a small Kuku Yalanji community. Paper bark is burning for a ceremonial welcome. Mooks invites us to walk around the fire, letting the smoke cleanse us while he welcomes us in his native tongue. We are about to enter a jungle older than the Amazon, with trees and plants that existed before there were dinosaurs.

'We call this the ghost tree,' says Mooks, pointing out a white-barked tree a few steps in. 'If you're lost at night, it glows in the dark.' I'm incredulous, but soon discover this will only be the first of many unusual wonders in Mossman Gorge. Mooks pulls several leaves of wild potato vine. 'It is said that two of these leaves will shrink cancers and kill bacteria, the rest won't work at all.'

He tells us stories of how his people believe these ancient plants heal the impossible, from terminal cancers to various diseases. Plants that must be ground up and prepared just so; plants you will not find anywhere else. Sap from trees that can be used to heal wounds,

act as glue, and also poison your spears. Stinging trees that will drive you crazy with pain for months, unless you quickly dig up the roots, crush them and rub them on the scratch. Medicine trees to cure toothache and upset stomachs and help insect bites, and other trees with poison thorns, razor-sharp stems and sap that will blister your skin. The Daintree houses a pharmacy of plants that can both heal and hurt; listening to the knowledge of elders, passed down through the millennia, is essential to help us determine which is which.

'The holes in these rocks date back tens of thousands of years, when women of the rainforest would grind seeds,' explains Mooks. They were short people, adapted for the environment in which they lived. We pick up a weighty boomerang, learning how these particular forest versions would not return to the thrower, but be deadly effective. Mussel shells from the coast are demonstrated to be sharp as knives, used for carving

More Bucket List Indigenous Experiences

NSW: Sand Dune Adventures, owned and operated by the *Worimi* people, takes you on quad bike, Hummer and cultural tours on their traditional land outside of Port Stephens, which comprises the largest coastal dunes in the southern hemisphere (see page 120).

WA: Wula Gura Nyinda Eco Adventures offers kayaking, four-wheel driving, stand-up paddle boarding, camping and cultural tours of Shark Bay (a region traditionally called Gutharraguda) by a descendant of the *Nhanda* and *Malgana* people,

SA: Aboriginal Culture Tours offers one to three-day tours of *Ngadjuri* Outbush country, encompassing Red Banks Conservation Park, the Clare Valley and Southern Flinders Ranges. Coastal tours explore *Adjahdura* land in the

Yorke Peninsula, the Point Pearce Aboriginal Community and Innes National Park.

VIC: Gulpilil's Australia offers full-day and half-day nature based eco-tour experiences at Lake Boort. Learn about the *Dja Dja Wurrung* people as you canoe or kayak among hundreds of scarred trees with bark removed for traditional shelters, shields and cooking.

TAS: The *wukalina* walk is a three-day, four-night Aboriginal owned and operated guided walk in the Bay of Fires and Mt William areas, the cultural homeland of the *Palawa* people.

NT: Nitmiluk Tours, owned and operated by the *Jawoyn* people, takes you on cruises, canoes and cultural bush tucker tours in Nitmiluk National Park.

and scarification. Having grown up in the bush, sleeping in huts and surviving exclusively off the land, Mooks learned a few tricks from the grandparents that raised him: how fresh water could be procured by digging up sand frogs, pricking their bloated pouches and sipping the water within; how driving sticks in the sand can detect the hollow sounds of a turtle shell buried beneath; how walkabouts within the rainforest would ensure the fruits grow back, the animals return, and humans and nature live in a state of environmental balance. The dense rainforest is in stark contrast to the fields of sugarcane I passed on my drive to Mossman Gorge, plantations that ultimately pushed Indigenous people off their ancient and sacred land.

We spot a Boyd's forest dragon perched on a branch in the sunlight and crack open a Daintree nut to taste the coconut-like seed inside. We see caterpillar vines and blush woods. We learn about decorative clay painting, and how the clay can be washed off the skin with certain leaves, creating a natural bush shampoo. We strip another medicine tree of bark and it smells like wintergreen – used, of course, to alleviate muscle pain.

'Is all this therapeutic stuff well known?' I ask Mooks, who has an endearing habit of calling everyone around him Mooks, or Mooksie, as well. 'It hasn't been studied much, Mooks. You know, the pharmaceutical companies, it's all about money.' That said, he tells us more stories about Dutch, German and English patients seeking him out to reveal the Daintree's miracles. Rupert Isaacson's book *The Long Ride Home* is about one family's quest to help their severely autistic

child through the wisdom of ancient traditions. There's a story about their visit to the Daintree, where a local healer smokes their son with paperbark, seemingly drawing out a mysterious liquid from his head. After three days of such treatment, their son's behaviour improved dramatically. The healer's name was Harold and – with a little bit of digging – I discover that Harold also goes by the name of Mooks.

We emerge from the forest for some tea and freshly baked damper. Mooks utters a blessing in Kuku Yalinji, translating it for us: 'We are all brothers and sisters, we are all welcome.' Mossman Gorge is like nowhere else on the planet – beautiful, hostile, fascinating and full of secrets waiting to be discovered.

START HERE:
aussiebucketlist.com/
mossmangorge

Go Rafting in the Wet Tropics

TULLY

The wild and invigorating excitement of whitewater rafting is a no-brainer on our bucket list, and there are really only two Australian rafting trips to consider: an expensive, multi-day expedition in the chilly waters of Tasmania, and conquering the Tully River in tropical North Queensland. This is where I find myself, booking a spot with the aptly named Raging Thunder tour company. Their full-day and world-renowned Classic Tully adventure will have me paddling 12 to 14 kilometres downstream through dozens of Class 3 and 4 rapids. Having whitewater rafted on four continents, I've learned that the success of the adventure is wholly dependant on: your location; the temperature and quality of the water; the rafting company and guide; the people in your raft; the rapids; and how much punishment you can take before wanting to curl up in a soggy ball.

Location: Tully Gorge National Park is located in the UNESCO World Heritage Wet Tropics, an ancient jungle where you half expect to see a T-Rex on the riverbank. Pristine water flows from the Misty Mountains, the wettest region in the country, into the Tully River. The Kareeya Hydroelectric Dam controls the full flow, enabling consistent rafting trips 364 days a year. Luminous butterflies and rainbow lorikeets flutter about, eastern water dragons bask on logs, white-bellied sea eagles patrol for fish and champagne waterfalls cascade down steep basalt canyons. It's rugged, unspoilt and, excuse my Italian, goddamn magical.

Temperature and quality of the water: You can safely drink from the Tully River; upstream, the hydroelectric dam ensures there's no farming run-off. The water is a refreshing relief from the region's infamous heat and humidity and it is warm enough that you don't need a wetsuit, and don't get frozen hands. The current is strong enough that you won't over-exert yourself paddling, and the first crocodile warning signs conveniently appear where your trip concludes (don't worry, estuarine

crocs don't come this far upriver). You can rock jump, splash and swim and, after a few choice rapids, your sinuses will get a thorough rinsing. Oh, and brace yourself for a mighty baptism beneath Ponytail Falls.

The company and guide: Operating for more than 30 years, Raging Thunder has guided over a million people down the Tully River. They know it like the back of an oar, and have the exclusive rights to operate on the best parts of it. Our guide, Paul, has rafted *everywhere:* Colorado, Canada, the Himalayas, New Zealand, the Franklin. He's been guiding on the Tully for twelve years, and he's fun and firm and completely in control (unless he doesn't want to be, which is the fun part). All the guides crack jokes that are so sharp I'm convinced they've done a theatre workshop. The safety briefings are thorough and safety is paramount: there's a trained first responder with every group, medical kits, satellite phones and easy-to-follow emergency procedures. Sure, there might be a cut or bruise, but you're hurtling down a raging river for Allen's sake, you're not in a waterpark.

The people in your raft: Sitting up front in my raft, Allen is an

electrician from the Blue Mountains and he's just departed the boat in a particularly challenging series of rapids called the Theatre ('this is where the drama and comedy happens,' Paul had warned us). After dropping hard into a Class 4 rapid, we banged up against a large boulder, causing Allen to lose his grip and bounce under the cascade. We quickly hauled him into the boat and seconds later we're in calm waters discussing our great rescue and Allen's awesome adventure. There are only four 16-foot durable rafts operating today (there can be double that during the busy season), each with six or seven people and a guide. Teamwork is essential, and we need to paddle forwards, backwards, shift weight and quickly sit in the centre together. Whether you're travelling solo or in a group, you'll get to know your rafting team well, rely on each other and laugh a lot, too.

The rapids: Satan's Toilet Bowl is 'an evil place to get stuck'. Alarm Clock will wake you up, Foreplay only lasts two minutes, Ninja Shute is sneaky, Double D Cup is named after a bare-chested incident, Birth Canal is a tight squeeze and Dogs Balls is, well, what you get when the name Devils Marbles is already taken. By now you've probably guessed the sensibilities of river guides when it comes to naming rapids. On the Tully River, there are corkscrews and zigzags, full stops and lemon squeezes. There are technical rapids like the Boulder

Garden Maze and hold-on-for-dear-life rapids like the Staircase. The river serves them up with enough frequency to keep things spicy and the guides ensure that you will get – as one explained in the briefing – 'very very very very very very very *very* wet.'

How much punishment you can take before wanting to curl up in a soggy ball: Look, anyone over the age of thirteen can and should go whitewater rafting. I took my 72-year-old Dad on this trip and, while he passed on a 4-metre rock jump, he didn't fall out of the raft and now has the mandatory hero photo (taken by professional photographers along the river) as his screensaver. One woman in our group said she was scared stiff by the safety video demonstration but ended up taking every opportunity to jump in the water and float feet-first with the current with absolute delight on her face. Raging Thunder feeds you a hot BBQ lunch, you don't have to worry about the state of the weather and, unlike previous rafting experiences, my hands didn't turn into icypoles. All this to say, you can take a lot of punishment on the Tully River and – as the guides will probably demonstrate later – a lot of punishment when you get back to the El Arish Tavern bar at the end of the day.

Ticking all the boxes, the Tully River is a world-class adventure, accessible from Cairns or Mission Beach. Hold that T-grip, smile, and when the jokes start flying, remember to go with the flow.

START HERE:
aussiebucketlist.com/tullyriver

Brave the Franklin River Rapids

An eight- or ten-day whitewater expedition down Tasmania's Franklin River is regarded as one of life's great rafting adventures. With steep gorges and treacherous obstacles, rapids range from Class I (easy) all the way to Class 5 (maximum thrill). A number of rafting companies guide visitors from around the world along the Franklin. As you raft across the Gordon Franklin Wild Rivers National Park and World Heritage area, campsites are located along the river, with tents or communal camping under tarps set up for the evening. All food is brought in and out on the rafts, which can carry a lot of weight. Rafting takes place October to April, through pristine and especially remote wilderness, with opportunities to hike to legendary peaks like Frenchmans Cap, spot wildlife, and conquer epic passes.

Do the
Great Barrier Reef

There's no question that the Great Barrier Reef belongs on any Australian bucket list. The world's largest living thing is a chain of reefs that stretches 2300 kilometres and covers an area of approximately 348,000 square kilometres. It consists of 2900 reefs and 900 islands, and is home to more than 1500 species of fish, 400 species of hard coral, 4000 species of mollusc and 240 species of birds. It's a sure-fire hit, an all-season summer blockbuster, Australia's biggest natural drawcard and a true natural wonder of the world. No question it belongs here, but the question is: How do you do it?

Quicksilver's high-speed catamaran is cruising towards the company's stationed pontoon on the outer Barrier Reef. Departing from Cairns and operating every day of the year, the boat is taking me and busloads of other passengers on the reef's most popular day-trip, where we'll partake in a host of fun aquatic activities. I snorkel, hop below a semi-submersible boat and check out an underwater observatory. My favourite activity is the Ocean Walker, on which I descend to an underwater platform with a weighty Cousteau-like glass bowl on my head. Every bucket list should include the opportunity to pet an unnervingly large yet friendly Maori wrasse named Wally. From Cairns and Port Douglas there are many day-trip options to visit the reef, from luxury catamarans to high-speed Reef Sprinters. More pontoon options are available further south in the Whitsundays (see Reefsleep, page 203). But what about those who want to spend a little more time on the reef?

From Cairns, I hop aboard a small plane for the hour-long flight to Lizard Island National Park. Home to an important marine research station, Lizard Island is also a five-star all-inclusive resort, with 48 luxurious villas facing a turquoise bay and white sandy beach. It is the epitome of

elegance – white walls, wooden boardwalks, palm trees, an azure pool, fine dining and a spa. Seemingly everyone who works here is young, tanned and attractive, from the resort staff to the international scientists at the marine research station. The island is also on many a diver's bucket list, especially the Cod Hole, where giant potato cod swim with curious sharks and technicolour fish on the outer reef. Descending beneath the surface, I chase reef sharks, stare into the eyes of giant fish and navigate reef canyons. 'Damn!' I exclaim back on the dive boat. 'The Great Barrier Reef delivers!'

From the Gold Coast, I hop aboard another small plane to explore the most southerly island of the reef, Lady Elliot Island. Owned and operated by the Australian government, Lady Elliot is famous for manta rays and turtles and is the most accessible reef island for those visiting from Australia's southern capitals. Far less glitzy than Lizard Island, the beach cabins are popular with families, divers, weekenders and backpackers. I pick up snorkel gear at the dive shop, take a few steps from my cabin into the lagoon, and the reef explodes with colour. The small, coral cay island offers excellent visibility, and year-round activities. On a dive that afternoon I swim through the Blue Hole, an underwater tunnel that opens up into a marine world teeming with life. Look at the size of that white-tipped reef shark! Hello Mr Curious Turtle! Check out the grace of that manta ray! Snorkelling from the Coral Garden to the lighthouse is so rich with turtles, coral, fish and manta rays it will leave you gasping for air, no scuba certification necessary. There are a dozen other resorts located on islands along the reef, and many more along the mainland. You might try Heron Island, Dunk Island, Magnetic Island or the Whitsundays, which is so rich and wondrous it gets two sections to itself in this book. Still, it's impossible to appreciate just how large the reef actually is, which is why you might want to consider taking to the air.

Helicopter flights never grow old and never get stale. The sensation of being on the ground one second and cruising at speed and altitude the next is worth every penny, especially in a helicopter with large viewing windows for scenic flights. My pilot Judd, from GBR Helicopters, is pointing out a hammerhead shark that seems to be swimming directly towards a

Not So Fantastic Plastic

No wonder the ocean has problems. The Great Pacific Garbage Patch is larger than the United States. It is an area of the ocean where bottles, straws, cigarette filters, cans, bags and other rubbish gather, travelling with the currents for more than five years from North America, and a year from Asia. Fish in the region ingest between five and seven tons of plastic every year. And the plastic is not going anywhere. Scientists estimate that it takes 20 years for plastic bags to break down in the ocean, 50 years for a tin can, 450 years for a plastic bottle and more than a million years for a glass bottle. Great strides are being taken in Australia to ban plastic bags and especially plastic straws, which continue to have a devastating effect on marine life.

dugong. We're flying 500 feet above Batt Reef and the shallow waters of low tide reveal eagle and manta rays cruising on the 18-kilometre reef. From above we can see the southern tip of the larger Tongue Reef, as we fly over the lighthouse on Low Island and various boats anchored off the mangroves of Woody Island. The thirty-minute scenic flight is so vivid with stunning shades of blue I think it cracked my mirrored sunglasses. GBR Helicopters also offers ten-minute flights from a helipad on the Quicksilver pontoon. High above the ribbons of the Agincourt Reef, the coral gardens appear to stretch on forever.

Despite evidence of widespread bleaching, ocean acidification, pollution and rising water temperatures, the Great Barrier Reef is not dead. Parts are definitely battered and bruised, while others are largely unaffected. Declaring the

Barrier Reef dead (as one writer did, garnering world news headlines) is like saying the United Kingdom doesn't exist anymore because an arsonist burned down Wales. Recognising just how important the reef is for both the environment and tourism, the Queensland and Federal governments are investing more than two billion dollars to repair and protect the reef, along with an additional $500 million pledged by the Federal Government (the reef supports more than 64,000 jobs, generates over $6.4 billion dollars in revenue, and attracts more than two million visitors a year). Organisations like the Great Barrier Reef Foundation and the Reef Restoration Foundation are cultivating heat-tolerant coral to mimic nature and allow damaged reefs to recover faster and become more resilient. After 25 million years of life on earth, nobody should be presumptuous enough to write an obituary for the Great Barrier Reef just yet. Whether we decide to experience it under water, from a helicopter, on a day-trip or on a week-long island getaway, rest assured that this natural wonder will be around long after we've kicked the bucket.

START HERE:
aussiebucketlist.com/
greatbarrierreef

Zip Through the Daintree

CAPE TRIBULATION

It takes just a few minutes by ferry to cross the crocodile-infested waters of the Daintree River, but when your wheels touch the ground on Cape Tribulation Road, it feels like you've been transported millions of years into the past. The narrow road meanders between dense rainforest, through tree tunnels of ancient ferns, figs, cycads and palms, and alongside impenetrable mangroves. Between the unpredictable weather, crocs, snakes, bugs and toxin-laced plants, no wonder Captain Cook named it Cape Tribulation. It's the kind of remote, tropical wilderness you'd expect to find in the jungles of Borneo or Central Africa, only the Daintree is far more accessible than either of them. And in the world's oldest rainforest, I'd recommend you head for the trees.

Operating out of Cape Trib, Jungle Surfing offers six tree platforms and seven ziplines in the heart of the Daintree – no mean feat considering we're in a protected UNESCO World Heritage Site. It's adventure eco-tourism with an emphasis on *eco*; solar and micro-hydro turbines power the facility and no heavy machinery was brought into the area during construction. A system of blocks and chains hold each platform to the trees so there is no need for a single nail or bolt, and a top-belay system means you can fly hands-free. I can confidently say *anyone* can zipline, as joining me today is my five-year-old daughter and her grandfather visiting from Canada. Three generations climb inside an ingenious human hamster wheel – a world-first conceived and engineered right here in the Daintree – which will tow us up to the first platform. Using our legs to rotate the giant treadmill, we get the cable moving and send our lead guide up to the first 16-metre-high platform. Then we take turns on the wire, until we're safely connected to a giant tree within the rainforest canopy. Our guide Brydehn reveals

some facts about the fascinating flora and fauna that lives within the Daintree, and what makes it such a unique and cherished biosphere. He also explains why it's definitely not a good idea to go swimming in the ocean or rivers of Cape Tribulation (estuary crocodiles!) or wander too far off the beaten track in the forest (stinging trees!). As my daughter safely launches off the platform on a 42-metre ride to the next tree, I'm quite happy we're in the air while the jungle does its thing below.

Over the next hour we happily make our way through the canopy, sometimes hanging upside down, sometimes going fast, always having fun. The region's famously wet weather holds off, although the tours operate rain or shine; this is, after all, a rainforest. If you've ziplined before, you'll appreciate the sheer diversity of the ecosystem,

the opportunity to be immersed in an environment unlike any other on the planet. If this is your first time, you'll quickly understand why ziplining is so popular, safe and ideal for bucket listers of all ages. On the longest line, Brydehn brakes us in the middle so we can spend a few moments dangling above a fast-flowing river, completely immersed in the magic of the Daintree. I breathe that moment in, cherish it, and back it up in the memory card of my travel highlights. The Daintree is an extraordinary place, and this is a bucket list moment well worth hanging around for.

START HERE:
aussiebucketlist.com/
junglesurfing

Exotic Tastes of the Daintree

On your drive up to Cape Trib, pull over at the Daintree Ice Cream Co. for a taste of something tropical. The 22-acre organic orchard grows fruit you might have heard of – mangoes, lychees, durian, passionfruit – and a few you might not know about: jaboticaba, capuassa, araca, mamey sapote, Davidson plum. The sampler bowl dishes up four scoops of whatever fruit is in season, all made on-site. If you're still hungry after that and feeling adventurous, pull over at Mason's Cafe for an exotic taster plate of kangaroo, emu, crocodile, boar, camel and buffalo.

Make Your Own Tracks

FRASER ISLAND

On the face of it, not much has changed on the world's largest sand island since 1770, when Captain James Cook first spotted it. It remains remote and undeveloped, 1840 square kilometres of unspoilt coastal paradise. That's what the island's Butchulla people called their home – *K'gari* means paradise. Unfortunately, the arrival of Europeans meant a great deal of change for them. Indigenous resistance to the arrival of settlers led to raiding parties and massacres. There have been sand mining disputes and fierce environmental battles, the introduction and removal of wild brumby horses, protection for the purest dingoes left in Australia and, after several attacks, a dingo cull, too. All of this matters deeply, yet little of it sticks when you finally step foot on the sand. Fraser Island is too damn big, raw and beautiful to accommodate the trials of history.

Heritage listed by UNESCO for its shifting sands, freshwater dune lakes and tropical rainforest, Fraser Island tops many an Australian bucket list. Crystal clear waters, light-turquoise seas and talcum-soft beaches bask under a big sky that curves around you like an umbrella. There may be limited options to get onto the island, but there are unlimited options once you do. Drive or rent an all-wheel-drive vehicle, catch a barge and the island is your oyster. Although there are some hotels on the island, many visitors choose to camp, packing everything in and out. Alternatively, there are dozens of companies that will gladly take care of the logistics, offering all-wheel-drive coach tours and multi-day itineraries. In high season, a lack of roads doesn't mean you won't find traffic, as vehicles whizz up and down the beaches and towards the island's biggest attractions. There's Lake McKenzie, with its crystal waters and pure silica sands. Central Station, once the island's logging centre, now a tall rainforest with rare vegetation. Pile Valley and the Hammerstone Sandblow, the doomed SS Maheno wreck and swimming in the green waters of Lake Wabby.

The Myth of Eliza Fraser

In 1836, an uppity British woman named Eliza Fraser was shipwrecked and taken in by the Butchulla people on an island called K'gari. After her eventual rescue and return to London, she told an enthralled public about her terrifying ordeal with the savages. She claimed she was stripped of her dignity and treated 'with the greatest cruelty'. The Butchulla version of events – and the truth – was a long way off.

As renowned historian Professor Iain McCalman explains: 'The Eliza Fraser myth is a foundational myth that says when a poor white woman is wrecked on an island, she is mistreated, terrorised, tortured and defiled by Aboriginal people for no reason.' He goes on to deconstruct the myth, showing how and why Eliza Fraser told 'essentially, a pack of lies' that was exploited by politicians at the time to justify dispossession of Aboriginal land. Fraser herself also financially profited from her experience, and her embellished saga has caused irreparable harm to relations between Europeans and Indigenous Australians ever since. In 2017, Great Sandy National Park was renamed K'Gari, and descendants of the Butchulla hope the island itself will follow. With any luck, the dubious legacy of Eliza Fraser will yield to the lasting power of Paradise.

'Most people will visit 30 per cent of the island, and then there's the other 70 per cent,' says the captain of the MV Whalesong, Ben Harper. We're motoring across the shallow channel from Hervey Bay, on the mainland, to the west coast of the sandy isle. Ben grew up in the area and has worked here for decades. 'There's simply no place on the planet like Fraser Island,' he enthuses, to which his first mate quickly agrees. Ideally, you'll want to spend two to three days on the island, although there's nothing wrong with a day-trip to Coongul Creek on the outskirts of Great Sandy Marine Park. Calm ocean waves tickle the beach like a kitten's tongue at a milk plate. Spotting dolphins in the distance, we set up fishing lines and bring out sea kayaks. My wife takes our two-year-old for a dip in the adjacent warm, tea-coloured creek, while my delighted five-year-old daughter quickly snags a baitfish with her fishing rod. Two teenage girls are kayaking along the shore, an all-wheel-drive vehicle cruises past. Not for the first time on my journey, I take it all in with a deep appreciation for such distinctly Australian opportunities. Unlike the coastal dunes I discovered in Port Stephens (see page 120), Fraser Island does not resemble a desert. There are more than eight-hundred and fifty species of plants, including forests of beach oak and towering pines. Many visitors hope to see a dingo in its natural habitat, a unique wildlife encounter that is still a major drawcard for the island. There are only around two hundred dingoes remaining on the island, isolated from domestic dogs for millennia and said to be the purest-breed dingoes still in existence. The

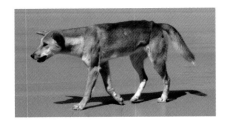

impact of humans on the island includes contamination of pristine lakes with sunscreen and soap, leaking dune latrines and littering. Reassuringly, legislative protection is in place to ensure the island will continue to stay a rugged outdoor paradise and a unique Australian ecosystem. Technology might be pushing us towards a science-fiction future but, with any luck, nothing will change on Fraser Island.

START HERE:
aussiebucketlist.com/fraserisland

Canoe the Aussie Everglades

NOOSA

'**H**ey guys, *bitte*, can we please take a moment to reflect?'
I say this as I sit in a canoe behind two German
backpackers paddling deeper into a tea-coloured
waterway. While I might be an adopted Canadian — and Canadians
are famously known to do *everything* in a canoe — we're nevertheless ping-ponging between the river banks of the narrow canal.
It's a perfectly acceptable thing to do in the Noosa Everglades,
where emerald foliage and blue skies reflect on tranquil, silent
waters. There are only two places on Earth where you can encounter such a setting, and the Florida Everglades are better known
for hungry alligators.

Protected by the Great Sandy
National Park and its World
Heritage-listed biosphere, the
Noosa Everglades comprise a
60-kilometre-long lake system in
south-east Queensland. Everglade
is an American term for a tract of
low swampy land with tall grasses
and spidery waterways. Australia's
own Noosa Everglades is a wetland
that is home to 44 per cent of all
the country's bird species, more
than 1300 different plants and
700 native animals. It is vast and
simply impenetrable on foot but – as
any visitor to the Amazon jungle
knows – you'd rather be exploring
this type of terrain on a river
anyway.

The town of Noosa Heads is
your entry point to the everglades,
which are typically accessed via
daily boat rides. Alternatively, you
can opt for hourly or multi-day
kayak rentals from Boreen Point.
Hoping to experience the best of
both experiences in the limited
time I have, I sign up for Discovery
Group's Bar-B-Canoe day trip,
which departs daily from their
river jetty. From a custom-built
vessel designed for the unusually
shallow waters of the everglades,
we gaze out the windows at Noosa's
eclectic houseboats and huge
shorefront houses. One house has
a large mango tree growing right
in the middle of it, with a sign

out front that names it, unsurprisingly, Mango Landing. With its outstanding weather, lifestyle and proximity to Brisbane, Noosa is a major destination for retirees – and the rich and famous, too. For I quickly realise there's rich, and then there's *boat* rich. We pass large yachts and flashy catamarans and then peer curiously into Richard Branson's private resort and celebrity hideaway, Makepeace Island. It has hosted royalty, rock stars and

Stay on the Water

With its renowned surf beaches, fine dining, markets, golf, fishing and boating, it's pretty obvious why Noosa has one of the best lifestyles in the country. If you want to spend more time on the water here, consider renting a six, eight or ten-berth houseboat. Fully equipped with kitchens, barbecues, bedrooms, a living area and your own dinghy to get around, houseboats let you navigate along the channels to Lake Cooroibah or Lake Cootharaba, casting your fishing line as you go. No boat license is required.

world leaders, accommodating up to twenty people at a cost of around $15,000 a night.

'I've visited several times,' laughs our wisecracking guide, Trevor. 'Made it to the pool before security tackled me.'

Our powerful outboard motors roar to life as we cross the brackish shallow waters of Lake Cooroibah. At an average of just 1 metre deep, the Noosa River is shallow enough to cross by foot, although too large, dark, and wide for anybody in their right mind to want to do it. We see the relics of boats that have been damaged in storms, and Trevor tells us he has participated in more than one rescue of kayakers stranded by currents in the middle of the lakes. We learn stories about the area – how it was deforested and used for cattle and dairy farming before being reclaimed and protected – and about some of the families who have owned land here for generations. The waters are so shallow in Lake Cootharaba that Trevor has to carefully slalom the boat between channel markers or risk being beached. Although the southern Pacific Ocean is just beyond the hills to our right, the lake funnels into a channel towards

Noosa Heads, back where we started 20 kilometres away.

Windsurfers are enjoying today's strong breeze, although those who rented kayaks would be wise to stick close to the shoreline until they reach the Kinaba Information Centre. Here they'll find illustrated boards detailing the everglade's myriad flora and fauna. Beneath us swim mullets, Australian bass, long finned eels, native honey blue-eyes and snake-necked turtles. Bull sharks are said to patrol the shallow river system, although there has never been an attack and swimming is regarded as perfectly safe. We disembark for morning tea at Fig Tree Point and divide into groups for a

canoe adventure into the pristine channels of the upper Noosa River. My new German friends are a little concerned we might capsize, but I remind them that canoes have been used for thousands of years because they are easy to master and tend to work very well.

'Keep your balance in the middle, grip your paddle and I'll do my best to ensure we don't impale ourselves on the grass trees,' I tell them. Not long after, we've been poked by sharp grass trees, hit another canoe and I've almost lost my paddle to a low-lying tree. All of which is taken in good humour and, as we float up a section called the Narrows, I politely request a moment for reflection, using one of only four German words I know. 'Wow! I've never seen anything like this beauty!' says Marnie up front.

'Incredible!' agrees Sebastian.

Tannins darken the still waters, creating the impression that we're floating on a smooth, black mirror. While we can't see any animals, we can certainly hear them beyond the melaleuca trees, banksias, reeds, tea trees and bushes. From this point on, our one-hour paddle up the Narrows is punctuated by short bursts of comically inefficient paddling and longer pauses to silently drift within a rare and magical natural environment. We reunite with the boat, moored at a jetty alongside a camping and day-use area, just in time for the essential reward of a steak and barramundi barbecue. Some of us decide to swim in the river, although not without reassurances about safety.

'It just feels like there should be crocs or hippos or piranhas or bull sharks,' I tell Trevor. 'After all, this *is* Australia.'

Whether you're camping, canoeing, day-tripping or kayaking, everyone will be able to reflect that indeed, this is Australia, and a very special part of it.

START HERE:
**aussiebucketlist.com/
noosaeverglades**

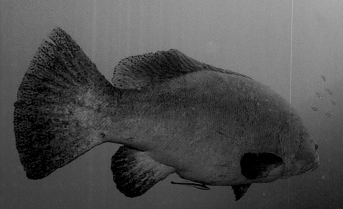

Dive the
SS Yongala

It is known as Townsville's *Titanic* and one of Australia's worst maritime disasters. On 23 March 1911, a luxury passenger steamship en-route from Melbourne to Cairns hit a Category 5 cyclone and vanished with one hundred and twenty-two people on board. The *SS Yongala* had almost a hundred successful voyages under its belt, but as it departed Mackay it failed to see last-minute warnings that it was headed into a monster storm (the ship's new wireless transmitter had yet to arrive from England). When the storm eventually passed, wreckage began washing up along the coast. An unsuccessful rescue effort was launched but no ship or survivors were found.

While a navy minesweeper detected a mysterious shoal in the area during World War II, it was not until 1958 that the *Yongala* was officially discovered by salvage divers, along with the skeletons of passengers washed into the bow. More than half a century later, the *SS Yongala* is the largest, most-intact shipwreck in Australia. Located within the protected waters of the Great Barrier Reef Marine Park, the top of the ship's main structure is just 14 metres below the surface, the base at 28-metres deep. The result is an artificial reef disco dancing with marine life, and a sure-fire bucket list adventure for novice and experienced divers. Although I've had the opportunity to dive in Papua New Guinea, the Philippines, the Cook Islands and in the cold dark waters off Vancouver Island, I still count myself in the former category, drawn to the promise of one of the world's best dives.

Based on Alva Beach about fifteen minutes from the town of Ayr, Yongala Dive is the best and closest operator to the wreck, with a full dive centre offering certification, equipment rentals and daily two-dive excursions. Boarding from the beach, their powerful skiff heads out into today's mildly choppy seas and I try to imagine the 20-metre swells and cyclonic winds that would have

sunk the 110-metre *Yongala*. It's a forty-minute cruise to the buoys that mark its burial site, where we're briefed about the dive. We must remain alongside the wreck and entry is strictly forbidden. The wreck is heritage-protected, subject to deterioration, and nobody wants to add more bones to the many that have been relocated to the inaccessible bow. Strong currents are common and all descents and ascents must be done on the safety line. Since I am here in April, we can expect visibility to be around 10 to 15 metres. Yongala Dive is an advanced ecotourism operator so there will be no touching the wreck, coral or wildlife. We will use a backwards roll entry, turn around with 120 bar in our tanks and must exit, by Queensland law, with 50 bar remaining in the tank. The average dive time will be forty minutes, with an hour-long interval before the second dive. Our group of divers from Australia, Germany and the US display the nervous energy of people on the cusp of a bucket list experience. The sky is blue, the currents are calm, the waters clear. Large batfish and a Hawksbill turtle breach the surface around us. The *SS Yongala* patiently awaits.

As with all wildlife excursions, you never know what you're going to get, but let me assure you, you will see *a lot* of fish. More fish in one place than any of us – hardcore

Australia's Bucket List Shipwreck Dives

Divers love wrecks because they look great underwater, attract scores of marine life and offer up intriguing history. With more than 8000 wrecks in Australian waters, here's a shortlist of the best.

- *SS Yongala*, Ayr, QLD: 110-metre passenger ship sunk during storms in 1911, now one of the world's best dives.
- *SS Orizaba*: Rockingham, WA: Sunk in shallow waters, great for beginner divers.
- *Usat Meigs*, Darwin, NT: A 131-metre-long transport ship sunk during World War II.
- *SS Nord*, Tasman Peninsula, TAS: Cold water and strong currents reserve this 82-metre steamship strictly for experienced divers.
- *Barcoola*, Gladstone, QLD: Fishing trawler sunk in 1994 off the Southern Great Barrier Reef, famous for marine life.

divers included – have ever seen. Coral cod and orange-pink coral trout, bluespine unicorns and banded angelfish, luminous blue and yellow fusiliers and huge schools of stripy snapper. Giant trevally and red bass, moray eels, bullet-quick tuna, barracuda, anemone, and we're just getting started! Green and hawksbill turtles, guitar, ray and bull sharks, venomous banded and curious olive sea snakes, flowery cod, roundface batfish, colourful Maori wrasse, eagle and manta rays, and too many more.

For over a century, the *Yongala* has become an island of life located in a stretch of sandy ocean desert. It is an important feeding and cleaning station, a reef with soft and hard corals that have penetrated just about every nook and cranny. No sooner do I leave the line below than a large and bizarrely shaped guitar shark cruises by. An olive sea snake dances next to me and, out of the corner of my eye, I spot a submarine approaching. Only, this submarine has big eyes and rubber lips and dozens of fish hanging off it, like thugs surrounding a Mafioso boss. It's

an enormous Queensland groper and, barring sharks, it is easily the biggest fish I have ever seen. All this within the first five minutes, mind you. Open-water certified divers are assigned a divemaster by Yongala Dive, and Trent guides me over the collapsed aft mast. I peer into the engine room and the coral-encrusted galley and check out the decks, which are slowly losing all semblance of being man-made. The *Yongala* nameplate is no longer visible, but I do peer into a glass port window and spot a blackened toilet. Large schools of small cardinals are everywhere,

with giant silver trevally and black turrum snatching them despite their safety in numbers. Several times I find myself disorientated, encircled by shimmering schools. There are red emperors, damsels, darktail snappers, java rabbitfish, blackspot tuskfish, estuary cod, mangrove jacks, small and large mouth nannygai. After two safety stops, we surface for an hour, snack on cakes and fruit, and prepare for our second dive. This time I'm more relaxed, more familiar with the lay of the wreck. In the shadows of the bow and stern hide the massive, 500-pound gropers, not the least bit perturbed by our presence.

Several dive reports call the *Yongala* an open-water aquarium, and easily one of the world's greatest dives. Back at the dive shop, our group discusses the experience and concurs. Of course, this is a dive story, and divers tend to exaggerate. That groper, was it 2, no 3, no 4 metres? Did you see the manta ray, the blacktip reef shark, or was it a bull shark? Bringing this diversity of marine life together is the wreck that divers the world over dream about. While nobody knows what happened, the

going theory is that the *Yongala* hit a reef, quickly took on water and, in the fierce storm, sank so abruptly no lifesaving vessels were deployed. In the ensuing tragedy, this ship and so many lives simply vanished. Many generations later, all is not lost. Australia's bucket list wreck remains off the coast of Queensland, waiting to be discovered.

START HERE:
aussiebucketlist.com/yongala

The Aussie Art of Getting High

Australians love being on top. Building and bridge climbs are found in unique locations, often have slick marketing and a pretty hefty pricetag and, less cynically, offer the chance to do something unusual. Depending on your age, interests and physical abilities, your experience will range anywhere from 'Wow, that was one of the most thrilling adventures of my life!' to 'Wow, I can't believe I just paid money for . . . *that*?' Here's a handy round up:

Sydney Harbour Bridgeclimb

The most iconic climb in the country is one slick operation, capable of funnelling in dozens of tour bus customers at one end and successful bridge climbers clutching souvenirs at the other. Processed through a series of efficient stages, you get suited, briefed and safely attached to the bridge, and then walk a series of ladders, gangways and arches. The view of the Opera House and the Sydney CBD is definitely worthwhile and, if you're a visitor, you'll learn much about the city and history of the bridge from the running commentary. You can climb at dawn, twilight, night or during the day, with a variety of flexible packages designed to eliminate whatever excuse you have for not climbing atop the world's largest steel-arched bridge. Millions of people have done it, more than 4000 couples have got engaged here, and the oldest climber was 100 years old.

Adelaide Oval Roofclimb

It probably wasn't fun dealing with the insurance company on this one, as they must have imagined every conceivable scenario of silliness one could get up to on a stadium roof. Climbers have to strap themselves into a harness, cover their rings in medical tape, remove every other object from their clothes, take a breathalyser test and wear overalls to climb up the ladder to Adelaide Oval's roof. The Oval is fetching, however, particularly if you take the tour and spend the extra cash to climb up during an AFL or cricket match. Enjoying a few minutes on the seats overlooking the pitch *is* totally bucket list. I did a two-hour twilight climb, watching the Adelaide Riverbank light up and the fruit bats fly across the city. All I could think of was: a) do we *really* need all this safety stuff, and b) it would have been great to have done this on a game day.

QI Skypoint Climb

Queensland's Gold Coast has long sandy beaches and meandering canals that shape the city's character. The best place to see them is from the QI Observatory or – better yet – stepping outside for the highest external building climb in the country. I followed the typical routine as dictated by the stringent requirements of insurance liability: light jumpsuit, safety harness, breathalyser, and cameras and phones in a lock box. Extra points here for the high-speed elevator that gets you to level 77 in just 42.7 seconds. From the Observatory, you take 140 steps up a walkway to the summit, where you are safely locked onto a railing. Here you can lean over the beach of Surfers Paradise, gaze down a 270-metre vertical drop, and wonder why no-one is climbing to the top of the other tall buildings that frame the coastline. It's a 90-minute experience (including the safety briefing) and your ticket includes access to the less exposed but just as scenic Observatory.

Eureka Skydeck's The Edge

The Eureka Skydeck is another observation deck, boasting the fastest elevator trip in the southern hemisphere and floor-to-ceiling 360-degree views of the city from 285 metres above the ground. There's an outside area to grapple with Melbourne's erratic weather, a kiosk and some touristy-activities. Perhaps recognising its lack of edge in the thrills department, Eureka Skydeck also offers The Edge, a moving glass cube that extends out from the 88th floor of the building and suspends those inside above the city streets. Ron Burgundy from the *Anchorman* movie might say you've been trapped in a 'glass cage of emotion'. My young kids didn't have any scary problems when the frosted windows cleared (with a sound-effect *crack* for good measure) to reveal Melbourne beneath their feet. Then again, they *are* my kids. Couples have been known to propose inside The Edge, and those with a fear of heights, well, they shouldn't be doing stuff like this in the first place.

Story Bridge Climb and Abseil

Brisbane's storied landmark is the only bridge climb that lets you abseil your way down. The three-hour tour operates at dawn, dusk and twilight, and lets you scale to the top of the Story Bridge for 360-degree views of the twinkling city, the Glass House Mountains and south to the Scenic Rim. Suitably impressed, you'll head over to the southern pylon for a thirty metre-abseil down into Captain Burke Park. The adventure, of course, is tailored for 'bucket list enthusiasts'.

INDIAN OCEAN

Broome

WESTERN AUSTRALIA

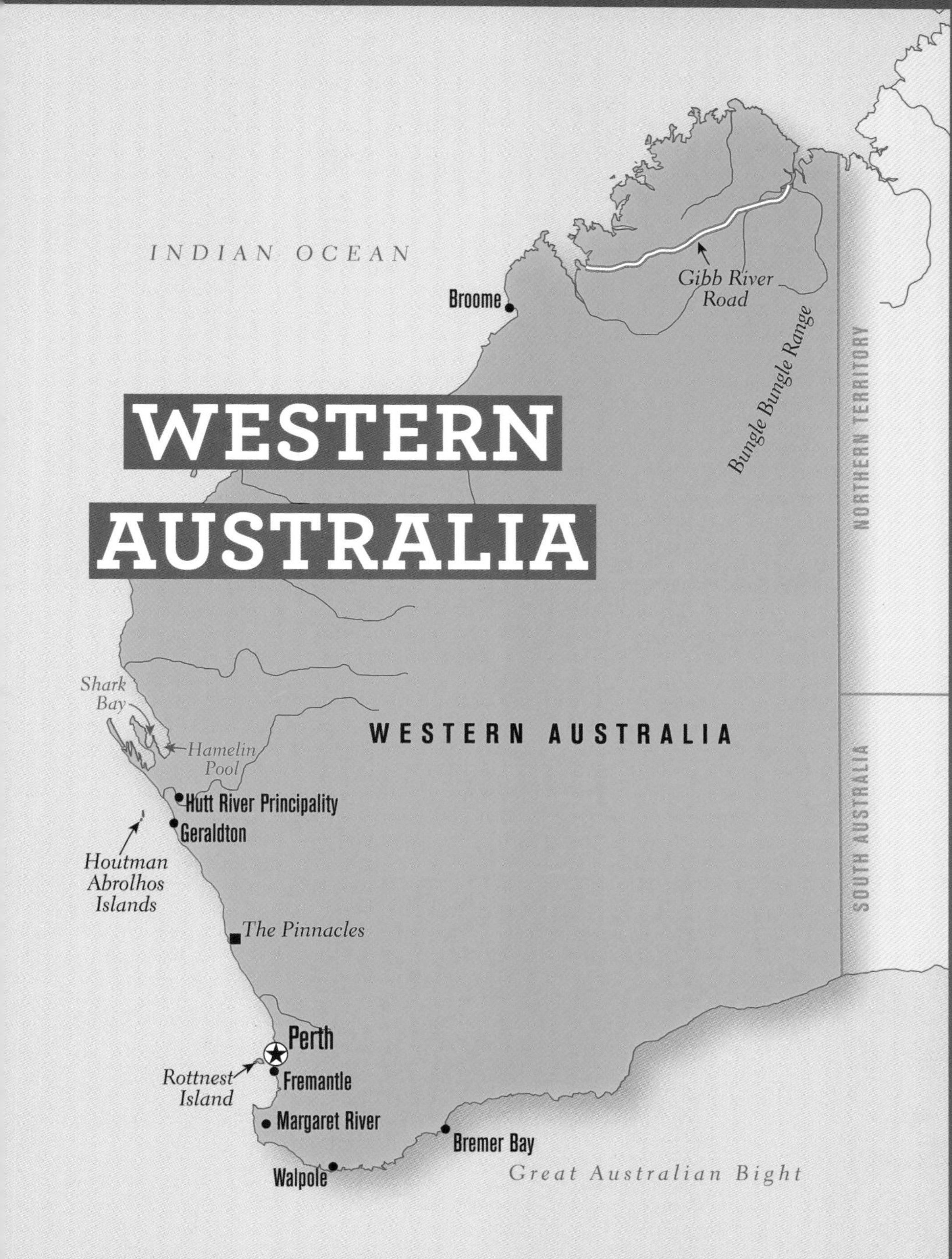

Gibb River Road

Bungle Bungle Range

NORTHERN TERRITORY

Shark Bay

WESTERN AUSTRALIA

Hamelin Pool

Hutt River Principality

Geraldton

SOUTH AUSTRALIA

Houtman Abrolhos Islands

The Pinnacles

Perth

Rottnest Island

Fremantle

Margaret River

Bremer Bay

Walpole

Great Australian Bight

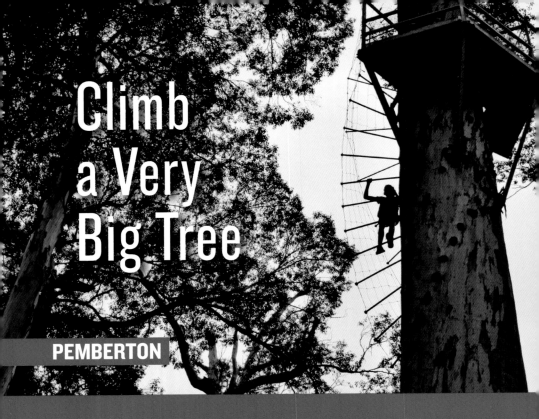

Climb a Very Big Tree

How is this a *thing*? In the same state where I was forced to wear a lifejacket and take a breathaliser test to paddle a boat in waist-deep water (see Fremantle Prison), I find myself climbing a 75-metre tree with no ropes, no safety harnesses and no way to stop my knees shaking. Located in Warren National Park, the Dave Evans Bicentennial Tree is the tallest of three regional fire lookouts, with a sweeping 360-degree view of the surrounding karri forest. The platform at the top is the place to spot bushfires, propose marriage, question your sanity, and conquer the world's tallest tree climb.

There are no liability waivers or ground staff, just a helpful sign from the Department of Environment and Conservation advising sturdy footwear, no backpacks, and to avoid the climb if you have a heart condition or fear of heights. The text at the bottom of the sign is bolded: **If in doubt, do not climb**. In which case, nobody would ever climb this tree, because if you don't have any doubts then something is probably wrong with you.

One hundred and sixty-five steel spikes poke out of the tree in a spiral formation, with unnervingly large gaps between them. It's not like a ladder, where you can simply look up. Lurching forward with white-knuckle grasps, I feel like there's too much air around my body, my heart immediately accelerates and my adrenalin skyrockets. A bunch of kids are coming down, so I shift to the outer side of the spike as they take the inner line closest to the tree. I have never wanted to hug a tree more in my entire life, although you'd need about five people to hug the girth of Dave Evans – the tree, not the guitarist also known as The Edge in the rock band U2.

The kids are fearless, of course, lacking the imagination to see how a body might splinter falling from just ten metres, never mind forty, fifty or sixty. When I reach the first platform, a cheery, unhelpful sign says: 'That was the easy part!' Now the spikes get steeper. My wife and kids below become very small indeed, and I find myself muttering, repeatedly, 'How is this a thing ... in *Australia*?' Sure, you'd expect to find something nutso like this in Laos, or Ivory Coast, or a bunch of overripe banana republics – but in Australia? Perhaps the reason is that you'll only find karri trees in the south of Western Australia and nowhere else. Or, could it be that anyone who attempts to climb Dave Evans,

Arboreal Aussie Giants

Eucalypts are among the tallest tree species in the world; in fact, Australia's mountain ash only looks up to the Californian redwoods. The tallest mountain ash ever officially measured was 114 metres high. In 2008, a 99.8-metre tree known as the Centurion was discovered by air in the Arve Valley of Tasmania. Having somehow survived logging and forest fires, the Centurion continues to grow at a rate five times faster than redwoods. No matter how long they might live, trees can't grow beyond 130 metres, as gravity eventually prevents water from reaching the leaves at the top.

along with the nearby Gloucester Tree (61 metres) and Diamond Tree (51 metres), takes a measure of personal responsibility last seen in the days before public liability insurance. According to reports, there has never been a single fatality on any of the trees. This is reassuring, but you can't help but wonder if you're going to be the one who changes that.

At the top, there are three platforms, linked by wobbly vertical ladders. On the viewing deck, I can see the forest for the trees, and then some. It's a glorious spot to make an epic announcement, write a poem, commit to a resolution, chat to strangers, or stall the reality that you're going to have to descend the same way you came up.

'Did you know that the Dave Evans Bicentennial Tree was only pegged in 1988 and there were once nine lookout trees in the region, but a bunch have been lost to cyclones and fires?' I tell nobody in particular. 'Maybe they named it after Dave Evans because this is the very Edge of adventure tourism, and U2 can do it?' The wooden floorboards are moaning too, so it's time to head down. In truth, it's a lot easier than going up; your head is forced to look at your hands and each step brings you a little closer to a cold beer in Pemberton. Hugging the tree on the inside of the spike, I crack jokes with those on the way up. Everyone has the same look of amazement, fear and uncertainty on their faces. It's like the relevant authorities were supposed to put an end to this but, fortunately, someone didn't get the memo.

For those who'd prefer to appreciate the impressive regional forests without the risk of, say, death, consider the Valley of the Giants Tree Top Walk near Denmark. There are also local campgrounds, hikes and bike trails. However you choose to explore the forests of the southwest, there's no doubt these tall, regal trees are a worthy *thing* on the Great Australian Bucket List.

START HERE:
aussiebucketlist.com/treeclimb

Float in a Prison Tunnel

I'm descending a 20-metre ladder beneath one Australia's most notorious former prisons. Dressed in gumboots, white overalls and a hard hat, I'm on a daily tour that explores tunnels burrowed deep into the limestone beneath the prison. Like many visitors, I assume prisoners dug the shafts as a means of escape. Scaling walls, hiding under planks, hammering through walls – Fremantle Prison has a long history of escapees. Yet the story of the tunnels, like the history of Fremantle Prison itself, is far more interesting.

In the late 1840s, the free settlers of the Swan River Colony petitioned the Colonial Office in London to send convicts to help build vital infrastructure and work as free labour. When the first transports arrived in 1850, prisoners were immediately put to work constructing their own convict establishment, using the limestone found on the hilltop site. When wells were sunk, a large aquifer of fine drinking water was discovered, just the sort of luck the settlers needed as water was in desperately short supply. More male convicts arrived – nearly ten thousand men by 1868 – and, with the addition of new blocks, Fremantle Prison grew into the largest convict-constructed building in the southern hemisphere. It continued to be utilised as a maximum security prison until 1991, when it was decommissioned, repurposed, and turned into one of the eleven living museums that make up the Australian Convict Sites, collectively a UNESCO World Heritage Site. Daily tours focus on Fremantle's convict past, modern penal history and the transportation era. A torchlight visit also investigates the prison's darker past. The adjacent

Australia's 11 Unesco World Heritage Convict Sites

- Cockatoo Island, NSW
- Great North Road, NSW
- Hyde Park Barracks, NSW
- Old Government House and Domain, NSW
- Kingston and Arthurs Vale Historic Area, Norfolk Island
- Brickendon and Woolmers Estates, TAS
- Cascades Female Factory, TAS
- Coal Mines Historic Site, TAS
- Darlington Probation Station, TAS
- Port Arthur, TAS
- Fremantle Prison, WA

women's barracks have been turned into a backpacker hostel, so you can honestly say you've spent the night in a prison cell (with your criminal record intact). Since the small, two-bunk cells are a little too crowded for families, I stayed in the adjacent colonial cottages, built by prisoners for the wardens, and blessed with a better psychic ambience.

From the first days of the prison, inmates kept a highly regimented routine that revolved around hard work and regular religious instruction. After hearing about the regular lashings, diets of bread and water, solitary confinement and the ever-present threat of the gallows, I'm not surprised to learn that few prisoners stepped out of line. At the gallows, I stare down at the trapdoor that swallowed at least 44 nasty souls, the last being a serial killer in 1964. Ironically, a prison riot in 1988 almost burned the place down and ultimately led to the end of Fremantle as a modern prison. Like many visitors, I wonder why it took so long. One block demonstrates how cells evolved from the 1850s through to the 1990s. Strikingly, they didn't evolve much. Hammocks made way for cots and

beds, but prisoners still ate meals in their cells, and used one bucket as a toilet and another for fresh water. I'm sure they crafted a very different type of bucket list. As for ours, Fremantle Prison is well worth ticking off, especially when you add in the unusual underground adventure.

It's 1845, and fresh water sources are limited in the budding Western Australian colony. Without it, the port town of Fremantle is stagnating. 'We are always thirsty,' wrote one settler at the time. The discovery of a massive aquifer with a seemingly unlimited supply of water beneath the prison is a

lifesaver. The fact that unpaid convict labour can be used to drill and manually pump the water to the surface is also pretty convenient. It's back-breaking work in horrendous conditions, so much so that prisoners are made to pump water as a form of punishment, some while wearing heavy chains. There are reports of several prisoners literally pumping themselves to death, which speaks volumes about the cruel and unusual forms of colonial punishment. In 1888, a steam pump finally relieved the convicts of the manual labour, but it quickly drained the aquifer of fresh water. As the aquifer was unable to fill up quickly enough, and minerals and salt were leaching through the porous limestone, the authorities decided to create horizontal tunnels that could drain the water into a catchment. Under the guidance of civil engineers, prisoners were forced to carve 1.5-metre-wide by 1.5- to 3-metre-high tunnels by hand. Unlike gold miners, convicts were not being paid by the yard for their tunnelling, nor were they blasting rock in search of personal fortunes.

WESTERN AUSTRALIA

'Imagine, you're down here with some nasty fellow prisoners, working with pick-axes in horrendous conditions,' explains our guide Courtney. 'So many things could go wrong, although we don't have any records that show they actually did.'

Deaths were simply noted down as *misadventures*. There will be no misadventures today, however. Prior to the tour, each visitor is given a breathalyser test and a life vest, a courtesy perhaps to the one lunatic who might show up drunk and drown themselves in waist-high tunnel water. We are led to a chain of narrow boats, hardy replicas of the wooden vessels convicts might have used in the tunnels. With our paddles, we head off on a circular route, the water perfectly still. I'm tempted to drink it, but Courtney tells us about the 85,000 litres of diesel that leaked into the tunnels from a ruptured oil pipeline. Since the tunnels hadn't been accessed for decades – they

had been concealed from prisoners during the modern era for obvious reasons – the leak was only discovered accidentally when the tunnels were tapped to water new gardens. It took several years and the help of a diesel-eating fungi to restore the tunnels, which look much like they once did, although you do get a faint aroma of diesel every once in a while. Courtney asks us to extinguish our headlamps and use our hands to ping-pong our boat against the walls of the shaft in complete darkness. Theme parks might strive for this kind of effect, but this is something far more authentic: floating in a pitch-black tunnel painstakingly carved into ancient limestone by hardened colonial convicts. You don't need to be a history buff to want to tick this off the national bucket list.

START HERE:
aussiebucketlist.com/
fremantleprison

Sail among the Dugongs

This chapter was originally going to be titled 'Feed the Dolphins at Monkey Mia', an iconic WA experience. In the 1960s, local fishermen began to feed and interact with friendly dolphins on the placid beaches of Monkey Mia. Half a century later, tourists come from around the world to repeat this experience, but they're in for a disappointment. Marine biologists discovered that these friendly bottlenose dolphins have been negatively impacted by human contact, with low survival rates in the wild. By 1994, just four of the fifteen nursing calves born to the beach-visiting dolphins survived, where the number should have been closer to fifteen. The solution was to employ strict controls on feeding and interaction, and by 2010 the survival rate was restored.

Great for the dolphins, but a little upsetting for kids who've flown in from Sydney or driven all the way from Perth with the promise of being able to feed a dolphin.

Gathered at the beach each morning for two sessions – around eight o'clock and nine o'clock – rangers greet dozens (and in busy season, hundreds) of visitors. The dolphins that choose to interact swim very close to shore, soliciting *oohs*, *aahs* and space on your memory card. After rangers explain more about dolphins in the area and the local conservation efforts, four buckets are brought out. The rangers randomly pick out four visitors to give a small fish to the dolphin – the quantity is carefully measured to make up just 10 per cent of its daily diet. It's over quickly.

Tipping their buckets in the water, rangers signal that the feeding is over, the dolphins swim off, and many a parent has some explaining to do and, likely, some ice cream to buy. With the recent expansion of the adjacent resort to accommodate hundreds more visitors, I don't believe the Monkey Mia dolphin feeding is the bucket list experience at all. That honour belongs solely to nearby Shark Bay. A UNESCO World Heritage Site, Shark Bay has the largest and richest area of seagrass meadows in the world. This makes it home to the world's largest population of dugongs, as well as a thriving population of sharks, turtles, whales, rays and dolphins. It supports 26 threatened Australian mammal species, 230 species of bird, 150 species of reptile, and some

fascinating creatures drinking beer in Denham's legendary Old Pub (aka the Shark Bay Hotel) as I type these very words.

I enter the protected marine reserve after driving up the bullet-straight Brand Highway, relieved to stretch my legs at the stromatolites of Hamelin Pool (see Text Box) and walk on the gazillion tiny white cockleshells that make up 60-kilometre-long Shell Beach. We don't stop at the Useless Loop (for obvious reasons), but do check out the worthwhile Ocean Park Aquarium. Guided by marine biologists, my kids loved the hourly shark feed, and learning about the secret lives of sea snakes, turtles, rays and other creatures.

There's so much more to keep you busy: taking a four-wheel

What's with the Stromatolites?

It is widely believed that life on Earth began with a bacterial organism on a microbial reef that pumped oxygen into the sea and, over billions of years, into the atmosphere itself. Or, we're the product of robot alien monkeys, but the first theory sounds more likely. These reefs were called stromatolites and, while they've basically vanished with the ages, Western Australia's Hamelin Pool has the planet's most extensive living stromatolite system (and one of only two stromatolite systems remaining worldwide). Thriving in hyper-saline water protected by the seagrass of Shark Bay, these splotch-like living rocks can be viewed from a boardwalk that lets you ponder the humble beginnings of life, and why robots would fashion themselves after monkeys.

drive excursion into the nearby Francois Peron National Park, visiting Dirk Hartog Island, or fishing for whiting in the local lagoon. From my base at the Shark Bay Hotel, I pop over to Monkey Mia for both a sunset and morning wildlife cruise on the Wildsights Shotover catamaran. In turquoise waters that are so calm Wildsights guarantee no seasickness, we spot dolphins, turtles and half a dozen dugongs breaching. According to the University of Western Australia's Ocean Institute, a marine heatwave in 2011 decimated seagrass in the region, causing 'mass mortality events' for a wide range of species. Locals say the dugong population is only just beginning to recover, but the threat of climate change and ocean acidification continues to rattle these fragile and remarkable ecosystems. The scales that balance conservation and recreation are constantly adjusting, especially in Shark Bay. That both dolphin and dugong populations appear to be healthy is an encouraging sign for bucket listers exploring a remote, truly unique slice of Australian coastline.

START HERE:
aussiebucketlist.com/sharkbay

Shake Hands with Royalty

BORDER
HUTT RIVER
PROVINCE

HUTT RIVER PRINCIPALITY

The Hutt River Principality is a self-proclaimed, independent sovereign state that seceded from Australia in April 1970. I've driven almost 600 kilometres from Perth to cross its modest border, as the idea of visiting an independent nation landlocked within Western Australia – albeit one that has not been recognised by the Australian government – is intriguing. Who is Prince Leonard? Why has he legally fought the government for decades, taking his 18,500 acres of land all the way to the Supreme Court, international trade organisations and the Queen of England herself? The Principality even declared war on Australia, claimed victory, and invoked the Geneva Convention. Is this a case of hubris, or madness, or is there something far more meaningful going on?

All are welcome to visit the principality, get their passport stamped, post a letter, view the museum, or perhaps pick up a souvenir. The affable Prince Graeme, the current ruler and son of founder Prince Leonard, greets me in the red-brick Government Offices, as he does about two-dozen visitors each day.

'Ah, Prince Leonard is waiting for you!' he tells me, and I wander along the dirt road to an adjacent building. Ninety-three-year-old Prince Leonard is Leonard Casley, a wiry man wound up like a jack-in-the-box. No sooner do I enter the room than he springs from his chair and launches into a tour of artefacts, official letters (including one from Buckingham Palace), passports, souvenirs, gifts from foreign governments, medallions and knick-knacks. I try taking notes but my fingers can't keep up. After leaving the air force after WWII, Leonard founded a successful copper mine in Fremantle, and eventually moved north with his family to grow wheat on a large property. This is where Leonard's story takes a dramatic turn, one that just might have far-reaching consequences for international law.

It all started with the establishment of a wheat board in Western Australia, which determined how many acres each farmer could use to grow wheat. This presented two immediate problems for the Hutt River farm. Firstly, they were allocated just 100 acres on an 18,000-acre property. Secondly, the announcement was made at the end of the harvest. Supported by his wife Shirley, Leonard appealed for more acres, and then for compensation. After exploring other legal alternatives, Leonard – a man who practices complex physics for fun – uncovered a loophole in state legislation. If your land and livelihood are under threat in a specific manner that has not been recognised or addressed by the existing government, you can formally secede. Of course, this doesn't mean much unless anyone recognises the secession and, after declaring first a Republic and then a Principality, Prince Leonard has been on a four-decade-long quest for full independence ever since. He stresses it has nothing to do with tax evasion or a quest for a power but to save his freehold land. It was born out of necessity, to save the farm, provide for his family, and, ultimately, pursue justice.

'Why a principality?' I ask Prince Leonard, who is seated in front of a whiteboard with mathematical calculations.

'If you're a principality, you cannot be tried for treason. A principality offers protection for our supporters,' the Prince explains.

'We're broadly based on Monaco. They have a few more billionaires there,' jokes Prince Graeme.

There have been legal victories and punishing defeats. In 2017, the principality was ordered to pay $3 million in outstanding taxes, which made national headlines. Prince Graeme explains how these taxes included seven years of GST on their campground, even though it had only been open for four. There is no love lost between the Australian government and this micro-nation.

Other Australian Micro-Nations

With a lot of land and no shortage of eccentrics, Australia has one of world's highest number of micro-nations. According to the Montevideo Convention on the Rights and Duties of States, a micro-nation is a permanent population in a defined territory governed by an authority exercising control and with a capacity to enter into relations with other states. Beyond Hutt River, you can find micro-nations at Tasmania's Grand Duchy of Avram, NSW's Empire of Atlantium and Principality of Wy, Queensland's Yidindji Tribal Nation, and the Gay and Lesbian Kingdom of the Coral Seas.

'If they recognise you, wouldn't that allow anyone to just declare their own kingdo ... sorry, princedom?' I ask.

Prince Leonard explains: 'The desire to secede is one thing. If your economy has been taken and there has been loss to the preservation of your land, you are entitled to secede by international law. The government has the right to rectify the situation, and in our case they refused. You have to have knowledge of how and when to do it, and the financial ability to do it too.

There are lots of technicalities, and there has been a big cost.'

Princess Shirley stood by her husband Leonard every step of the way, until her passing in 2014. A shrine has been built on the property to honour her. I ask Prince Leonard if fighting for his principles has been worth it, and where it will all end.

'It has everything to do with the truth,' he says. 'I believe in the truth of nature, as you can see by my love for the truth of mathematics. This has led me towards the truth of judicial process and politics. It's not fighting, it's dealing with truth. I don't think I'll win in my lifetime, but this will live past my lifetime. Truth is a hard one to beat.'

With more than 13,000 honorary citizens scattered around

the world, several mentions in legal theses about international sovereign law, documentaries, and invitations for Leonard to speak at universities and even the Vatican, Hutt River Principality joins other self-proclaimed micro-nations in challenging existing, recognised states and the laws that govern them.

Hutt River has its own mint, issues honorary rewards for community service or scientific advancements, and has its own diplomats.

'We have a symbolic army and navy. We used to have an air force, but the bloke flew home in his plane,' quips Prince Graeme.

As to what would happen if they were formally recognised, Prince Graeme talks about immigration, building a community and working with local government for everyone's mutual benefit.

As for our bucket list, the opportunity to get your passport stamped in a self-declared independent nation within Australian borders, have a chat to remarkable and thought-provoking characters and turn off an endless highway to amble down a lovely country road – well, that's a royal opportunity nobody should pass up.

START HERE:
aussiebucketlist.com/huttriver

Admire the Karri on Boranup Drive

Allow me to familiarise you with the concept of *dayenu*, pronounced '*die-yay-noo*'. It is one of the more beloved songs that Jews sing at Passover, with an easy, catchy refrain everyone really gets behind. *Dayenu* roughly translates from Hebrew as: 'It would have been sufficient.' Each verse of the song essentially runs through the story of Exodus, capped with a mightily proclaimed '*dayenu!*' For example: 'If God had parted the sea for us, and not taken us out on dry land . . . *dayenu*! If God had taken us out on dry land and not drowned our oppressors . . . *dayenu*! If God had drowned our oppressors and not supplied our needs in the desert for forty years . . . *dayenu*!' You get the gist.

Now, indulge me, if you will, as I apply the concept of *dayenu* to Margaret River. You see, if this region at the southern end of Western Australia *only* boasted some of the world's finest showcaves ... *dayenu*! If it boasted some of the world's finest showcaves and didn't have some of the world's finest wineries ... *dayenu*! If it had some of the world's finest wineries and didn't have one of the best and biggest surf breaks anywhere ... *dayenu*! If it had one of the best and biggest surf breaks anywhere and didn't allow you to hand-feed stingrays on the shoreline of Hamelin Beach ... *dayenu*! And if it allowed you to feed stingrays on the shoreline of Hamelin Beach and didn't boast a spectacular drive through forests of giant karri trees ... *dayenu*! If you knew the tune, right about now we'd bust into the foot-stomping, table-banging part.

What I'm trying to say is: it's no easy task nominating just one bucket list activity in Margaret River. I encountered surfers ticking off their bucket list at Surfers Point, foodies revelling in some of the finest wineries not only in Australia, but on the planet. The six-day Cape Naturaliste to Cape Leeuwin track is as good a hike as they come. The five publicly accessible showcaves would be a sufficient global tourism

drawcard on their own. So let's begin by raising a glass or seven to Margaret River, which is why Dirk Hos of Margaret River Nature Tours is driving. A geologist, botanist and highly knowledgeable local, Dirk has agreed to show me around, which primarily consists of driving a series of spectacularly scenic roads book-ended by spectacular attractions. Like many people who don't know much about the region, it was the wine that first drew my attention.

'Margaret River produces only 3 per cent of Australia's wine, but accounts for 25 per cent of the premium wines, and 20 per cent of Australia's total wine export value,' explains Dirk. In other words, this region produces wines of distinct quality, prized by collectors and connoisseurs. Adds Dirk, rather seriously: 'I'd call a lot of stuff made in other regions an 'alcoholic beverage.' It tastes like wine, and it becomes drinkable after the third glass, but it's not wine. Here, we make wine.'

Although the region has major producers, Dirk takes me to several boutique wineries, where passion (and often some form of off-farm income) is infused into every bottle.

'Our little patch is unique and so different from the rest of the country,' says winemaker Jessica Worrall of Firetail, a small award-winning estate that produces just 1500 cases a year, sold mostly through their cellar door. 'We have bush, caves, surf and beautiful growing vines that produce unique and consistent wine.'

Brew Sensation

Craft breweries have exploded in Margaret River, offering similar tasting experiences in similarly beautiful settings as the region's renowned wineries. With gorgeous gardens designed to attract families, breweries are leading the charge against the perceived elitism of upmarket wineries. Australia is a nation that loves its beer, and the impact of this new business model is being felt. Perhaps it won't be long before we see waterslides and playgrounds drawing the crowds into the local wineries.

In the upmarket tasting room at Vasse Felix, it's hard to believe that this was the first winery in Margaret River, founded only in the 1960s. Leeuwin, Voyager, Cape Mentelle – there are now more than 175 wineries in the region, but it's not all smooth sailing.

'Doctors, bankers, lawyers . . . they've all bought into the dream, but it's a tough business; you can only lose money for so long,' explains Greg, owner of Bettenays Winery. They've branched out into quality nougat, and it's working.

It's a cracker of a summer day as Dirk pulls into Hamelin Bay, located about half an hour's drive from the centre of Margaret River. Protected as a marine reserve, the bay has a lovely white-sand beach with an additional natural attraction: smooth and eagle stingrays swim right up to the beach to feed on scraps from local fishermen. Local kids are handing out baitfish, and next thing I know I'm hand-feeding a large stingray, with another swimming over my feet! 'This is so . . . bucket list!' I tell Dirk, but there's so much more.

He takes me to Temper Temper, a fantastic chocolate store where it's free to sample high-quality cacao from around the world. Adjacent is Yahava, where coffee and tea has been elevated into artform. I feast at Morries on the main strip of Bussell Highway and marvel at the crown jewel of the showcaves, the aptly named Jewel Cave. Big waves, magnificent coastline, natural 'spas' where the Indian Ocean washes over you in rock pools – it's enough to make your head spin. But it's the Boranup Drive that steals my heart.

Hardwood karri and jarrah trees are only found in south-west Western Australia. The original giants were logged in the 1800s but even the second-growth trees of Leeuwin-Naturaliste National Park are some of the tallest on the planet. After an introduction to Boranup Drive from Dirk, I return alone in my powerful Ford Everest to race along the 14-kilometre dirt road that cuts through the forest. Each bend delivers another postcard, with towering trees framing the kind of road you only see in dreams and car commercials. Pulling over numerous times, I yell into the forest, my voice echoing amidst birdsong and beams of golden sunlight. *Dayenu!* Margaret River is a destination *more than sufficient* to add to our bucket list.

START HERE:
aussiebucketlist.com/ margaretriver

Salute the Past

I t's too easy for the great stories of the Second World War to disappear in the fog of time, forgotten by younger generations in our digitally enhanced modern world. Two such stories are set in Western Australia. After the fall of Singapore and the Japanese attack on Darwin, the Allies identified the port of Fremantle as the key port for all shipping activities in the Indian Ocean. Transport, convoy, military and merchant ships were assembled, maintained and loaded up for crucial journeys to India, Africa and the Middle East from Fremantle. Of course, this fact did not escape the attention of the Axis powers and defence of the area was therefore essential. While the strategic placement of artillery along the coast was an excellent deterrent, it did not prevent the deadliest man-made disaster in Australian history.

Every Sunday morning, a group of volunteers from the Royal Australian Artillery Historical Society greet visitors in a parking lot off the Stirling Highway in Perth. David Carter, the president of the RAAHS, is guiding me into the intriguing past of the Leighton Battery Heritage Site. One of seven such artillery stations built along the coast, Leighton Battery had two six-inch breech-loading MkVII guns to deter an attack, which were manned twenty-four hours a day. With their ranges carefully coordinated, the Allied artillery covered a wide coastal area. Any enemy ship could be quickly sighted, targeted and blown out of the water. On Rottnest Island, I visited Oliver Hill (see page 282) to learn more about the largest weapon in the defence system. At Leighton Battery, David takes me beneath Buckland Hill into a series of service tunnels that stretch more than three hundred metres. After the war, the tunnels were largely hidden from public view, and became the domain of squatters and local kids. When developers started eyeing the land, the RAAHS was formed to protect and showcase Australia's military heritage. A ten-year volunteer effort was required to clear the tunnel debris, restore the twelve rooms, research how the tunnels and artillery operated, and produce interpretative displays. Designed to shelter the gun crew

Lest We Forget

Around 41,000 Australians departed for the Great War from the shipping port of Albany, WA, bidding farewell in two large convoys comprised of more than 50 ships. Many never made it home. Albany's National ANZAC Centre honours their memory with outstanding exhibits located in a striking building overlooking the King George Sound. Award-winning interactive exhibits and audio displays illuminate the personal and tragic history of the ANZAC story. The ANZAC Centre is located within the grounds of the historic Princess Royal Fortress, where visitors can also explore a military museum, gun emplacements, a naval gun collection and underground magazines.

and keep projectiles cool, the rooms are damp, cool and eerie. I imagine the stale air and tension in the Stand Easy Room, where the crew would take turns catching some sleep on the bunk beds. It warms up considerably in the above-ground Defence Observation Post, which has been carved into the limestone hill. State-of-the-art equipment was used to monitor the horizon, with the seven station crews in constant wire communication. Since the instruments were soon made obsolete with the introduction of radar, I ask David how accurate the heavy guns would have been.

'Better than aiming a dart at a board, although the ships would be manoeuvring, so it would also be like trying to throw a stone at a flying bird.'

For history and military buffs, these World War Two tunnels are a fascinating glimpse into the past. The guns were never used in battle, and, once the war ended, the equipment was scrapped or sold. Were it not for the important work of the RAAHS, the tunnels and their stories would be forgotten altogether. The same cannot be said for the fate of the *HMAS Sydney II*.

Part two of our military history bucket list begins some 425 kilometres north of Perth, atop

Mount Scott. From here I can see the port town of Geraldton, a hazy horizon and a storm working its way down the coast. The morning tour has concluded and I'm alone with my thoughts at the striking HMAS Sydney II Memorial. Etched into the memorial are the names of 645 men who sank with the Leander-class light cruiser on November 19, 1941, never to be seen again. The *Sydney II* was the pride of the Australian navy, a hero vessel that had seen battle in the Mediterranean, sunk two Italian warships, and pounded the Libyan coast. Returning to Australia, she was a vital armed escort vessel for convoys, and was returning to

Fremantle from a successful voyage when she encountered a German raider – the *Kormoran* – disguised as a merchant ship. It would take investigators some time to piece together what happened next, and to this day there is still some controversy. After being lured into close proximity, the *Sydney II* took part in a cat-and-mouse game before a fierce battle ensued. The lighter, faster *Kormoran* was well prepared to inflict maximum damage on the unsuspecting *Sydney II*, and the ship took a number of serious hits. Torpedoes were eventually fired by the Sydney, and enough rounds landed to ensure both ships sealed each other's fate. As the disabled warships floated apart, the burning *Sydney II* disappeared over the horizon, and the Germans eventually abandoned ship. Several days later, a large search and rescue mission rounded up 318 survivors of the *Kormoran's* 399 crew. As for the *Sydney II*, all traces of the ship and crew simply vanished. Other than the flu pandemic of 1918 and a polio outbreak in the late 1940s, it is the single deadliest disaster in Australian history.

In a nation that deeply respects the personal sacrifice of war, the fate of the *Sydney II* captured and continues to hold the country's imagination. When the ship was eventually discovered in March 2008, then-Prime Minister Kevin Rudd was the one to make the announcement. Much has been written about the *Sydney II,* including three official inquests, and you can read all about it online. The brilliant design of Geraldton's HMAS Sydney II Memorial brings the loss and sacrifice into sharp relief. Our bucket list wants you reflect beneath the Dome of Souls, made up of 645 stainless steel seagulls. To feel the sorrow and longing embodied in the sculpture of the Waiting Women, and watch the sea breeze create ripples in the Pool of Remembrance.

For younger readers, the idea of epic naval battles or hand-digging tunnels might seem as antiquated as the rotary telephone. Engraved on a wall, the names of those lost appear wastefully tragic. Yet the legacy of the past is essential to our future. We will never appreciate what we have unless we know how close we came to losing it. For six long years, the coastline of Western Australia presented a potentially deadly threat. Thousands of Australian men and women stepped up to meet it. The rest is silence.

START HERE:
aussiebucketlist.com/hmassydney

Get *the* Quokka Selfie

ROTTNEST ISLAND

I t's been said that quokkas are the world's happiest animals. Certainly, any wild animal that lets you get close enough to pull out a phone and take a damn selfie with it must be pretty content. *Especially* as the small marsupial has been known to look directly into the camera, ripping a goofy smile as it does so. This is why #quokkaselfie has become a social media sensation, and why Rottnest Island is booming. Located off the coast of Perth, Rottnest is home to these dependably adorable creatures, and is an island destination like no other.

For starters, no one is allowed to drive a car on it. Fast ferries leave daily from Perth, taking foot passengers, bicycles and luggage to the main settlement area, Thomson Bay. A strong south-westerly ensured my half-hour crossing lived up to its reputation as one of the roughest in the southern hemisphere. Luckily, Rottnest Express designed its ferries specifically for such tumultuous action. On arrival, we pick up our rental bikes and start exploring the island. It is not a resort island in the traditional sense; there are no mega hotel chains, no glitz or bean-shaped swimming pools. While public and tour buses circle the 11-kilometre-long island, the primary means of transport is a bicycle.

When Dutch sailors first explored the island in the 1600s they named it *Rotte nest*, confusing the abundant quokkas for rats. Not much else happened until European settlers arrived centuries later, failed in their attempts to plant crops, and subsequently turned Rottnest Island into a penal colony for Aboriginal people – the dark past of this sunny holiday destination. Biking down Vincent Way and Abbott Street, I see families and couples chilling on the patios, their bikes parked outside. Locks are unnecessary, although two policemen are telling kids

without helmets to get off their bikes and walk. There are a handful of casual restaurants and the local supermarket is well stocked with everything from fresh fruit and veggies to snorkelling gear. I park my bike at the Settlement Railway Station and hop on board a train to the Oliver Hill Heritage Site. The railway was built during World War II, when Allies installed two massive 9.2 inch artillery guns on Rottnest with a 28-kilometre range. Twenty-two men were needed to operate the site twenty-four hours a day, and a network of tunnels were hand-dug to accommodate the engine, fuel, men and shells.

The guns were never fired in anger, although they came close when a suspicious ship appeared on the horizon. Permission to fire came too late from Canberra, and the ship disappeared from range.

'That might have been the *Kormorant*,' speculates our volunteer guide, referring to the German ship that sunk the *HMAS Sydney II* just a few days later (see page 277). History buffs will love the tunnels and gun tour, but Rottnest Island is really one for nature lovers. The island has sixty-three beaches and nearly two-dozen bays, many secluded and quiet enough to feel like it's yours for the day. To get to

the quiet spots you'll have to pedal out, or use the hop-on hop-off bus that circles the island. Parker Point and Salmon Bay, protected by the adjacent marine reserve, have white sandy beaches. Sand dunes provide a windbreak in stunning Parakeet Bay. Armstrong Bay has outstanding snorkelling, Fish Hook Bay is framed by limestone cliffs. Strickland Bay offers wild waves for surfers, while Henrietta Rocks has a wreck to snorkel. There's a beach and a bay for everyone, which is why you need a few days to find the one you love most. As for the quokkas, they love everyone. There

are some ten thousand quokkas on the island, protected by law and with no natural predators. The only thing they really need to worry about are distracted cyclists and drunk kids who invade the island for Schoolies Week.

This chapter is titled 'Get *the* Quokka Selfie' as opposed to 'Get a Quokka Selfie' because it's no big shakes to get a selfie, but with your friends on social media watching, you want to get *the* selfie. Perhaps one with a smiling quokka, her eyebrows raised and cheeks full. Tennis star Roger Federer visited the island and his quokka selfie generated more than 500 million views. My wife took a photo of my attempted selfie, a *meta-selfie* as it were, as I tried to keep my kids from touching their new favourite living soft toy. Authorities strongly advise visitors not to pet, feed or make fun of the quokka, as it is detrimental to conservation efforts (and probably hurts their feelings). As always, the quokkas themselves are more than accommodating. I'm convinced these guys are one Pixar movie away from global superstardom, and clearly love the paparazzi. They might be the stars of Rottnest Island, but Rotto is a star unto itself.

Australia's Macropods

The first time I heard the word pademelon I assumed it was some kind of tropical fruit. Outside of Australia, nobody knows much about pademelons or wallaroos, tree-kangaroos, hare-wallabies or quokkas. Native only to the Australian continent, macropods are plant-eating marsupials characterised by strong hind legs, long tails, thin necks and small heads. Six species have become extinct since European settlement in Australia, with a dozen others severely threatened.

START HERE:
aussiebucketlist.com/rottnest

Drive into Mars

THE PINNACLES

Bucket listers love unusual natural rock formations. Not only do they make great visuals, they can make you feel like you're on another planet. Case in point: the hundreds of limestone peaks that jut out of the desert sands of Nambung National Park. They look like the inverted incisors and molars of a giant, and since geologists can't quite agree on how they formed, it's as good a theory as any. The Pinnacles might have formed anywhere between 80,000 and 500,000 years ago, as sand dunes possibly stabilised over hardened caps of calcite, causing plants to grow, roots to crack through, and wind and rain to do the rest. Calcified teeth of extinct giants sounds better.

The Pinnacles opened to the public in the 1960s and today are a must-see for road trippers on the West Coast. If you want to avoid the 200-kilometre drive from Perth and see other attractions in the area as well, consider Swan River Sea Planes' Pinnacles – Taste of WA tour. As we taxi along, I couldn't ask for a more scenic runway than the glimmering Swan River with the Perth skyline in the background. Seaplanes offer the most gentle of take-offs and, after looping around Rottnest Island, the plane traces the seemingly endless WA coastline, where green bush and golden beach contrast with the turquoise Indian Ocean. The seaplane lands with wheels on a dusty track outside the town of Cervantes, where we are met by a blissfully air-conditioned coach. Summer temperatures hover around the high 30s in Cervantes, so we did what most tourists do: beelined it to the family-owned Lobster Shack. Western Australian rock lobster (aka crayfish) is a prized dish, especially in Asia. This explains the Chinese signs, staff and coach tours parked outside. A post-lunch tour of the fishery reveals just how important crayfish is to the local economy, generating millions of dollars a year and one-fifth of Australia's total fishing industry catch. Personally,

Bucket List Geological Marvels

We'll meet other unusual formations in this book, like the Remarkable Rocks of Kangaroo Island, the Twelve Apostles in Victoria and the Painted Cliffs in Tasmania. Here are a few more to add to our bucket list.

☑ **Wave Rock, WA:** This 15-metre-high, 110-metre long granite rock carved by millennia of erosion resembles a wave frozen in stone.

☐ **The Three Sisters, NSW:** Meehni, Wimlah and Gunnedoo are iconic sandstone pillars formed by erosion, and perhaps the best-known site in the Blue Mountains.

☐ **Hanging Rock, VIC:** Formed six million years ago by vent magma congealing into place, these unusual rocks inspired an iconic Australian murder mystery (*Picnic at Hanging Rock*) and now host major concerts.

☐ **Karlu Karlu/Devils Marbles, NT:** Weathering and erosion have carved large granite boulders into strange shapes and sizes, which are bunched into groups and often perched atop one another.

☐ **Black Mountain, QLD:** Otherworldly black granite boulders overlook a surrounding lush landscape – the legendary home of mythical creatures, alien visitors and mysterious underground chambers.

I'm more of a northern-hemisphere claw lobster guy, although seeing the twenty-ton holding tanks with live crays ready to be flown to China proves I'm probably in the minority.

The Pinnacles themselves offer little shade from the day's afternoon heat. Since the self-drive trail is off-road and off-limits to coaches, we continue onwards to Yanchep Wildlife Park for traditional afternoon tea. All in, a grand day out, but I was determined to return to Nambung National Park on my own to see if I could turn my Ford Everest into a Mars Rover. Admittedly, Mars does not have an air-conditioned visitor centre, but it's considerably more expensive to get to and you'll have to leave your vehicle behind. You don't need an all-terrain vehicle to drive the 4-kilometre rock-lined unsealed loop around the Pinnacles. With scenic lookouts dotted along the route, it's a great opportunity to cruise around and in between the formations, stopping to take photos as you go. It's a one-of-a-kind drive of a lifetime, especially since it's publicly accessible. On my return visit there was a different glow of colour over the sand and rocks, although peak hour is sunset or sunrise, when golden hues work their magic. The rocks themselves resemble teeth, sea lions, ghosts, turd emojis, crowns, phalluses, chimneys and mushrooms. Visitors used to scramble all over them, but today they are protected with 'Falling Rocks' warning signs. Stopping the car frequently, I wander about each section, stung by the fine sand blowing from the nearby coast. Whether you choose to fly over or drive among the Pinnacles, Nambung National Park truly does feel like another planet – hot, dry and out of this world.

START HERE:
aussiebucketlist.com/pinnacles

Spot Seabirds and Shipwrecks

THE ABROLHOS ISLANDS

Off the coast of Geraldton sits a chain of small and desolate islands, connected by a stunning shallow reef system. It is the centre of Western Australia's lucrative rock lobster fishing industry, which generates over $40 million a year for the hardworking folks who haul in a catch that is quickly and primarily shipped off to Asia. Sailors have known about the Houtman Abrolhos Islands for centuries, mainly because they have a tendency to wreck a good ship, and also because they inspire tales that captivate and terrify. As Geraldton Air Charter's GA8 Airvan leaves the mainland behind, I'm invited to take it all in.

Abrolhos comes from a Portuguese naval term for spiked obstructions, but sounds very similar and just as relevant in Spanish as *abre ojos*, which translates as 'open your eyes.' One moment your ship is in deep waters and the next you're wrecked on the most southerly coral reef in the Indian Ocean. As for the islands themselves, split over one hundred kilometres between the Palseart, Easter and Wallabi groups, they're not the kind of place you want to be marooned. No trees for shelter, little if any freshwater, and hell on earth if you are stranded with, say, one of naval history's most notorious psychopaths. This was the fate that befell the Dutch merchant ship *Batavia*, a legend so sordid and outrageous it has inspired books, movies and pretty much every *Lord of the Flies/Heart of Darkness* tale since. Other ships and passengers fared slightly better. For a small chain of islands, the Abrolhos boasts a bounty of shipwreck history.

Our pilot Jason has just signalled we're going to turn back. The tail-end of a cyclone up north

The Batavia Incident

First there was mutiny, then there was a shipwreck, and then things got really nasty. In 1628, the Dutch East India Company sent a ship named *Batavia* with 322 passengers on a trade mission to Batavia (now Jakarta) for spices. Along the way, a junior merchant named Cornelisz conspired a sordid mutiny that included molesting a high-ranking female passenger and steering the ship off course. But before the mutineers mutiny could enact their plan, the *Batavia* wrecked on the shallow reefs of the Houtman Abrolhos. Along with a few passengers and soldiers, Pelsaert, the ship's commander, set out in a long boat in search of water, leaving the survivors of the wreck under the control of Cornelisz, who was apparently a full-blown delusional psychopath.

Cornelisz had plans to hijack any rescue attempt, steal the loot and set up a kingdom of his own. Surrounding himself with henchman, he abandoned the ship's soldiers on a neighbouring island to die, and then purged anyone he thought would betray him. As Cornelisz descended into madness and paranoia, 110 men, women and children were brutally murdered. A full-blown battle with the soldiers eventually took place on West Wallabi Island, with the soldiers triumphing over the mutineers (you can still see their makeshift fortress today). Once Pelsaert returned with a rescue party, the mutineers were tried and executed in a variety of gruesome ways. In the end, only 68 passengers of the doomed *Batavia* made it to port.

has brought in heavy clouds and, while there's little chance of us crashing into a mountain (the highest point of the Abrolhos is just 15 metres), he still has to see the dirt runway to land on East Wallabi. It's the only island tourists are allowed to visit, with others fully protected as A-Class Reserves, or only accessed for the exclusive use of commercial fisheries and aqua-culture operations. I don't argue with the Weather Gods anymore, because they never listen. Or maybe they do, because suddenly a gap opens up in the clouds, Jason banks left and my bucket list breathes a sigh of relief. Soon a patch of blue sky reveals waters

so crystal clear I can see manta rays swimming from my window. We touch down on East Wallabi and walk to a shelter overlooking Turtle Bay. It's been centuries since a turtle was spotted in the bay, but we are welcomed by a bottlenose dolphin swimming at the shoreline with her pup. It's an ideal spot to snorkel a reef teeming with life. Without the warm Leeuwin Current keeping the sea temperature a constant 20 to 22 degrees, there wouldn't be a reef here at all, much less tropical fish. Soon enough I'm surrounded by luminescent wrasse, goby and parrotfish, who are most likely delighted not to have been born as rock lobsters.

After lunch under the shade of the shelter, we walk along rocky cliffs that once formed the seafloor, stepping over coral rubble and spotting shells in the limestone. Large, spiny-tailed skinks dart between the rocks, doing a particularly fine impression of a carpet python, another protected and rare reptile found on the islands. The Abrolhos serves as one of the world's key breeding sites for seabirds. I spot an osprey and white-bellied sea eagle hunting for fish, as well as wedge-tailed shearwaters and various terns. We walk past a large, decades-old osprey nest that eventually toppled in the strong winds, and a small wallaby shyly nibbling under a low bush in the shade.

This abundance of marine life allowed survivors of the *Zeewijk* shipwreck in 1727 to survive an astonishing ten months on Gun Island before they were rescued (although far from everyone made it). Jason will later fly us over the wrecks of the *Ben Ledi* (1879) and the *Windsor* (1908). For those navigators who didn't open their eyes, the Abrolhos presented treacherous waters with razor-sharp reefs ready to ruin a profitable excursion. For visitors today, opening our eyes to the natural and historical wonders from air and ground, we're guaranteed a far more successful adventure.

START HERE:
aussiebucketlist.com/abrolhos

Soak in the Wilderness

THE KIMBERLEY

et's begin with some perspective. England is a nation of 53 million people living on an island of approximately 130,279 square kilometres. The Kimberley is a *region* of Western Australia with 40,000 people living across 423,517 square kilometres. Its striking landscape of red cliffs, rivers, mangroves, creeks and outback desert comprise one-sixth of Australia's landmass. Other than the Canadian Arctic, it offers the most remote wilderness escape of any developed nation. Heck, the Kimberley is bigger than Germany.

We'll start on its western edge in the gateway town of Broome, with a sunrise or sunset camel ride on the 22-kilometre-long white sands of Cable Beach. It's an iconic bucket list experience unto itself, especially since dromedary (one-hump) camels have essentially adopted Australia (see page 295). A camel ride is certainly not the only thing to do in Broome, but it's the one thing most visitors gravitate towards. After exploring the city's historical legacy, enhanced by a strong 18th-century Asian influence, the Kimberley itself beckons. You might choose to rent a high clearance four-wheel drive for a land-based

adventure on the 660-kilometre Gibb River Road linking Wyndham and Derby. The Gibb is one of the world's great remote road trips, requiring resourcefulness and endurance and, of course, a high quality vehicle. You'll discover El Questro Wilderness Park, where you can stop for a swim in the Emma Gorge and get some climate relief in the air-conditioned visitor centre. Arrive early for a dip in the thermal Zebedee Springs, which is only open in the morning. As the sign says: 'If the parking is full, so are the springs.' Since you're essentially driving along private land, various permits are required to stop and visit the sparse but worthwhile attractions along the Gibb's bumpy track of red dirt. Pull up to puffed-up boab trees, hike to Manning Gorge, spot crocodiles in Windjana Gorge National Park, boat along the Ord River and Lake Argyle, or take a helicopter or horse ride. The Gibb is a big sky, high-heat and hard-core camping adventure that requires careful planning. Or not, if you have the budget for the luxurious end of the Kimberley spectrum.

While campers might pop their tents in El Questro Wilderness Park, the exclusive Homestead located in the park is a nine-suite luxury hideout perched on a sandstone bluff over the sparkling Chamberlain River. The white-linen gourmet meals, pampered, comfortable excursions and five-star accommodation can set you back as much as $3000 a night. Alternatively, you can take a small cruise expedition along the Kimberley coast, threading through the region's 2600 islands while fishing for barramundi, watching for whales, taking skiffs or an on-board helicopter for scenic flights and excursions. Swimming in crystal billabongs, anchoring at the mouth of the King George Falls, exploring rock art and slurping back fresh-shucked black-lip oysters – it's easily on par with a small cruise experience in the Galapagos. Bear in mind that a ten-night itinerary on the True North vessel can set you back as much as $25,000 – and that doesn't include the cost of getting to the boat, or the optional heli-excursions.

The eastern agricultural town of Kununurra is blessed with an abundance of water and is serviced with flights from Broome, Darwin and Perth. Here you can hop aboard

Lawrence of Australia

With an estimated 750,000 beasts roaming the outback, Australia is home to the world's largest herd of camels. Originally imported in the 19th century for transport in the outback, several thousand were released into the wild when trucks – less smelly and a lot less thirsty – motored onto the scene. With no natural predators (a camel fart is more than enough to deter an ambitious dingo), feral camels have bred like rabbits; only rabbits don't drain waterholes or cause as much damage to farm infrastructure. A controversial culling program and round-ups for sales to the Middle East have helped, but feral camels continue to roam across a 3.3 million square kilometre wilderness that spans Western Australia, Queensland, South Australia and the Northern Territory.

a light plane or helicopter to visit Purnululu National Park, more popularly known as the Bungle Bungles. The park's distinctive orange-and-black striped karst sandstone 'beehive' domes were only brought to widespread attention in 1983, by a documentary film crew. Four years later the area was declared a national park, and in 2003 a UNESCO World Heritage Site. Exploring the Bungle Bungles by land is possible; ideally from May to August when the temperatures are bearable, although it does come with the usual challenges of remote northern outback travel. However you choose to explore the Kimberley – camel, four-wheel drive, camping, exclusive retreat, luxury cruise, helicopter or plane – your experience is sure to be as unique and unforgettable as this vast landscape itself.

START HERE:
aussiebucketlist.com/kimberley

Spot an Orca in the Southern Ocean

BREMER BAY

Great white sharks may be the big bad wolf of the ocean, but consider this: researchers at the University of Western Australia are reproducing the sounds of a marine mammal to scare them away. Yep, no matter how big you think you are, there's always someone bigger. For sharks, it's the magnificent *orcinus orca*, aka the killer whale. There's only one place you can see pods roaming the waters of Australia, and it's off the coast of Bremer Bay.

The sun has just risen as we catch an early morning ride with the Busy Blue Bus, a company that arranges transfers from Albany. For the next two hours, we'll learn about the region's natural and cultural history. If you're going to encounter the ocean's apex predator in a challenging natural habitat, it's best to kick things off with a leisurely drive. We arrive in Bremer Bay and are greeted by the marine-biologist staff of Naturaliste Charters, and soon find ourselves powering into the 2-metre swells of the Southern Ocean. Our destination is the Bremer Canyon, where the ocean floor gives way to a 3.5-kilometre-deep abyss, creating ideal conditions for orca pods to feed on riches flushed off the shallower waters. Rough waves also help whale watching expeditions, as pods use swells to conserve energy. Not a bad day to hit the sea-sick tablets, then.

It doesn't take long to see the first of what will be many orcas – baby orcas, bull orcas, orcas feeding on whatever unlucky creature happens to be

Whale Sharks in Ningaloo

My own efforts to swim with whale sharks have been thwarted on numerous occasions in numerous destinations around the world, the result of poor weather or whales not showing up. Yet snorkelling with the largest fish in the sea is totally bucket list and, by all accounts, the outer Ningaloo Reef is the best place to do it. These gentle giants gather off the coast of Exmouth to feast on plankton, and whale shark excursions depart daily from May to August. Interaction is heavily monitored by the Department of Parks and Wildlife, and only ten people can swim with a shark at a time. The reef itself, which is fast developing a reputation as 'a better Great Barrier Reef', also presents opportunities to see humpback whales, manta rays, dugongs, dolphins and colourful coral gardens shimmering with life.

swimming nearby. Orcas got their *killer* moniker from their generalist dietary habits. They'll eat sharks and dolphins, sea lions and seabirds, rays and – most famously – other whales. Missing from this list are humans, which might explain why tourists are paying hundreds of dollars to see orcas, and not hunting them to the verge of extinction. Not that you'd want to jump into a pool with an orca. Bulls can weigh up to nine tons, swim up to forty-eight kilometres an hour in short bursts, and have rows of conical teeth designed to shred prey. They are also incredibly social, with hunting techniques passed down the generations and an intelligence that has been admired (and exploited) in aquariums worldwide. French

Best Places to Spot Whales in Australia

WHERE	WHAT	WHEN
Exmouth, WA	whale sharks	May to August
Great Australian Bight Marine Park, SA	southern right whales	May to October
Hervey Bay, QLD	humpback whales	August to October
Bremer Bay, WA	orcas	January to March
Warrnambool, VIC	southern right whales	June to September
Port Stephens, NSW	humpback whales	June to August and September to November
Eden/Merimbula, NSW	humpback whales	June to November
Bruny Island, TAS	southern right and humpback whales	May to December
Cairns/Port Douglas, QLD	dwarf minke whales	June/July
Perth/Perth Canyon, WA	blue whales	March/April and September to December
Victor Harbor, SA	southern right whales	July/August
Byron Bay, NSW	humpback whales	June to November

scientists recently announced that orcas could even mimic human speech, capable of saying 'hello' and counting to three. They believe that one day we might be able to have basic conversations with orcas. I expect the first conversation will include orcas berating us for centuries of whale hunting and overfishing.

Our on-board marine biologists explain the life cycles and habits of orcas with far less speculation, and it's rewarding to be on a

vessel that is part tourist boat, part research boat. With a photographer taking photos to help identify the members of the pods (and happy to share those snaps), we can concentrate on the experience as opposed to our viewfinders. Thrillingly, the whales swim close enough to the boat for us to hear them take a breath. Over the eight-hour excursion, you might also see pilot whales, pods of dolphins,

sharks, sperm whales and giant sunfish – all of whom might be unlucky enough to encounter a pod of hungry orcas. As for bucket listers in search of a unique wildlife encounter, spending a day on the water with these incredible ocean predators is very lucky indeed.

START HERE:
aussiebucketlist.com/orca

Work Out on the Stairway to Heaven

It's seven o'clock in the morning at the top of Cliff Street, just a stone's throw from Perth's Kings Park. Sane people are making breakfast, having a shower, getting dressed, feeding the kids. *Really* sane people are still sleeping. Instead, I'm watching dozens of people running up and down 242 concrete steps without stopping to pause and appreciate the view. They come in all shapes and sizes, ages and levels of athleticism; people who are in-step, in-shape and partaking in a rather unique Australian urban experience. It's a 46-metre staircase with 18 landings called Jacob's Ladder, and I've arrived this morning to see what the fuss is about.

In a gym, you don't get fresh air. On a Stairmaster, you rarely see fabulous examples of the *gluteus maximus* at work, and definitely not this close to your nose. Even the very best fitness clubs cannot offer a view quite as stunning as the Swan River, the Darling Scarp, and the Perth skyline. It's a view shared by some of the city's priciest real estate. Years ago, it inspired a local real estate agent to erect a sign at the bottom of Mount Eliza's public staircase, naming it 'Jacob's Ladder'. The name has endured far longer than, say, my calf muscles, which after two circuits are threatening to pack up and move to Sydney. My local cousin Ron does ten circuits

of Jacob's Ladder three times a week, and has been doing this for more than twenty years. He tells me it's a spot to socialise *and* exercise. Ron points out one of the regulars with a rather large infant on his back. After six circuits, Super Dad finishes up with ten push-ups for good measure, the kid still attached to his back. Another regular is in his eighties. Ron steams ahead of me, chatting to some friends along the way, one step at a time.

I once took on an obstacle course at the Royal Canadian Mounted Police academy, which was designed to test new recruits. Located in a gymnasium, the four circuits of the Physical Abilities Requirement Evaluation didn't look like much. Jump over this, duck under that, roll into this. After three rounds, my tongue was swollen, my lungs were heaving, and my eyeballs were sinking to the back of my neck. This is what you might feel if you do enough circuits of Jacob's Ladder. Ron tells me the staircase gets plenty of action throughout the day, including during lunch breaks. Regulars have developed various strategies: take every two steps for the first five platforms, then every one. Or take

two steps on the way up, and every step on the way down. Stretching before and after is essential.

Explains Ron: 'I've had marathon runner friends come and tell me this is no big deal, until a few days later when they're cursing the ladder. You're using different sorts of muscles and you'll *know* about it!'

A gateway to Kings Park (see Text Box), Jacob's Ladder is a quirky attraction that offers amazing views, active company and a healthy challenge for locals and visitors alike. In the Bible story, the patriarch Jacob has a dream of angels climbing a ladder from earth to heaven. Maybe they were just working out too.

START HERE:
aussiebucketlist.com/
jacobsladder

A Park Fit for a King

At just over 4 square kilometres, Perth's Kings Park is the largest inner city park in the world. Located on Mount Eliza with million-dollar views of the city, Swan River and Darling Scarp, it is the most popular attraction in Western Australia. Entering the park between the massive lemon-scented gum trees on Fraser Avenue, I was instantly struck by the manicured lawns and haunting war memorials. The adjacent botanic garden celebrates the flora of WA and beyond, with an elevated glass-and-steel walkway and a striking centrepiece boab transplanted from the Kimberley. Kings Park is also home to an Aboriginal art gallery, excellent kids' play areas, a grass amphitheatre, restaurant, lovely walking trails and, in September, Australia's largest flower show.

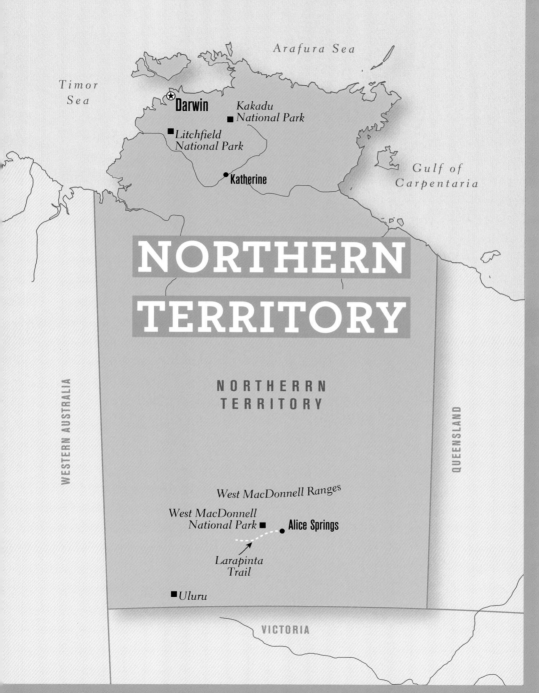

Timor
Sea

Arafura Sea

★ **Darwin**

Kakadu
National Park

■ *Litchfield*
National Park

Gulf of
Carpentaria

● **Katherine**

NORTHERN
TERRITORY

NORTHERRN
TERRITORY

WESTERN AUSTRALIA

QUEENSLAND

West MacDonnell Ranges

West MacDonnell
National Park ■ ● **Alice Springs**

Larapinta
Trail

■ *Uluru*

VICTORIA

Train Across the Red Centre

THE GHAN

No self-respecting bucket list can possibly remain on track without a great train adventure. The Oriental Express, the Trans-Siberian, the Canadian, the Maharajas' Express – these are epic journeys that roll to a rhythm that our bigger-better-faster modern world often leaves behind. Australia is blessed with two of the world's great rail experiences, and one of them has beckoned me to Darwin for a 2979-kilometre journey south to Adelaide. Not only will it capture the romantic essence of rail travel, daily off-train excursions will provide a tantalising glimpse into the essence of the outback. All aboard The Ghan Expedition! Our carriage is waiting.

'Good morning everyone and welcome to The Ghan. We are 902 metres long today, with 38 carriages and 2 locomotives serving 260 guests and 55 crew.' Over the next four days, I will get to know this calm and friendly voice on the loudspeaker. She will greet me each morning as I witness an orange sun rising at my feet, remind me of mealtimes in the Queen Adelaide Restaurant dining car, and provide helpful information about the day's itinerary. The dry, unforgiving interior of Australia lies in stark contrast to the comfort of my well-appointed ensuite cabin, the delicious gourmet meals and the constant opportunity to slake my desert thirst with ice-cold beer or fine Australian wine. Early

pioneers would be rolling in their dusty graves.

Cameleers first arrived in South Australia in 1839, equipped with the perfect beast for far-ranging expeditions into the Northern Territory. As land opened up with the lucrative promise of coal, minerals and agriculture, a narrow-gauge track was initially commissioned from Port Augusta to Alice Springs. It took more than three decades before the inaugural journey of a train from Adelaide to Alice Springs, at first dubbed the Afghan Express, later shortened to The Ghan. No-one is certain whether the nickname was to honour or deride the cameleers (who were largely replaced by the steam locomotive), but the name stuck. In the ensuing decades, faster diesel

locomotives and sleeper berths were added, but floods, mechanical breakdowns, wood-eating termites and shifting sands continued to punish the stationmaster's time-table. The narrow gauge was finally replaced in 1980, using more robust rail materials and following a more dependable route. It was not until 2004 that the final 1420-kilometre link between Alice Springs and Darwin was completed. Today, Great Southern Rail leases the track to offer two passenger itineraries: a 54-hour one-way journey aboard The Ghan, or a 76-hour Ghan Expedition with excursions along the way. Which is how I find

myself gently floating between the auburn sandstone cliffs that line the Katherine River, looking for crocodiles.

As one would expect on a train journey of this calibre, everything runs like clockwork. Buses greet passengers at each stop and we have several options for the day's activity, mostly included with our ticket. Do I take a Rock Art Cruise in Nitmiluk National Park, learning about the history and culture of the local Jawoyn people, or opt for the Katherine Outback Experience to visit horsemen on a working cattle station? Do I upgrade for a scenic helicopter or fixed-wing flight, or simply enjoy the striking Nitmiluk Gorge, learning about the region with an Indigenous guide? I never did spot a crocodile, but there is much to discuss with fellow passengers in the dining car that evening, toasting glasses of wine over grilled saltwater barramundi or braised beef rib with potato *spaetzle*. Cocktails, scotch and conversation continue to flow in the adjacent Explorers Lounge until it is time to retire for the night, finding our ensuite cabins magically converted from the day's bench-seat configuration to beds with soft duvets and, of course, a chocolate on the pillow.

A perfect egg-yolk sun peeks over the horizon, lighting up scrubby bush and orange sand as we approach Alice Springs. It is the start of the dry season, when the dusty roads of the Northern

Territory open for tourist business. We're 200 kilometres from Australia's geographical centre and a wet season of solid rainfall has the Alice Springs landscape looking more mint than cinnamon. When we alight the train, I choose to take a scenic flight to Uluru with a view to absorbing the sweeping vastness of the outback from the cockpit of a small, single-engine Cessna. Skirting the MacDonnell Ranges, I see the giant golf ball shapes of a distant American satellite base before the plane levels at 8000 feet and heads west towards the country's most recognisable geological landmark. Below us, the landscape resembles the back of a red crocodile. Hundreds of millions of years of erosion has resulted in striking ridges, outcrops and the dry remains of meandering rivers.

'That's the Finke over there, the oldest river in the world,' crackles the pilot in my headset. The landscape reminds me of the African Rift Valley, a vista I also viewed from above while writing a story about the Flying Doctors in Nairobi. Back in Alice Springs, our Cessna departed from a hangar next door to the Royal Flying Doctors, bringing me full circle. Witnessing Uluru from above leaves a powerful impression, as do the shifting shapes and shadows of Uluru-Kata Tjuta National Park. I look forward to returning for a closer look.

We rejoin The Ghan passengers under a clear evening sky in the grounds of the Old Telegraph Station that kicked off the modern history of Alice Springs. Fire pits and lanterns illuminate white-linen-covered tables set for dinner under the Milky Way. A local band entertains us with timeless classics as we devour steak (grilled with a perfect red centre as one would expect in the Red Centre) and vegetables. Returning to the train, passengers share the day's experiences – exploring Simpsons Gap, climbing ANZAC Hill and wildlife encounters at Alice Springs Desert Park. Soon enough, The

Ghan continues its ramble down the tracks at an average of 85 kilometres per hour, crossing the South Australian border in the middle of the night.

Once again, I awake to catch a magical sunrise outside my cabin window. A steward knocks on my door to deliver fresh coffee. After a quick shower, I join now-familiar faces for another sumptuous breakfast in the Queen Adelaide dining

Up, Down and Across Too

While The Ghan crosses the continent north to south, the Indian Pacific tracks east to west. Operated by Great Southern Rail with the same level of comfort and service, the Indian Pacific is the longest rail trip in the southern hemisphere (at 4352 kilometres) and one of the longest domestic routes in the world. It includes the world's longest straight track – 478 kilometres across the remote Nullarbor Plain. The Indian Pacific departs all year round from Sydney to Perth or vice versa, and follows a four day, three night itinerary with stops along the way.

car. Our final excursion deposits us quite literally in the middle of nowhere, alongside a remote station called Manguri Siding. Air-conditioned tour buses greet us for a dusty 42-kilometre drive to Coober Pedy, the remote desert town that produces most of the world's precious opal. Entering the town along the same road featured in that striking scene from *The Adventures of Priscilla, Queen of the Desert*, we spend the day exploring this unusual desert town, where many locals and businesses are housed in underground dugouts. You can read more about this remarkable town on page 86.

Canapés, wine, beer and a large bonfire greet us back at the train before we continue the journey, arriving in Adelaide the following morning. Passengers are raving about the memorable excursions, the quality of the meals, the excellent staff. Families, retirees, friends and single travellers like me have all enjoyed the region's greatest experiences, the companionship and the ever-changing panorama outside the cabin windows. Since launching in 2015, The Ghan Expedition continues to exceed all expectations as one of the world's great rail journeys. As for our Great Australian Bucket List, we're definitely on board.

START HERE:
aussiebucketlist.com/theghan

Stare Down a Saltie

Growing up to six metres in length, estuarine (aka saltwater) crocodiles are the world's largest living reptile. Over hundreds of millions of years, salties have evolved into apex predators and killing machines. They can swim fast, creep quietly and lunge high to snatch prey with the mightiest bite of any creature alive (more than ten times the force of a great white shark, or equivalent to dropping a three-ton truck on your foot). Over-hunting once threatened these crocs with extinction but, since becoming protected in 1970, numbers have rebounded and there are now an estimated 150,000 salties in Australia, two-thirds of which prowl the coast and rivers of the Northern Territory. Clearly, these beasts are best observed from a distance. You certainly don't want to get close enough to gaze into their reptilian death stare – but that is exactly what I'm about to do.

Located in downtown Darwin, Crocosaurus Cove is home to several massive salties, the country's largest display of reptiles, various feeding sessions, educational programs and the notorious Cage of Death. It's something a Roger Moore-era James Bond villain might have thought up: you enter a circular Perspex tube by ladder, a monorail crane lifts you up and places you into a pool with a giant beastie. It's too unusual an experience for our bucket list to pass up although – having earlier listened to the loud 'whomp' of a croc's jaws slamming together during the Big Croc Feeding Show – it's enough to make a sane person reconsider. I notice the handlers use a very, very long stick with food on the end. Even though the handlers are fond of the crocs and have worked with them for many years, it's safe to say the love all flows in one direction. The crocs wouldn't hesitate to add trainer meat to their strictly monitored diet. I meet Burt, arguably Australia's most famous crocodile, having starred with Paul Hogan in *Crocodile Dundee*. Weighing 700 kilograms, Burt has been in captivity for three decades and has appeared in many

documentaries and films. The rest are considered problematic crocs because of their aggression or penchant for attacking boats and cars. Unable to peacefully cohabit with others in a crocodile farm, they have been brought here instead. Like Burt, Chopper is also estimated to be more than 80 years old, and he's missing an arm from a territorial tussle in the wild days of his youth. There's Wendell and Denzel and Axel, but I've got a date with the royal couple, William and Kate.

The park's successful breeding pair was originally named Houdini and Bess but crocodiles don't get too attached to names. They were renamed after the royal couple in 2011. Apparently, the petite 110-kilogram Kate holds

700-kilogram William's wild ways in check. Sounds more like a Harry and Meghan scenario if you ask me.

After signing the prerequisite waiver, I slip on my bathing suit and meet the handlers at the monorail.

Ain't He a Sweetheart?

Not far from Darwin there lived a 5-metre-long, 780 kilogram croc that liked to chase after boats in Sweets Lookout Billabong. A dominant male, the endearingly named Sweetheart was notoriously aggressive, with a taste for outboard motors. Attacks were becoming more frequent. In 1979, Parks and Wildlife decided it was best to relocate him to a crocodile farm but Sweetheart unfortunately drowned in the botched capture. He was transported to the Museum and Art Gallery of the Northern Territory and handed over to the resident taxidermist. Pig bones, two long-necked turtles and a large barramundi were found in his stomach. Decades later, Sweetheart remains one of the most popular exhibits in Darwin, an iconic and fearsome croc with the most tender of names.

A ladder is lowered into the 5-inch-thick clear Perspex cylinder and I climb inside wearing a pair of goggles. Immediately I notice scratch marks on the plastic, caused by gnashing teeth and sharp claws. Unlike shark cage diving, the crocs are not merely curious about my presence; they are literally eager to tear me to pieces and add me to the menu. Water comes up to my neck, and the handler starts slapping the water to arouse the interest of William and Kate. Slowly, they float closer, eyeing me the way kids look at a new vegetable. From below, I observe their seemingly soft white bellies, and from small open slits in my plastic tube I see armour-hides glistening in the sunshine. I'm strongly advised that under no circumstances should I put any part of my body through those slits. It's like advising someone not to stick their tongue into a high-speed fan, but I suppose there will always be idiots who do it anyway.

After a few minutes, the handler ties chicken to a long stick and splashes it close to my head. As big as they crocs are, they only eat about 3 kilograms of food a week (these feedings make up part of that diet). William swims over and

becomes far more interested. He scratches the cage, bangs against it. I observe his sixty-six white and shiny pyramid-shaped teeth and the soft pink recess of his triangular mouth. He flashes me that famous crocodile smile. Through the holes in the cylinder, we then have a real human-crocodile moment. I look him straight in his golden eyeball and he looks deep into my soul. I wonder what he's thinking, but he's probably just wondering how to eat me. Every time he bangs the plastic I almost jump out my skin. Soon, my fifteen minutes are up, the crane raises the cage, transports me over Chopper's lair and back to the load ramp. I'm relieved to get out the tube. Just being in the same water as those crocs was enough to give me the heebie-jeebies.

While horrifying to visualise, crocodile attacks are extremely rare; there are only about two deaths a year in Australia, many involving people swimming or crossing in areas they have been specifically warned not to. Still, more crocs mean that attacks are increasing, and Crocwise is a serious campaign in the Top End and northern Queensland that is trying to educate people about the dangers. Unless cleared for swimming, you must assume that beaches or rivers have crocs patiently waiting to pounce. It's much safer, and more thrilling, to encounter them at Crocosaurus Cove on Darwin's busy Mitchell Street, where you can shower off, get dressed and hit a local bar to ease your nerves.

START HERE:
aussiebucketlist.com/cageofdeath

Relive the Day War Came to Australia

DARWIN

The world might have been at war, but February 19, 1942 was just another morning in tropical Darwin. People greeted each other on their way to work; the weather was hot and sticky. With Japanese forces advancing unchecked in the Pacific, Allied powers recognised the strategic value of northern Australian ports and chose Darwin as the base for major operations. Forty-nine warships and merchant vessels were in the harbour that day, a significant deterrent for any foreign attack, or perhaps an invitation for the same. The dramatic assault on Pearl Harbour just a few months prior had resulted in the precautionary evacuation of most women and children, but all essential services were operating. Still, there had never been a foreign invasion on Australian soil. Darwin was as sleepy as ever. It was just another morning.

Norman Cramp, the director of the Darwin Military Museum, leads me through the interactive galleries of the Defence of Darwin Experience. 'It's an important story that many Australians simply don't know,' he tells me.

At 9.58am, one hundred and eighty-eight Japanese attack aircraft flew over Darwin, dropping more bombs and sinking more ships than they did at Pearl Harbour. No air raid siren was sounded, as reports of a large group of approaching aircraft were assumed to be a squadron of American planes returning to base because of bad weather. Darwin's defences were caught completely off-guard. A second wave of land bombers followed two hours later and the result was devastating. Thirty-one Allied aircraft were destroyed, including ten of the twelve USAAF planes flying in defence. Eleven ships were sunk, most buildings were levelled and the death toll, well, that is *still* being debated. It is estimated more than two hundred and fifty people died that day, ranging from Wing Commanders to teenage civilians. Many of the casualties were American servicemen stationed

in Darwin (the sinking of the USS Peary cost ninety lives alone). A direct hit on a trench shelter wiped out nine people who worked at the post office, including the Postmaster and his family. With few steel or concrete structures in Darwin, incendiary bombs burned what explosions didn't flatten. The Japanese reportedly lost only four aircraft and retreated in triumph. They had crippled Darwin, but they certainly did not break its spirit.

Through a combination of archive photos, videos, computer graphics, flashing lights and booming sound design, I relive this eventful day inside the museum's Defence of Darwin Experience. When the doors open and the lights flicker on at the end of the show, I am left with many

questions. Fortunately, this is the best place in the country to find answers. 'Many people think the Japanese were planning a ground invasion, but that was never the case,' explains Norm, a passionate student of military history currently researching his PhD. The goal was to cripple Allied plans to build a base that could counter Japanese aggression in Portuguese Timor, Papua New Guinea and other theatres in the Pacific. The Japanese knew that Australia's northern coast would inevitably be used against them and so they took the initiative. They continued to pepper the Top End with nearly one hundred bombing raids, right through to mid-1944. Darwin alone withstood another sixty-two air raids, although none were as destructive as the initial raid. It forced the Allies to double down. The military completely took over the town, defences were improved and better infrastructure built. British, Dutch and a large contingent of US forces joined the Australian defence. Eventually, the Japanese were pushed out of Portuguese (now East) Timor and Indonesia and the tides of war turned.

Of course, there's so much more to this story – it is the personal stories of those involved that bring the Defence of Darwin Experience to life. 'We have the Bible belonging to the famous commander who led the Japanese raid,' Norm tells me. Mitsuo Fuchida led the attacks on both Pearl Harbour and Darwin, clocked over 3000 hours of combat flying, survived the war and became

The Mother of all Cyclones

Three decades after surviving the Japanese bombs, Darwin was levelled by the most destructive storm in Australian history. Cyclone Tracy hit the city on Christmas Eve 1974, killing seventy-one people and causing more than $7 billion (in today's figures) in damage. Blasted by winds of up to 240 kilometres per hour, it is estimated that 70 per cent of the city's buildings and more than 80 per cent of its houses were destroyed. Hundreds were injured and, within a week, two-thirds of the population had been evacuated south. It remains a seminal event in Darwin's history, with a permanent exhibition at the Museum and Art Gallery of the Northern Territory. Don't miss the room that lets you hear the roaring sound of the cyclone (a sign warns Tracy survivors that it might be upsetting). Darwin was rebuilt to endure future cyclones and continues to thrive as the capital and most populous city in the Northern Territory.

an evangelist who toured the United States and Europe. I'm captivated by the honest video interviews and stories of Australian civilians and soldiers, the interactive maps and various objects on display. Bringing it home are the physical legacies of war waiting for me outside the blissfully air-conditioned gallery.

During the war, Darwin's East Point became the most heavily fortified military base in Australia. More than one hundred thousand military personnel were based in the town, which became – as the Japanese had feared – a major centre for Allied forces in the Pacific. Outside, in the adjacent

Darwin Military Museum, I walk among hundreds of army, navy and air force artefacts, including vehicles and armoured carriers, massive guns, equipment and original documents from the war. In the shade of large tropical fig trees, a six-inch gun is still in its original placement, installed at great cost after the attacks had ceased. I enter a concrete building to view a vast collection of machine guns and firearms. A display of swords and bayonets includes a 15th-century samurai sword, and some of the press clippings and original documents here are deeply moving. Visitors are invited to try on authentic army-issue clothing, explore sections relating to other conflicts, and view plaques honouring the names of Northern Territory servicemen and civilians claimed by the war. Regardless of your interest in military history, it will likely keep you outside long enough to reapply sunscreen (which the museum thoughtfully provides at the entrance).

There is one more twist in Darwin's wartime story. 'In the mid-1960s the Australian government put out a tender to dismantle and remove World War II shipwrecks and other equipment,' Norm tells me. 'The irony is that it was awarded to a Japanese company. They destroyed all our stuff and then we paid them to come over and take it away.' Irony it is, and progress too. Today is just another day in Darwin – hot, sticky and still. A peaceful day, something you can very much appreciate after visiting an outstanding museum dedicated to February 19, 1942: the day war came to Australia.

START HERE:
**aussiebucketlist.com/
defenceofdarwin**

See the Sun Rise on the Rock

ULURU

'Checking in please, my name is Robin Esrock.'
'Excuse me, Robin . . . Ayers Rock?'
'Yes, Esrock.'
[Blank Stare]
'E-s-r-o-c-k'
'Oh . . . that's cool!'

It's cool because I'm checking in to Ayers Rock Resort and, with an accent, there's not a lot to distinguish my surname – of Lithuanian descent – from the name of the resort. Like the airport that services it, the resort still goes by the former name of the most iconic geological formation in the country, the beating red heart at the centre of Australia. Today, Ayers Rock is better known as Uluru, and no bucket list could possibly be complete without seeing it.

My first glimpse of this sandstone inselberg (literally, an island mountain) is from the cockpit of a small Cessna (see page 309). Towering over the flat outback plain and tinged with its famous red hues,

The Many Heads of Kata Tjuta

Repeat visitors to the area often claim the real star is Kata Tjuta. Comprised of thirty-six steep rocky red domes, the tallest of which sits 546 metres above the plain, Kata Tjuta is also deeply significant for the Anangu and climbing on the rocks is prohibited. Formed by the same geological processes as Uluru, the domes are the surviving hard rock of an alluvial fan subjected to hundreds of millions of years of erosion. Depending on your viewpoint – air or ground – the domes (formerly known as the Olgas) appear to constantly change shape and colour. As well as tours and a scenic viewpoint, there are two walking trails: the 2.6-kilometre Walpa Gorge and 7.4-kilometre Valley of the Winds.

Uluru was bigger than I expected. Having seen so many photos and videos over the years, I thought I had a solid grasp on the sacred rock so integral to the traditions of the local Anangu people, and the tourism industry of central Australia. Yet there it loomed, its surface marked like flaking red skin, further eroded into distinct holes, caves, ribs and ridges. From above, surrounded by the peppercorn-like scrub of the early dry season, Uluru looked like the back of a giant rocky creature crawling on hands and knees in search of something down below. This 'back', it turns out, is actually the top of a huge slab of arkose sandstone that continues underground for 5 or 6 kilometres. It's the result of hundreds of millions of years of erosion, the impact of a disappearing inland sea and powerful geological thrusts. Fascinating if you're into geology, but this is a place of undeniable spiritual energy, from above or below.

Ayers Rock Resort is owned by the Indigenous Land Corporation and managed by its Voyages subsidiary. An oasis in the desert, 443 kilometres from the nearest major centre (Alice Springs), the resort offers accommodation that ranges from the plush five-star Sails in the Desert to the Ayers Rock Campground. With a permanent population of around one thousand people, the resort is the fourth-largest settlement in the Northern Territory, operating as a small town. It is located about 20 kilometres from the great rock itself, and 50 kilometres from the domed heads of the lesser-known yet just as magnificent Kata Tjuta (formerly referred to as the Olgas). As if anyone needed an excuse to revere the rocks, UNESCO awarded Uluru-Kata Tjuta heritage status in 1987 for its outstanding natural and cultural status. With hundreds of thousands of tourists arriving from around the world, the resort and associated tour operators offer a variety of means to tackle the iconic formations. Dine with a view under the stars, take a scenic flight or helicopter ride, hire bicycles, take a guided hike or motorcycle tour, skydive, mount a Segway, jump on a hop-on hop-off bus. There are free daily activities that include a bush food experience, learning about Anangu culture and history, guided nature walks and Indigenous art programs. The Wintjiri Arts and

Museum will tell you everything you need to know about the region, and dining ranges from your campground BBQ to cafes and high-end restaurants. Visitors must purchase a park pass, with most choosing the three-day pass that provides ample opportunity to tick off the experiences that appeal to you most.

Having taken in Uluru from the air, I hop on a SEIT Australia bus for a tour to the base. Our guide explains the ecological history of the rock and its spiritual significance. The Anangu have been living in this region for many thousands of years, with Uluru serving as an important spiritual site for male initiation rites. The first non-Aboriginal visitor was William Gosse in 1873 and, other than dingo hunters and gold prospectors,

there was little reason for anyone else to visit for decades after. With the opening of a graded dirt road from Alice Springs, the first wave of tourists arrived in the mid-1940s. The area was declared a national park in 1958 and the campgrounds and hotels, which were originally much closer to the rock, were gradually relocated to the Yulara town site by the 1970s. In 1985, the park was handed back to its traditional Indigenous owners, who leased it back to the National Parks and Wildlife Service for ninety-nine years. It continues to employ and support the 300-strong Anangu community – based in a nearby settlement – and the Anangu co-administer the park.

Depending on weather conditions, the bush flies and your physical ability, you might choose to stroll the full 10.6-kilometre loop. I take the Kuniya Walk to the watering hole at the foot of Uluru, learning how the Anangu travelled the region in search of food, adeptly burning the landscape to ensure fresh growth and the return of animals. Nearby, shaded from the sun inside the Mutitjulu cave, my guide points out rock art that dates back decades to centuries.

Unfortunately, early visitors to Uluru damaged large portions of this priceless rock art. These days, the impact of visitors is carefully regulated, although some controversies remain. While the Anangu implored tourists for decades to respect their traditions and not climb the pathway to the top, some people still did. But climbing Uluru is officially prohibited as of October 2019.

Stargazing is incredible under the expansive outback sky. On a must-do Astro Tour, the resort's resident and visiting astronomers point out various constellations and nebula, focusing their telescopes onto the Galilean moons of Jupiter. Like most visitors, I go to bed early and awake with the stars still twinkling above. The distinctive colours of Uluru and Kata Tjuta are most brilliant at sunrise and sunset, and most tours will be operating early or late to allow you to experience both. I opt for sunrise with Uluru Camel Tours, sitting on a tall shaggy beast with charming batty eyelids. As the sky begins to brighten, our camel train is led into the bush, with guides enthusiastically telling stories about the history and impact of camels in the outback. We park on a dune just in

time to watch the morning's first golden rays strike the iron-rich ribs of Uluṟu. They make a big deal about the changing colours of the rock here – and for good reason. I witness the blush of a delicate rose, the juice of a blood orange, the rust of an old tractor. Within a few short minutes, the bright colours of Uluṟu have awoken. I feel something shift in the parched desert air and a bucket list miracle being ticked off.

In 1873, William Gosse ignored the Indigenous name Uluru, meaning 'immense rock rising abruptly from the plain'. He named it Ayers Rock, after the Chief Secretary of South Australia, Henry Ayers. In 1995, Ayers Rock-Mount Olga National Park officially became Uluṟu-Kata Tjuṯa National Park, finally recognising the Anangu people's ownership and relationship to the area. Visitors, however, still fly into Ayers Rock Airport and stay at the Ayers Rock Resort. Perhaps that will change and future generations of Esrocks won't get funny looks when checking in. As for Uluṟu, it will forever and always be a standout on *The Great Australian Bucket List.*

START HERE:
aussiebucketlist.com/uluru

325

Swim in the Buley Rockholes

LITCHFIELD NATIONAL PARK

Two iconic national parks dominate most itineraries to the Top End. Kakadu — the better known of the two — is blessed with a high concentration of Indigenous rock art, pristine bush, stunning waterfalls and rugged cliffs. Closer to Darwin, Litchfield National Park is known for waterfalls, hikes, trails and four-wheel drive tracks. Both are shoo-ins for our national bucket list, although neither are without their challenges. There are vast distances to cover and the environment can be challenging. If you visit in dry season — when the bugs clear off and the crocs clear out — the remoteness and beauty in both parks is something to behold. With limited time to tick off both Kakadu and Litchfield, I opted for the latter, a two-hour drive from Darwin and the ideal overnight trip. Driving along the highway with a 130 kilometre-per-hour speed limit, I watch as all evidence of civilisation disappears and the bush takes over.

The Batchelor Butterfly Farm, located on the outskirts of Litchfield, felt like a great fit for overnight accommodation for my family. Kids love butterflies and there would be farm animals, too. Our plan was to drop off our stuff and head straight into the national park. But along with the butterflies we meet the Hornes, a boisterous Irish and Filipino couple with a passion for **b**unnies, **b**abies and **b**utterflies. Chris and his wife have hand-built a homely temple that celebrates their love for the three bs, creating a hotel/restaurant that's a riot of stuffed animals, reptiles, rabbits, frogs, farm animals and large toys. Pink floatie flamingos greet us in the pool beneath a rock waterfall.

A black-faced python dances the cha-cha in a terrarium, and Chris gleefully sweeps up my daughter to put a large butterfly on her nose.

'I . . . guess we can stay for lunch,' is my only reply, which is music to my daughter's ears. Lunch turns out to be outstanding – chicken cooked with ginger, nuts and basil and the authentically Filipino dish of beef kaldereta. We leave our bags in a cabin, but lose our daughter in the pens, where she is playing with newly born bunnies. With all the Asian influences about, it feels like we've wormholed into Bali. It's a reminder of the unplanned randomness you often encounter on the road. Eventually, I tear my

kids away from the butterfly farm with promises of our return that evening, and we continue the drive into Litchfield National Park.

You can't miss one of the park's key attractions because towering termite mounds are easy to spot from the road. Two species of termite are responsible for the two different types of mounds, and while both creatures are tiny, their homes are massive. About 17 kilometres from the park's eastern boundary are the Magnetic Termite Mounds, looking very much like grey tombstones perfectly aligned north to south. Nearby, the

Cathedral Termite mounds look like an organic version of Gaudi's La Sagrada Familia: colossal, orange-caked columns that grow up to eight metres tall and are constructed over many decades. Cathedral termites engineer these mega-structures with mud, plant material, saliva and faeces and they are strong enough to withstand the elements as well as predators. They even build ventilation shafts to keep the mounds cool in the baking heat. Relative to their tiny size (less than one centimetre long) both species of termite build some of the tallest non-human structures

Highlights of Kakadu

Considering it's the size of a small country, it's not difficult to lose yourself in Australia's largest national park. Accessed via the sealed, all-year Arnhem Highway, the park is serviced by various tour operators, scenic flight companies and outfitters for one-day or multi-day expeditions. Among the many highlights, don't miss:

- **Jim Jim Falls**: The image most often associated with Kakadu, with its crystal clear cascades from the southern escarpment.

- **Ubirr/Nourlangie**: Some of the most famous Indigenous rock art sites in the country, with galleries dating back thousands of years.

- **Yurmikmik Walks**: A series of waterfalls and swimming holes linked by a chain of connected walking tracks.

- **Gunlom**: Kakadu's natural infinity pool, with a wonderful view from the top of the falls.

- Jabiru's **Bowali Visitor Centre** or Cooinda's **Warradjan Aboriginal Cultural Centre** are great resources to learn about the park from its cultural custodians.

in the world. Given their accomplishments, let us glad be glad they pile up the red dirt of the Top End and not the wooden beams of our houses.

Waterfalls and sandstone formations are the park's bigger rock stars and, depending what time of the year you visit, you'll be spoiled for choice. Wangi Falls and Florence Falls are sizable cascades for unforgettable swims, accessed via easy trails. My personal favourite – and particularly family friendly – are the Buley Rockholes, where a series of descending cascades fill deep and shallow rock

pools, creating a variety of relaxing water features. We could rock-jump safely into the deeper pools, park ourselves in shallow plunge pools for some therapeutic hydrotherapy or roll down the slippery rocks from one pool to the next. Along with bushwalking, bird watching, an adventurous four-wheel drive trip to the striking sandstone formations of the Lost City, Litchfield represents nature in the Top End at its finest – and most accessible.

START HERE:
aussiebucketlist.com/litchfield

Hike the Larapinta Trail

CENTRAL AUSTRALIA

In the bush, along the beach, through the forests, and over the mountains – Australians love a good hike. It is a country spoiled for choice in hiking options, so I set out to find the iconic bucket list trek that encompasses and perfectly captures the unique wonder of the continent. Issue number one: I'm not an experienced hiker and have never planned a multi-day hike. Issue number two: the most spectacular hike in the country is also spectacularly remote. Completed in 2002 and running a total of 223 kilometres, the Larapinta Trail in the West MacDonnell Ranges presents the essence of the parched, striking outback, front and centre.

Commencing in Alice Springs, it is a rugged path that cuts through striking rocky ridges, creeks, canyons, bone-dry riverbeds and dense bush. It's a mighty endeavour for even the most experienced hikers and should only be attempted in winter, when the scorching sun won't cook you through to your red centre. You'll have to carry in all your food (or carefully plan food drops), survive severe temperature swings and forego the little things like showers and toilets. Well, that's one way to do it. Another is to sign up to World Expeditions' Larapinta Trail in Comfort, a six-day journey that finds me sleeping in safari tents, sipping single malt under the stars and salivating over perfectly grilled lamb chops. Guided by trail experts and hosted in three bush camps, the tour allows anyone in modest physical shape to experience the sheer joy of bushwalking and revel in the unmistakable magic that permeates central Australia.

We begin at the Old Telegraph Station in Alice Springs, where the town's namesake springs more accurately resemble a barren sandbed. Among our group is a large contingent of walkers from New South Wales who have left their husbands and kids at home.

Before leaving, we stock up on supplies and, judging by the volume of wine and beer procured for the week, I immediately discern I am in fine company. *In Comfort* means we will hike with only a daypack, while the rest of our luggage is transferred to that evening's bush camp. The Larapinta was designed with plenty of off-road access points to allow for just such convenience, and it means our days always end with delicious meals and chilled wine around the campfire. We join a narrow trail of red earth lined by buffel grass. Dingoes howl in the distance and a large wallaroo suddenly leaps across the trail. We cross beneath the Geoff Moss Bridge, which I'm told is named after the father of Ian Moss, who I'm told is from an iconic band called Cold Chisel, and who, being Canadian, I've never heard of. There's going to be a lot to learn this week.

By taking a twenty-day hike and condensing it into six days, World Expeditions has effectively packaged the Larapinta Trail's greatest hits. No two days are the same and each day leaves us glowing with a sense of a wonder and accomplishment. Day One takes us 13.5 kilometres, mostly atop Euro Ridge, introducing the sweeping valleys and rocky spines of West MacDonnell National Park. Three hundred and fifty million years ago, monumental geological shifts bent and folded quartzite and dolomite into mountains as tall as the Himalayas. Erosion has since created dramatic ridges of red rock, steep canyons and arid windswept valleys full of mallee

bushes and hardy, razor-tipped spinifex. Hiking along escarpments means few challenging hills and a constant view. After spotting a dingo stalking rock wallabies in the aptly named Wallaby Gap, we hop on our bus for a short drive to Nick's Camp. Located on Indigenous land, World Expeditions' semi-permanent camps have large, two-person canvas tents with stretcher beds and swags. We're encouraged to roll them out to sleep under the stars, which are reliably brilliant. Shortly before dinner, an Indigenous chef named Raylene Brown visits the camp to introduce us to the wonders of local bush tucker. We sample bush tomato and pepperberry, grilled kangaroo with bush lime, quandong chutney, and feta marinated in lemon myrtle. Harvested by local women, these ingredients are distinct to the region and have so much culinary potential. After our hearty dinner – each camp has a large kitchen and barbecue – we sit around the fire with a drink and get to know each other. What is apparent to all: this is bucket list living.

We awake before dawn to pack our things and have breakfast before rejoining the trail and

continuing the hike to Simpsons Gap. We're reminded that each canyon holds deep cultural significance for the local Arrernte people and, arriving in Standley Chasm after a 9-kilometre hike though bloodwood and ironwood forests, we're about to learn why. Deanella Mack is a local Arrernte woman who believes in the power of connecting cultures and has an uncanny knack for clearly communicating how to do so. Using analogies like corporate structures, sports teams and ecosystems, she explains the system of Skin and Kin, the idea of Dreamtime, the concept and importance of cultural volume, Indigenous

religion, respecting country, dance and song – and how simple, misunderstood customs create cultural chasms. Informal, funny, provocative and honest, Deanella provides the most fascinating and revealing Indigenous experience I've had throughout my journey. 'How did we not know this stuff before?' says a fellow hiker from the Hunter Valley. It gives us so much to discuss around the fire in Charlie's Camp, after a feast of barbecued barramundi with lemon and dill. Above us, a dark serpent seems to snake through the stars, symbolic perhaps of our exposure to the stories of Dreamtime and a precursor to the Serpentine Gorge.

Australia's Bucket List Hikes

Sue Badyari, CEO of World Expeditions, reveals her best hikes in Australia.

☐ **The Larapinta Trail, NT**: Incredible scenery, waterholes, big skies and the choice of walking different sections make this a must-do outback experience for hikers of all abilities.

☐ **The Overland Track, TAS**: Enjoy one of Australia's finest walks from the craggy spires of Cradle Mountain to the rainforest-clad shores of the deepest natural lake in the southern hemisphere.

☑ **The Walls of Jerusalem, TAS**: Tasmania's ultimate pristine wilderness trail with ancient rock cliffs, tarns and weird and wonderful flora and fauna making this a truly magical hiking area.

☐ **The Heysen Trail, SA**: The Flinders Ranges offer a rolling range of majestic peaks and rugged ridges, deep gorges and endemic plants and animals.

☐ **Bungle Bungles and Piccaninny Gorge, WA**: Western Australia's national wonder, a trail that follows the gorge as it winds its way between the red-and-black beehive-like sandstone domes.

☐ **Kakadu National Park, NT**: Immense waterfalls, tranquil waterholes, caves adorned with rock art, an array of birds and butterflies, Aboriginal culture – Kakadu has it all!

☐ **Blue Mountains National Park, NSW**: A playground for adventure with a network of walking trails winding through the famous Blue Mountains wilderness.

After a long, gentle ascent, we trek along a high ridge to a spot called Counts Point, which offers staggering views of the Territory's highest mountains. Water, so valuable in this parched country, pools at the base of towering red canyons, casting a shadow over ancient acacias and tall red gums. We breakfast in a dry creek and I notice my tired muscles are loosening up and strengthening, my knees and joints creaking less. We pop over to the Glen Helen Homestead Lodge, where I strip down for a swim in the surprisingly ice-cold waters of the Finke River. It's an easier day of hiking to prepare us for the climax of the journey: a tough 16-kilometre return hike up Mount Sonder to catch the sunrise. We wake at two in the morning, layer up and grab headlamps to help us navigate the challenging climb up the slope of the fourth-tallest peak in the Territory. Depending on which direction you're travelling, Mount Sonder is the official start or finish of the Larapinta Trail. I've never hiked beneath the stars, which

begin to sparkle like a disco ball around four o'clock, as the moon disappears beneath the horizon. Several times I stop, turn off my lamp and savour the cool outback breeze and magical feeling of isolation. We reach the breezy summit in time for the well-earned sunrise, marvelling at the astounding view in all directions. We also marvel at how steep and long the return hike is, the darkness having shielded us from the intimidating visual of the ascent, which most of us agree would have broken our resolve. We deserve that extra beer tonight and, hell, a bottle of champagne, too.

On our final day, we pack up camp and backtrack to Section 10 of the Larapinta Trail's 12 sections, a side hike called the Ormiston Pound Walk. It's a three and a half hour trek into spinifex-covered hills, culminating in a silent walk beneath the intense red cliffs of the Ormiston Gorge. Still pools of water reflect that special, crisp light you only see in the outback. Some of us choose to refresh in the deep waters of a permanent swimming hole, while others take refuge from the bush flies with a cup of coffee in the air-conditioned kiosk. Throughout the week, my fellow hikers have been wonderful company and I'd follow our friendly and seemingly superhuman guides into the bush anywhere. The Larapinta Trail has been

physical, it has been rugged, it has been sublime, and it is bucket list experience at its peak. Sure, through World Expeditions I opted for an easier route, but compared to the intense challenges of true pack-in, pack-out outback hiking, this once-in-a-lifetime opportunity is reassuringly comfortable.

START HERE:
aussiebucketlist.com/larapinta

Acknowledgments

Putting this book together, and the journey it recounts, was a master class in the creative management of ninja logistics, feverish communications, samurai strokes of luck, intense deadline stress and the warm generosity of strangers. Let me assure you that travelling across Australia with two young kids on a mission to tick off every iconic experience you can find is not for the faint of heart, or possibly the sound of mind. There are many people and organisations that made it possible.

Special thanks to **Ford Motor Company of Australia**, who provided a powerful 3.2-litre V8 Ford Everest in every port of call, a vehicle well equipped for everything Australia threw at it (including the projectile vomit of my toddler, Galileo). This entire project would be stuck in the mud without the vision of Jasmine Moberak and logistical wizardry of Eddy Sleiman. Special thanks to all the Ford dealers around the country who helped us truly Go Further.

We travelled by land, sea, train and air. Special thanks to Ingrid Nason, Simon Tsang, Kelly Ogilvie and all the exceptionally friendly staff and crew at **Jetstar Airways** for flying us to and fro.

We had comfortable, convenient, spacious and much-appreciated abodes in a dozen **Oaks Hotels and Resorts** properties around the country. Special thanks to Stacey Beckingham, Kira Klein, Barry Abkin and all the lovely Oaks staff we encountered along the way.

Outside the cities, we loved our time exploring **Discovery Holiday Parks**, where the kids ran riot in the waterparks, on the bouncy pillows and playgrounds. To all the park managers, and especially Jane Ford, a hearty g'day!

Special thanks to Larissa Duncomb, Brad Atwal, Danielle Flegg, Sue Badyari and all at **World Expeditions** for the ongoing support on their adventures of a lifetime. Speaking of which, special thanks to Deb and Tim at **Keen Footwear** for providing the footwear one needs to take on a country as vast and diverse as Australia.

Special thanks also to Rob Cowie and all the great staff at **Move Yourself**, who conveniently hitched us up with trailers around the nation.

Anthony Whittle and Jami Sutcliffe at **Sunshades Eyewear** kept our retinas safe and looking good, **Victorinox** provided luggage that stood the test, **Britax** car seats and **Valco Baby** kept our kids safe and easily transportable, with thanks to Teresa Thompson and the *menschood* of Jeffrey New. More on that in the next book!

Special thank you to Caitlin Jones and the team at **Journey Beyond**, a company whose mission is in absolutely perfect alignment with my own.

Special thanks to Jessica Schmidt and all at **Tourism Tasmania** for helping us discover the many wonders of my favourite state.

Katherine Droga was instrumental with her support, and we still dream of the most comfortable bed in the Blue Mountains.

ACKNOWLEDGEMENTS

Affirm Press had the foresight to recognise that storytelling in travel is just as important as providing buckets of information. So many people are needed to make a book idea become a reality. Special thanks to Keiran Rogers, Martin Hughes, Grace Breen, Laura McNicol Smith, Stephanie Bishop-Hall, my lovely editor Ruby Ashby-Orr, eagle-eyed copy editor Emma Miller, and all at Affirm Press.

Special thanks to Jaci Taylor for her companionship, creative eye and kindness for our kids. Thanks to the ever-optimistic Amy Markus for the big hearted home-front support. A warm and heartfelt shout-out to Erin Pimm, Brad and Tamar Resnik, Lance and Maxine Radus, Annette and Issy Liebenthal, Heather Lewin, Ron Gordon and Renicia Vilensky, Kenny and Melanie Baranov, and our long-lost cruisemates Kate and Shelly. Thanks to Rico, Duck, Rat and Doosh, as well as the Barons, the Aikens, Dennis and Paola Villagomez and Bonnie McCoy. Of course, as always, none of this would happen without the support of our family, the Kalmeks in Vancouver and Roberto and Gabi in Rio de Janeiro. Jon Rothbart continues to provide his special brand of sound council. Mary Rostad provided the great maps yet again – this is our ninth book together! Thanks to my good friend and fellow rock Dave Rock for the time and amazing videos.

In each state, special thanks (in no particular order) to:

Victoria
Glenn Harvey and Sharon Wells, Kellie Barrett, Roland Pick, Samantha Mackley, Brook Powell, Shane Brown, Tim Whittaker, Sheena Dang, the National Trust of Australia, staff at the Oaks on Southbank, Visit Victoria.

South Australia
Robert Main, The Barn, Tess Armfield, Suzanne Parisi and the South Australian Tourism Commission, Ben Neville, Dylan Beach at Monarto Zoo, Yasmin and Georgia Stehr, Cheryl Turner, staff at the Oaks Embassy.

Western Australia
Emily Andrews, Shark Bay Hotel, Wendy Mann, Fran Raven, Pam and Dirk

Hos, Stell Limnios and Chloe Lyons at the lovely Attika Hotel, Lily Yeang and Australia's Southwest, Beth and Rick Cowan at the homely Bridgewater B&B in Margaret River, Prince Graeme in Hutt River, Sean Stahlhut at Fremantle Prison YHA, Dean Kingi, Ron Gordon and Renicia Vilensky.

Tasmania
Maddy, Belle and everyone who joined me on the six-day east coast adventure, Mark and Claire Walsh at Discovery Parks Cradle Mountain, Anthony at Cradle Mountain Canyoning, Rael Dusheiko, Amanda Beck at Sullivan Cove (a toast of the French Oak is overdue), Narissa Armstrong at Devonport Discovery Parks, Harry Nichols, Felix Nelson, Genevieve Hall and Jaci Taylor.

New South Wales
Kristine McCarthy, Danielle Edwards, Joanna at Worimi, Kelly Seagrave, Sophie Turner at Experience Co, Peta Zeitsch, Brenda and Blake at Let's Go Surfing, Kellie Sommerville at Crystal Castle, Louise Wallace at Scenic World, Kirk Tutt, Michelle Baker, the staff at the Oaks Goldsbrough, Oaks Pacific Blue and Oaks Cypress Lakes.

Canberra
Donna Ciaccia and Joanne Barges at Visit Canberra, Glen Nagle, Heather Gow-Carey at Tidbinbilla Nature Reserve.

Queensland
Leigh Arredondo at Tourism and Events Queensland, Biccara Guerin, Georgie Sadler, the unstoppable Peter Hackworth, Peta Zeitsch, Merryn Andrews, Dave and Georgina at Discovery Parks Fraser Coast, Janelle Murray, Caitlin Jones, Brett and Hilton Abkin, Joe and Cheryl Kalmek (well travelled!), Discovery Parks Airlie Beach, Oaks Sunshine Coast, Oaks Charlotte Towers Brisbane, the Oaks Lagoons Port Douglas, and the Oaks Rivermarque Mackay.

Northern Territory
Leanna Boyd, Amanda Perry and the CaPTA Group, Stuart Lamont, the

ACKNOWLEDGEMENTS

Caravan Industry Association of Australia, Norm Cramp, Merryn Andrews, Karena Noble, Phoebe Smith, Caitlin Jones, Belle, Jess and Molly, the Group of Five, the Group of Eight, Margaret Beattie, Josh and Julie, and the Oaks Elan in Darwin.

I worked with so many fantastic people, tour operators and organisations. If my words inspired you, I encourage you to seek them out on your own journey and visit *www.aussiebucketlist.com* for links, lodging and meal recommendations, videos and further information.

The story of travelling across Australia with my young family will form the basis of my next book, but I certainly could not leave them out of this one. My wife and two children had no idea what they were in for when we left winter in Canada for our once-in-a-lifetime adventure in sunny Australia. The road has been long, emotional, unpredictable, and often lonely. Sleep was not forthcoming and there was always somewhere else we needed to be. I promise you a vacation from our so-called vacation and, with any luck, we might never travel again. At least . . . for a little while.

*The author acknowledges the many Indigenous owners
of the lands of Australia. This project aims to treat all
Indigenous people, their customs and beliefs, with respect.*

Photo Credits

NEW SOUTH WALES

Swoop through the Forest
108, 109, 110, 111: Robin Esrock

Cook Something Fishy and Fabulous
112: Jaci Taylor
113, 114, 115: Robin Esrock
116: Ana Esrock

Spend a Night at the Opera
117, 118: Pixabay
119: Robin Esrock

Learn about Country on a Sand Dune Adventure
121, 122, 123, 124: Robin Esrock
125: Jaci Taylor

Learn to Surf
126: Courtesy Let's Go Surfing
127, 128 (top): Robin Esrock
128 (bottom): Courtesy Let's Go Surfing
129: Robin Esrock
130: Courtesy Let's Go Surfing

Feel the Energy of Crystal Castle
131, 132 (both), 133: Robin Esrock
133: Pixabay
135: Robin Esrock

Freefall over Lake Macquarie
136: Courtesy Skydive Australia
137: Robin Esrock
138: Courtesy Skydive Australia
139, 140: Robin Esrock

Stop and Smell the Roses
141, 142, 143, 144 (left): Courtesy Hunter Valley Gardens
144 (right): Robin Esrock

Marvel at the Blue Mountains
145, 146, 147, 148,: Robin Esrock

Paddle Beyond the Pass
149, 150, 151: Courtesy Go Sea Kayaking
152: Robin Esrock

TASMANIA

Cycle, Kayak and Walk
154, 155, 156 (both), 157, 158, 159: Robin Esrock

Abseil off Gordon Dam
160, 161, 163: Robin Esrock

Go down a Rabbit Hole
Images of the museum courtesy of MONA Museum of Old and New Art, Hobart, Tasmania, Australia
164: MONA / Leigh Carmichael.
165: Matt Newton
166: Robin Esrock
167: MONA / Jesse Hunniford
168: MONA / Rémi Chauvin

Take a Sip of Liquid Gold
169, 170, 171: Robin Esrock

Plunge into Dove Canyon
173, 174: Courtesy Cradle Canyoning
175 (top): Jaci Taylor
175 (bottom): Mark Walsh
176: Courtesy Cradle Canyoning

Hear the Devils Grunt
178, 179, 180, 181: Robin Esrock

Listen for Ghosts
182, 183, 184, 185: Robin Esrock

Cycle Down a Mountain
186: EWM
187, 188, 189, 190: Robin Esrock

Marvel at the Painted Cliffs
191, 192, 193 (both): Robin Esrock

See Lavender Fields Forever
194, 195: Courtesy Bridestowe Lavender Fields
196: Ana Esrock

QUEENSLAND

Polish Jewellery in the Sand
198: Robin Esrock
199: Pixabay
200, 201, 202 (top): Robin Esrock
202 (bottom): Ana Esrock

Sleep on the Reef
203, 204, 205: Robin Esrock
206: Pixabay
207: Robin Esrock

Eat Your Heart Out
208, 209, 210, 211: Robin Esrock
212: Courtesy Tangalooma Island Resort

Walk in an Ancient Rainforest
213, 215, 216, 217, 218: Robin Esrock

Go Rafting in the Wet Tropics
219, 221: Courtesy Ben Webb, Raging Thunder

Do the Great Barrier Reef
223: Courtesy GBR
224: Courtesy Quicksilver
225: Robin Esrock
226: EWM
227 (top): SOURCE
227 (bottom): Robin Esrock
228: Courtesy GBR

Zip Through the Daintree
229, 230, 231(both): Courtesy Jungle Surfing
232 (all): Robin Esrock

Make Your Own Tracks
233: Ana Esrock
234 (top): Pixabay
234 (bottom): Robin Esrock
236 (both): Pixabay

Canoe the Aussie Everglades

237, 238: Robin Esrock
239: Courtesy Luxury Afloat
240, 241: Robin Esrock

Dive the SS Yongala
242: Courtesy Yongala Dive
243: Robin Esrock
244, 246, 247 (both):
Courtesy Yongala Dive

THE AUSSIE ART OF GETTING HIGH
248: Courtesy Sydney
Bridge Climb
249 (top): Courtesy Adelaide
Oval Roofclimb
249 (bottom): Courtesy Q1
Skypoint Climb
250 (top): Robin Esrock
250 (bottom): Courtesy Visit
Brisbane

WESTERN AUSTRALIA

Climb a Very Big Tree
252, 253, 254, 255: Robin
Esrock

Float in a Prison Tunnel
256, 258, 259: Robin Esrock

Sail among the Dugongs
261, 262, 263 (both), 264:
Robin Esrock

Shake Hands with Royalty
265, 266, 267, 268, 269: Robin
Esrock

Admire the Karri on Boranup Drive
270, 271: Robin Esrock
272: IntoTheWorld /
Shutterstock
273, 274 (both:) Robin
Esrock

Salute the Past
275, 276, 277, 278, 279: Robin
Esrock

Get the Quokka Selfie
280, 281, 282, 283, 284: Robin
Esrock

Drive into Mars
285, 286: Robin Esrock
287: Benny Marty /
Shutterstock
288: Robin Esrock

Spot Seabirds and Shipwrecks
289, 291, 292: Robin Esrock

Soak in the Wilderness
293: Marc Witte /
Shutterstock
294: John Crux /
Shutterstock
295: edella / Shutterstock
296: Alex Couto /
Shutterstock

Spot an Orca in the Southern Ocean
297, 298, 299, 301: Keith
Lightbody

Work Out on the Stairway to Heaven
302, 303: Robin Esrock
304: Ron Gordon

NORTHERN TERRITORY

Train Across the Red Centre
306, 307, 308, 309, 310, 311:
Robin Esrock

Stare Down a Saltie
312, 313: Paige Mattsson
Courtesy Crocosaurus
Cove

314: Robin Esrock
315: Paige Mattsson
Courtesy Crocosaurus
Cove

Relive the Day War Came to Australia
316, 317, 319: Robin Esrock
320: EWM

See the Sun Rise on the Rock
321, 322, 323, 325: Robin
Esrock

Swim in the Buley Rockholes
326: Ana Esrock
327: Robin Esrock
329: Ana Esrock
329, 330: Robin Esrock

Hike the Larapinta Trail
331: EWM
332, 333: Robin Esrock
334: Josh Petre EWM
335: Robin Esrock
336: O&M St John
337, 338, 339: Robin Esrock

340, 343, 347: Robin Esrock
351: Jaqui Taylor

Also by Robin Esrock

You've taken on Australia, now take on the world. During his remarkable journey to over 100 countries on seven continents, Robin Esrock uncovered unique adventures, fascinating histories, cultural spectacles, natural wonders, hilarious situations and unforgettable characters – proving that modern travel is so much more than just over-trafficked tourist attractions. From the Amazon jungle to the beaches of Zanzibar, *The Great Global Bucket List* presents the world we don't hear much about in the news: a planet that is strikingly beautiful, thought-provoking, incredibly diverse and sometimes just very, very funny.

With his trademark wit, photography and insight, Esrock introduces the inspiring experiences you'll be talking and dreaming about for many years to come.

Get ready to ...

- **cage dive with crocodiles in South Africa**
- **float in Colombia's mud volcano of youth**
- **cheer for a masked wrestling hero in Mexico**
- **discover space tourism in Russia's Star City**
- **zip-line off the Great Wall of China**
- **swim with sunken treasures in Papua New Guinea**
- **camp on the ice in Antarctica**

. . . and that 's just the tip of the proverbial metaphor!